STUDIES IN CHRISTIAN HISTORY AND THOUGHT

The Priesthood of Christ

Atonement in the Theology of John Owen (1616-1683)

STUDIES IN CHRISTIAN HISTORY AND THOUGHT

Series Editors

Alan P.F. Sell	Visiting Professor at Acadia University Divinity College, Nova Scotia
D.W. Bebbington	University of Stirling, Stirling, Scotland
Clyde Binfield	Professor Associate in History, University of Sheffield, UK
Gerald Bray	Anglican Professor of Divinity, Beeson Divinity School, Samford University, Birmingham, Alabama, USA
Grayson Carter	Associate Professor of Church History, Fuller Theological Seminary SW, Phoenix, Arizona, USA
Dennis Ngien	Professor of Theology, Tyndale University College and Seminary, Founder of the Centre for Mentorship and Theological Reflection, Toronto, Canada

STUDIES IN CHRISTIAN HISTORY AND THOUGHT

The Priesthood of Christ

Atonement in the Theology of John Owen (1616-1683)

Edwin E.M. Tay

Foreword by Carl R. Trueman

Copyright © Edwin E.M. Tay 2014

First published 2014 by Paternoster

Paternoster is an imprint of Authentic Media
52 Presley Way, Crownhill, Milton Keynes, Bucks, MK8 0ES, UK

www.authenticmedia.co.uk
Authentic Media is a division of Koorong UK, a company limited by guarantee

09 08 07 06 05 04 03   8 7 6 5 4 3 2 1

The right of Edwin E.M. Tay to be identified as the Author of this Work
has been asserted by him in accordance with the Copyright, Designs
and Patents Act 1988.

All rights reserved. No part of this publication may be reproduced, stored in a retrieval system, or transmitted, in any form or by any means, electronic, mechanical, photocopying, recording or otherwise, without the prior permission of the publisher or a license permitting restricted copying. In the UK such licenses are issued by the Copyright Licensing Agency, 90 Tottenham Court Road, London W1P 9HE.

British Library Cataloguing in Publication Data
A catalogue record for this book is available from the British Library

ISBN 978–1–84227–7997

Printed and bound in Great Britain
for Paternoster
by Lightning Source, UK

Series Preface

This series complements the specialist series of Studies in Evangelical History and Thought and Studies in Baptist History and Thought for which Paternoster is becoming increasingly well known by offering works that cover the wider field of Christian history and thought. It encompasses accounts of Christian witness at various periods, studies of individual Christians and movements, and works which concern the relations of church and society through history, and the history of Christian thought.

The series includes monographs, revised dissertations and theses, and collections of papers by individuals and groups. As well as 'free standing' volumes, works on particular running themes are being commissioned; authors will be engaged for these from around the world and from a variety of Christian traditions.

A high academic standard combined with lively writing will commend the volumes in this series both to scholars and to a wider readership.

For
Angela, Phoebe and Chloe

CONTENTS

Foreword by Carl R. Trueman	xi
Acknowledgements	xiii
Abbreviations	xv
Chapter 1 Introduction	**1**
Owen and the Atonement	2
Methodological Issues	6
Scope of Study	9
Conclusion	22
Chapter 2 The Agent of Redemption	**24**
Opera Dei: the Reformed Orthodox Context	24
Owen and the *Opera Dei*	27
The Internal Work of God in Redemption	29
The Divine Decree and Counsels	29
The Eternal Compact: General Observations	32
The Eternal Compact: Exegetical and Theological	
Considerations	36
The Eternal Compact: the Role of the Spirit	45
The Prominence of Christ's Priesthood	47
The External Work of God in Redemption	51
Conclusion	57
Chapter 3 The Means of Redemption: Christ the Mediator	**58**
The Christological Context	58
Christologia (1679)	63
Owen's Reformed Christology	72
Incarnation	72
Mediator According to Two Natures	76
One Common Work, Two Principles of Operation	80
Conclusion	85
Chapter 4 The Means of Redemption: Christ's Priestly Office	**87**
The Polemical Significance of Christ's Priesthood	87
Arminians, Saumurians, and Thomas More	92
Owen's Formulation of Christ's Priestly Office	102
A Display of Arminianism (1642)	102
Two Short Catechisms (1645)	104
The Death of Death (1647)	106

Exercitations Concerning the Priesthood of Christ (1674)	108
Conclusion	112
Chapter 5 The Means of Redemption: Satisfaction for Sin	**114**
Satisfaction and the Whole Obedience of Christ	114
The Matter of Satisfaction: Seventeenth-Century Background	114
The Obedience of Christ the Mediator	119
Unio Mystica and Imputation of Christ's Obedience	123
Christ's Suretyship and Imputation of Christ's Obedience	128
The Twofold State of Christ	133
Satisfaction and the Death of Christ	136
Owen's Debate with Baxter: the Nature and Effects of Christ's Death	136
Owen's Debate with Baxter: the Importance of Christ's Priesthood	142
Owen's Contradiction?	145
Owen's Commercialism?	147
Conclusion	149
Chapter 6 The End of Redemption	**151**
Owen's Teleology: Current Perspectives	151
The Supreme End of Redemption: the Glory of God	154
Foundational Issues	154
The Divine Attributes and the Work of Redemption	156
The Necessity of Christ's Priesthood	163
The Intermediate End of Redemption: the Saints' Perseverance and Salvation	170
Conclusion	178
Chapter 7 Conclusion	**179**
Bibliography	**186**
Primary Sources	186
Secondary Sources	192
Index	

Foreword

John Owen (1616-1683) was one of the central figures in the religious life of England during the turbulent middle years of the seventeenth century. He was chaplain to Oliver Cromwell, pastor, university academic and administrator, and finally one of the most significant non-conformist leaders after the Great Ejection of 1662. In addition, he was also a significant theologian, biblical exegete and polemicist who helped to shape and articulate the theology not only of English Puritanism but of European Reformed Orthodoxy.

Recent years have seen a welcome increase in interest in the life and work of John Owen, particularly with reference to his significance to the broader context of Reformed Orthodoxy. Indeed, one might say that Owen is only now being given the attention which his importance to Reformed theology and to the intellectual life of the Commonwealth and restoration really deserves.

Given this significance, it is a great pleasure to write this foreword to Edwin Tay's fine study of Owen on the priesthood of Christ. The topic was something which preoccupied Owen from his earliest anti-Arminian writings to the massive Hebrews commentary of his later years. The reasons for such a preoccupation are manifold.

First, the priesthood of Christ is an emphasis of Scripture, and Owen, as a Puritan, was above all a man of Scripture. Yet his exegesis was, of course, shaped both by past exegeses, contemporary linguistics and the pastoral and polemical exigencies of his day.

Second, it was perhaps the point of contention in English theology in the mid-seventeenth century. Amyraldians divided Christ's priesthood in a way that seemed to prioritise intercession over sacrifice. Arminians denied its efficacy. Socinians reduced Christ to little more than an inspiring example and thus had little need for his priesthood at all. Roman Catholics blurred the line between Christ's priesthood and that of earthly priests. Antinomians so emphasized the eternal objectivity of Christ's priesthood that the moral imperatives of the Christian life were seriously undermined. The last four of these groups each represented a significant challenge to orthodoxy in the England of Owen's day and thus it was to these that he responded.

In the world of seventeenth century English theology, this theme loomed large and Owen was without doubt the most significant expounder and defender of the Reformed Orthodox position. In addition, the claims made by contemporaries such as Richard Baxter, that Owen's own theology was antinomian in tendency, meant that there was a personal as well as a pastoral urgency to all that he wrote in this area.

For all of these reasons, this present book represents a significant contribution to our knowledge of Owen and the debates of his day. Dr Tay has done a fine job of studying Owen's contribution in this area. Setting his theology in historical context, he demonstrates how it connects both to discussions within Reformed Orthodoxy itself and to the various debates within the wider English theological world. This study is well-argued and an excellent addition to the growing literature on this man, who was quite possibly the finest theological mind that England ever produced and certainly the finest in the seventeenth century. This book will repay careful study.

Carl R. Trueman
Paul Woolley Professor of Church History
Westminster Theological Seminary, PA

Acknowledgements

This study is a slightly revised version of my doctoral thesis undertaken at the University of Edinburgh. I owe a debt of gratitude to a host of people without whom the completion of this study would not be possible.

The first serious conversation that began the whole process of theological training with the aim of doctoral studies occurred some twelve years ago with the Reverend Dr Quek Swee Hwa, then Dean of Biblical Graduate School of Theology, Singapore (BGST). Ever since that conversation over lunch, he has been deeply concerned with my development at every stage of the journey, giving support in ways too numerous to list here. To him I owe a special debt of gratitude.

Embarking on a prolonged period of training and research in the UK is a huge financial undertaking. Without the necessary funding, no amount of serious consideration and planning for doctoral studies is able to see to its realization. I want to especially thank the members of my family, both immediate and extended, friends, the BGST Council, members of my home church, Telok Ayer Chinese Methodist Church, all of whom gave so generously and consistently in my years abroad. Worthy of note is the contribution of my brother, Winston, whose timely financial support is deeply appreciated. I am very grateful to the trustees of *The Brash Scholarship*, whose enormous sponsorship covered a huge part of my tuition and living expenses. I would also like to thank the award committee of New College Edinburgh for the award of the New College Scholarship for three consecutive years.

I owe a special debt of gratitude to my *Doktorvater*, Susan Hardman Moore. Her availability as a supervisor, enthusiasm for my work, personal encouragements, and detailed feedback of every chapter that I have written have contributed to making this study a much better work than it otherwise would have been if left to my own devices. Any shortcomings are, of course, entirely mine.

I am also grateful for the community at New College Edinburgh. Research work can be a lonely experience. Fortunately, this is not the case for me. I am grateful to Christopher Ross, Joseph Chi, Hansang Lee, Timothy Bridges, John Tweedale, Susan Chapel, and Simon Burton, members of *The Conventicle*, all of whom have made life at New College socially and intellectually memorable. I especially want to thank the librarians at New College Library and the staff at the Inter-Library Loan department for rendering incalculable help during a period of physical inability due to an accident.

There is no doubt that the ones who have spent the most time in prayer for me in the course of my studies are my parents, David and Shirley Tay. I am extremely grateful to them for the spiritual support they have provided and indeed for so much more. Also noteworthy is the community and ministry of

Charlotte Baptist Chapel, my spiritual home for nearly half a decade. If not for her, the reality of Christ's priestly mediation would not have had the impact upon my consciousness as it now does, for which I will always be grateful.

My deepest thanks are reserved for my wife, Angela, and daughters, Phoebe and Chloe. Their presence and prayers have meant more to me than perhaps they realize. I freely confess that I could not have come so far without their unflinching support and love. This study is the result of their journey with me through the peaks and valleys of my life in the UK. Thus, it is to them that I dedicate this book.

Edwin E.M. Tay
Trinity Theological College, Singapore
February 2014

Abbreviations

ANF	*Ante-Nicene Fathers*, 10 vols., eds., A. Roberts and J. Donaldson (Reprint ed., Peabody, MA: Hendrickson Publishes, 1999)
BO	E. Millington, ed., *Bibliotheca Oweniana Sive Catalogus Librorum Plurimis Facultatibus Insignium, Instructissimae Bibliothecae Rev. Doct. Vir. Joan. Oweni, (Quondam Vice-Cancellarii & Decani Edis-Christi in Academia Oxoniensi) Nuperrime Defuncti* (London, 1684)
BT	J. Owen, *Biblical Theology or the Nature, Origin, Development, and Study of Theological Truth, in Six Books*, trans. Stephen P. Westcott (Morgan, PA: Soli Deo Gloria, 1994)
BTr	Banner of Truth
Commentary	*Calvin's Commentaries*. 46 vols. (Edinburgh: Calvin Translation Society, 1843-1855; reprint, in 22 vols., Grand Rapids: Baker, 1996)
CTJ	*Calvin Theological Journal*
DLGTT	R.A. Muller, *Dictionary of Latin and Greek Theological Terms Drawn Principally from Protestant Scholastic Theology* (Grand Rapids: Baker, 1985)
EQ	*Evangelical Quarterly*
GC	Owen, *Two Short Catechisms*, Greater Catechism
JEH	*Journal of Ecclesiastical History*
JTS	*Journal of Theological Studies*
LC	Owen, *Two Short Catechisms*, Lesser Catechism
LCC	Library of Christian Classics
LXX	Septuagint
MAJT	*Mid-America Journal of Theology*
NAKG	*Nederlands Archief Voor Kerkgeschiedenis*
*NPNF*1	*Nicene and Post-Nicene Fathers: First Series*, 14 vols., ed. P. Schaff (Reprint ed., Peabody, MA: Hendrickson Publishers, 1999)
NPNF2	*Nicene and Post-Nicene Fathers*: Second Series, 14 vols., eds. P. Schaff and H. Wace (Reprint ed., Peabody, MA: Hendrickson Publishers, 1999)
ODNB	*Oxford Dictionary of National Biography*, 61 vols. (Oxford: Oxford University Press, 2004) [*Oxford DNB Online* at http://www.oxforddnb.com, 2004 –.]

PRRD	R.A. Muller, *Post-Reformation Reformed Dogmatics*, 4 vols. (2nd ed., Grand Rapids: Baker, 2003)
SCJ	*Sixteenth Century Journal*
SJT	*Scottish Journal of Theology*
TJ	*Trinity Journal*
WMQ	*William and Mary Quarterly*
Works	*The Works of John Owen*, ed., W.H. Goold, 23 vols. (Reprint ed., Edinburgh: Banner of Truth, 1965-68, 1991)
WTJ	*Westminster Theological Journal*

CHAPTER 1

Introduction

In 1647, these words were found on the front pages of a certain book written by the pastor of a parish church at Coggeshall: "Read it diligently, and I doubt not but you will say with me, there is such variety of choice matter running through every vein of each discourse here handled, and carried along with such strength of sound and deep judgment, and with such life and power of a heavenly spirit, and all expressed in such pithy and pregnant words of wisdom, that you will both delight in the reading and praise God for the writer. That both he and it may be more and more profitable shall be my hearty prayers."[1] These are the words of the eminent Puritan, Stanley Gower, who was a member of the Westminster Assembly. It was written as an attestation to the immense worth of a certain soteriological masterpiece. The work to which he referred was *Salus Electorum, Sanguis Jesu, or The Death of Death in the Death of Christ*, and its author, John Owen (1616-1683), then thirty-one years of age.[2] Gower could

---

[1] John Owen, *Salus Electorum*, Preface, in *The Works of John Owen*, ed. William H. Goold, 24 vols. (London: Johnstone and Hunter, 1850-55), 10:147. This edition of Owen's works is by far the best. The twenty-one volume edition issued by Richard Baynes in 1826 is of an inferior quality with respect to textual accuracy. Owen, *The Works of John Owen, with Memoirs of His Life by William Orme*, ed. Thomas Russell, 21 vols. (London: Richard Baynes, 1826). In addition, it does not include Owen's *Theologoumena* and his commentary on the book of Hebrews. The most recent edition is published by the Banner of Truth Trust with sixteen volumes issued in 1967 and another seven in 1991. This twenty-three volume edition is essentially a reprint of the Goold edition except Owen's *Theologoumena*, along with some rearrangements of the materials in volumes sixteen and seventeen. In this study, references follow the volume number and pagination of the Banner edition on account of its accessibility to the scholarly community and the general public. The references to *Theologoumena* are based on the 1661 publication in Latin and the recent English translation by Westcott. Owen, *ΘΕΟΛΟΓΟΥΜΕΝΑ ΠΑΝΤΟΔΑΠΑ, Sive, De Natura, Ortu Progressu, Et Studio Verae Theologiae, Libri Sex Quibus Etiam Origines & Processus Veri & Falsi Cultus Religiosi, Casus & Instaurationes Ecclesiae Illustriores Ab Ipsis Rerum Primordiis, Enarrantur* (Oxoniae, 1661); idem, *Biblical Theology or the Nature, Origin, Development, and Study of Theological Truth, in Six Books*, trans. Stephen P. Westcott (Morgan, PA: Soli Deo Gloria, 1994). Citations from the 1661 publication will be by book, chapter, and page number.
[2] For biographical details, see Peter Toon, *God's Statesman: The Life and Work of John Owen* (Exeter: Paternoster Press, 1971); Andrew Thomson, "Life of Dr. Owen," in *Works*, 1:xxi-cxxii; James Moffatt, ed., *The Golden Book of John Owen* (London: Hodder and Stoughton, 1904), 1-96; John Owen, *The Correspondence of John Owen (1616-1683): With an Account of His Life and Work*, ed. Peter Toon (Cambridge: James

never have known the extent to which his prayers for the young Puritan pastor and his treatise were to become a reality in the English-speaking theological world.

Owen and the Atonement

In Anglo-American theological writings, the name of John Owen has come to be associated with the doctrine of limited atonement, a doctrine known to have been given significant and decisive expression in *The Death of Death*. When the Scottish pastor-theologian, John McLeod Campbell (1800-1872), sought to address critically his inherited Calvinistic doctrine of atonement in his acclaimed work, *The Nature of Atonement* (1856), it was Owen to whom he owed its definitive statement along with Jonathan Edwards (1703-1758).[3] With respect to Owen's writings, *The Death of Death* was Campbell's key source. In his estimate, both theologians have "set forth the modification of the doctrine of atonement (i.e. limited atonement)...to the greatest advantage of which it is capable."[4]

Campbell's estimate of Owen is still evident in current scholarly literature on the atonement. Already in 1886, Sheldon had alluded to the significance of Owen in the history of the development of Christian doctrine.[5] On the doctrine of Christ's work in particular, Franks' historical survey singles out Owen as a key figure in what he terms, "the older Protestant theology", which spans the sixteenth and seventeenth centuries.[6] Like Campbell, it was *The Death of Death* that captured Franks' attention and to which he devoted much of his efforts in elucidating. More recently, in Kennedy's study on Calvin's view of the atonement, he saw that it was necessary to engage with the position of those

---

Clarke, 1970); *Oxford Dictionary of National Biography* (Oxford: Oxford University Press, 2004), Richard L. Greaves, "Owen, John (1616-1683)", henceforth cited as *ODNB*; Sebastian Rehnman, "John Owen: A Reformed Scholastic at Oxford," in *Reformation and Scholasticism: An Ecumenical Enterprise*, ed. Willem J. van Asselt and Eef Dekker, Texts and Studies in Reformation and Post-Reformation Thought (Grand Rapids: Baker, 2001), 181-203; Carl R. Trueman, *John Owen: Reformed Catholic, Rennaisance Man* (Aldershot, England: Ashgate, 2007), 1-33; cf. also *The Oxford Orations of Dr. John Owen*, ed. and trans. Peter Toon (Cornwall: Gospel Communication, 1971).
[3] J. McLeod Campbell, *The Nature of the Atonement* (First published, 1856; Edinburgh: Handsel Press; Grand Rapids: Eerdmans, 1996), 65-80.
[4] Campbell, *The Nature of the Atonement*, 66. Words in parentheses added.
[5] Henry C. Sheldon, *History of Christian Doctrine*, 2 vols. (New York: Harper and Brothers, 1886), 2:49. Three of Owen's treatises were identified as especially significant: A *Display of Arminianism* (1643), *The Doctrine of the Saints' Perseverance* (1654), and *The Doctrine of Justification by Faith* (1677).
[6] Robert S. Franks, *The Work of Christ: A Historical Study of Christian Doctrine* (London: Thomas Nelson, 1962), 459-471.

who claim that Calvin taught limited atonement.[7] No apology was needed as to his choice of authority and source for the issue at hand: "I identify John Owen's *The Death of Death in the Death of Christ* as the classical expression of the traditional Reformed doctrine of limited atonement. This work had tremendous influence in Owen's day and continues to have a major influence upon English-speaking Reformed theologians."[8] Owen's continuing influence, Kennedy rightly points out, has been facilitated by the multiple reprinting of his works in general and of his 1647 treatise in the second half of the last century in particular.[9]

Given the abiding interest on Owen's formulation of the atonement, it is not unreasonable then to suppose that some basic account of his theology of atonement is available in the current scholarly literature. Yet this is not the case. There is yet to be a single major study to date that gives a coherent account of his theology of atonement.[10] While it is true that certain strands of

---

[7] Kevin Dixon Kennedy, *Union with Christ and the Extent of the Atonement*, Studies in Biblical Literature 48 (New York / Bern / Oxford: Peter Lang, 2002).

[8] Kennedy, *Union with Christ*, 8-9. However, this does not seem to be the case in the writings of modern continental theologians. There is, for instance, not a single mention of Owen in Barth's massive *Church Dogmatics*. See Karl Barth, *Church Dogmatics: Index with Aids for the Preacher*, eds. T.F. Torrance and G.W. Bromiley (London / New York: T&T Clark International, 2004). In Heppe's helpful compendium of selections from Reformed orthodox theologians, Owen is cited once in relation to the covenant of grace. Heinrich Heppe, *Reformed Dogmatics: A Compendium of Reformed Theology*, ed. Ernst Bizer, trans. G.T. Thomson (1950; reprint, London: Wakeman, n.d.), 378. Likewise, Owen is cited once in Pannenberg's acclaimed systematic work. Even then, it is merely a passing reference contained in a footnote within the context of ecclesiology. Wolfhart Pannenberg, *Systematic Theology*, trans. Geoffrey W. Bromiley, 3 vols. (Edinburgh: T&T Clark; Grand Rapids: Eerdmans, 1991-1998), 3:23. Although the Dutch theologian, Abraham Kuyper (1837-1920), was heavily indebted to Owen for his theology, the influence of Owen came from his writings on the Holy Spirit and not *The Death of Death*. See "Preface" in Abraham Kuyper, *The Work of the Holy Spirit*, trans. Henri De Vries (New York; London: Funk & Wagnalls, 1900), ix-xiv, esp. ix-xi.

[9] The first sixteen volumes of Owen's twenty-four volume work published by Johnstone and Hunter in the nineteenth century (1850-1853) were reprinted six times by the Banner of Truth Trust from 1965 to 1993. Owen's *The Death of Death* had a total of seven reprints between and inclusive of the years 1959 to 1995. See John Owen, *The Death of Death in the Death of Christ* (Reprint, Edinburgh: Banner of Truth, 1959). These figures, of course, do not shed light on actual readership and influence, but they do give some basic indication of the demand for Owen's writings, especially his soteriological treatise.

[10] The following is a list of monographs on Owen's theology up to the year 2011 in chronological order. Where doctoral dissertations are published, it is the published form that is referenced. William Ward Bass, "Platonic Influences on Seventeenth Century English Puritan Theology, as Expressed in the Thinking of John Owen, Richard Baxter, and John Howe" (Ph.D. dissertation, University of Southern California, 1958); Don Marvin Everson, "The Puritan Theology of John Owen" (Ph.D. dissertation, The Southern Baptist Theological Seminary, 1959); Dewey D. Wallace, Jr, "The Life and

Thought of John Owen to 1660: A Study of the Significance of Calvinist Theology in English Puritanism" (Ph.D. dissertation, Princeton University, 1965); Peter N.L. Pytches, "A Critical Exposition of the Teaching of John Owen on the Work of the Holy Spirit in the Individual" (M.Litt. dissertation, University of Bristol, 1967); Dale Arden Stover, "The Pneumatology of John Owen: A Study of the Role of the Holy Spirit in Relation to the Shape of a Theology" (Ph.D. dissertation, McGill University, 1967); Sinclair Ferguson, *John Owen on the Christian Life* (Edinburgh: Banner of Truth, 1987); Richard Mitchell Hawkes, "The Logic of Grace in John Owen, D.D.: An Analysis, Exposition, and Defense of John Owen's Puritan Theology of Grace" (Ph.D. dissertation, Westminster Theological Seminary, 1987); Gavin John McGrath, "Puritans and the Human Will: Voluntarism within Mid-Seventeenth English Puritanism as Seen in the Works of Richard Baxter and John Owen" (Ph.D. dissertation, University of Durham, 1989); Robert K.M. Wright, "John Owen's Great High Priest: The Highpriesthood of Christ in the Theology of John Owen, (1616-1683)" (Ph.D. dissertation, The Iliff School of Theology and University of Denver, 1989); Alan C. Clifford, *Atonement and Justification: English Evangelical Theology 1640-1790, an Evaluation* (Oxford: Clarendon Press, 1990); Randall C. Gleason, *John Calvin and John Owen on Mortification* (New York: Peter Lang, 1995); Michael William Bobick, "Owen's Razor: The Role of Ramist Logic in the Covenant Theology of John Owen (1616-1683)" (Ph.D. dissertation, Drew University, 1996); Carl R. Trueman, *The Claims of Truth: John Owen's Trinitarian Theology* (Carlisle: Paternoster Press, 1998); David Wai-Sing Wong, "The Covenant Theology of John Owen" (Ph.D. dissertation, Westminster Theological Seminary, 1998); Joel R. Beeke, *The Quest for Full Assurance: The Legacy of Calvin and His Successors* (Edinburgh: Banner of Truth, 1999), 165-213; Sebastian Rehnman, *Divine Discourse: The Theological Methodology of John Owen*, Texts and Studies in Reformation and Post-Reformation Thought (Grand Rapids: Baker, 2002); Henry M. Knapp, "Understanding the Mind of God: John Owen and Seventeenth Century Exegetical Methodology" (Ph.D. dissertation, Calvin Theological Seminary, 2002); Howard Griffith, "High Priest in Heaven: The Intercession of the Exalted Christ in Reformed Theology, Analysis and Critique" (Ph.D. dissertation, Westminster Theological Seminary, 2004); Richard W. Daniels, *The Christology of John Owen* (Grand Rapids: Reformation Heritage Books, 2004); Jon D. Payne, *John Owen on the Lord's Supper* (Edinburgh: Banner of Truth, 2004); Matthew Mason, "The Significance of the Systematic and Polemic Function of Union with Christ in John Owen's Contribution to Seventeenth Century Debates Concerning Eternal Justification" (M.Th. dissertation, Oak Hill College, 2005); Philip A. Craig, "The Bond of Grace and Duty in the Soteriology of John Owen: The Doctrine of Preparation for Grace and Glory as a Bulwark against Seventeenth-Century Anglo-American Antinomianism" (Ph.D. dissertation, Trinity International University, 2005); Alan J. Spence, *Incarnation and Inspiration: John Owen and the Coherence of Christology* (London / New York: T & T Clark, 2007); Kelly M. Kapic, *Communion with God: The Divine and the Human in the Theology of John Owen* (Grand Rapids: Baker, 2007); Brian K. Kay, *Trinitarian Spirituality: John Owen and the Doctrine of God in Western Devotion*, Studies in Christian History and Thought (Milton Keynes: Paternoster, 2007); Trueman, *John Owen*; Christopher H. Cleveland, "Thomism in John Owen" (Ph.D. dissertation, University of Edinburgh, 2011).

The edited volume by Oliver contains helpful articles from various authors on Owen's Christology, pneumatology, ecclesiology, and his doctrine of Scripture. The omission of his doctrine of God and salvation is regrettable. Robert W. Oliver, ed., *John

his atonement theology have been explored in the field of Owen research, however, they are carried out in contexts where the chief focus is not the atonement. This study is the first full-scale attempt to articulate Owen's atonement theology in which its various aspects are pulled together and their organic relatedness demonstrated.

Like all pioneering projects, this study is not without its antecedent. There is one significant precursor to date. Arguably, the closest attempt to date at a substantial explication of Owen's atonement theology is found in Alan Clifford's 1990 publication, *Atonement and Justification: English Evangelical Theology 1640-1790, an Evaluation*.[11] Clifford compares and critically analyses the views of John Owen and John Wesley (1703-1791) on the two distinct but interrelated issues of atonement and justification in the course of which the views of Richard Baxter (1615-1691) and John Tillotson (1630-1694) are explored as well. His task is not merely descriptive but involves an evaluation of their views against the teachings of Scripture. To this end, he sets his whole study against the backdrop of the Reformation tradition that stems from Calvin, arguing that Baxter's *via media* between Owen's particularism on the one hand, and Wesley's universalism on the other, best accounts for the Biblical material and is the rightful heir of Calvin.[12] Owen's doctrine of atonement, Clifford claims, departs from both Biblical teaching and that of the Reformers of whom Calvin's view was representative.[13]

Clifford's study is not without shortcomings. An apparent weakness is its overly ambitious scope. The sheer breadth of coverage on the lives and writings of four authors over nearly two centuries of English church history prevents him from adequately locating Owen within the broader intellectual and theological contexts of his day which informed his formulation of the atonement. With the exception of the doctrine of justification, Clifford also does not account for the way in which the broader doctrinal matrix of Owen's theology bears upon his statement of the atonement. He seems content to confine his locus of examination to the atonement's extent and the influence of Owen's alleged Aristotelianism upon it, based primarily on *The Death of*

Owen: The Man and His Theology (Darlington: Evangelical Press; Philadelphia: P&R Publishing, 2002).

[11] See list in footnote 10.

[12] See also Alan C. Clifford, *Amyraut Affirmed or 'Owenism, a Caricature of Calvinism'* (Norwich: Charenton Reformed Publishing, 2004), which covers the same ground and relies heavily on his earlier work. His apologetic for Calvin's "middle way" is found in idem, *Calvinus: Authentic Calvinism, a Clarification* (Norwich: Charenton Reformed Publishing, 1996).

[13] Clifford, *Atonement and Justification*, 82, 100-101: "Sufficient evidence has been adduced to indicate that the reformers would not recognize Owen's doctrine of atonement as their own"; "It is arguable…that Owen's Aristotelian theorizing and Wesley's total reluctance to theorize lead alike to anomalous conclusions, neither of which are Scriptural."

Death. Consequently, analyses of Owen's exegesis are prejudged by the supposed negative implications that arise from the use of Aristotelian categories.[14] Furthermore, in a work that purports to evaluate theological positions against the Biblical material, it is unfortunate that the most elaborate exegetical grounding for Owen's soteriology – *An Exposition of the Epistle to the Hebrews* (1668-1671) — is entirely neglected.

Methodological Issues

Notwithstanding its weaknesses, Clifford's work raises some issues of methodological significance for this study. First, it raises the question of the theological context in which Owen is to be situated for an accurate understanding of his theology of atonement. This is part of a larger question on the nature of the relationship between Reformation thought and that of the late sixteenth- and seventeenth-century Protestant orthodoxy. The scholarship that argues for discontinuity between the two understands the breach to consist in the influence of Aristotelian rationalism upon Protestant orthodoxy, which manifests itself in deductive systems of theology derived from a central dogma such as predestination or the doctrine of God.[15] A trajectory of this argument is the "Calvin against the Calvinists" thesis of which Clifford's study is an instance.[16]

---

[14] In his chapter entitled, "The Verdict of Scripture", Clifford does not assess the merits of each theologian's exegesis against a fresh exegesis of the relevant texts in question, but compares them against the standard of Calvin's exegesis on the basis of the unsupported assumption that Calvin's is the right one. This assumption, coupled with the negative association of Owen's limited atonement with Aristotelian categories, constitute the norm for Clifford's evaluation. For instance, on Owen's particularistic reading of the parable of the good shepherd in John 10, Clifford comments: "Owen cannot demonstrate his exegesis of the parable without the *questionable tactic* of relating it to another, the parable of the sheep and the goats (Matt 25:31ff.)." Emphasis added. Here, Owen's exegesis is prejudged negatively before the legitimacy of his hermeneutic is examined in any significant way. That the "questionable tactic" was based on the widely accepted interpretive principle of *analogia Scripturae* in Reformed orthodoxy does not seem to have crossed Clifford's mind. Cf. the criticism of Clifford's thesis in Trueman, *Claims of Truth*, 52ff., 233-40.

[15] An extensive survey of the relevant scholarship is found in Richard A. Muller, "Calvin and the 'Calvinists': Assessing Continuities and Discontinuities between the Reformation and Orthodoxy. Part One," *CTJ* 30, no. 2 (1995), 345-359.

[16] The phrase is first found in Basil Hall, "Calvin against the Calvinists," in *John Calvin: A Collection of Distinguished Essays*, ed. Gervase Duffield (Grand Rapids: Eerdmans, 1966), 23-27. Others include R.T. Kendall, *Calvin and English Calvinism to 1649*, Oxford Theological Monograph Series (Oxford: Oxford University Press, 1979); Holmes Royston III, *John Calvin Versus the Westminster Confession* (Richmond: John Knox, 1972); James B. Torrance, "Covenant or Contract? A Study of the Theological Background of Worship in Seventeenth Century Scotland," *SJT* 23 (1970), 51-76; James B. Torrance, "Strengths and Weaknesses of the Westminster Theology," in *The Westminster Confession in the Church Today*, ed. Alisdair Heron (Edinburgh: St.

Recent reappraisals of the relationship between Reformation and post-Reformation thought have found this line of scholarship to be seriously inadequate.[17] Not least there is the overly simplistic and indeed misleading construal of intellectual and theological developments in a static and monolithic fashion, as the "Calvin against the Calvinists" slogan suggests, when measured against the rich diversity of the Reformed tradition in the sixteenth and seventeenth centuries. Instead, proponents of the reappraisal argue that there is essential continuity between Reformation thought and that of Protestant orthodoxy, affirm the presence of discontinuous elements, albeit of a non-essential nature, and acknowledge the fluidity of intellectual and theological thought in a way that allows for a tradition to be expressed in a plurality of ways within an ongoing process of development.

If Owen's theology of atonement is to be accurately understood, it is necessary, in light of the recent reappraisals, not only to situate him in his immediate theological context of seventeenth-century England, but also to widen the boundaries to locate him within the broader ongoing development of the Western theological tradition in general, and of Reformed orthodoxy in particular. In other words, the interpretation of Owen's thought will have to be approached synchronically and diachronically.[18] Trueman and Rehnman have taken the lead in this direction in their recent monographs with insightful results, giving concrete expressions to the otherwise unexplored terrain of Owen's trinitarian theology and prolegomena respectively.[19] Obviously, with a

---

Andrew Press, 1982), 40-53; Thomas F. Torrance, "Predestination in Christ," *EQ* 13 (1941), 108-141; *The School of Faith: The Catechisms of the Reformed Church, Trans. And Edited with an Introduction by T.F. Torrance* (London: James Clarke, 1959), xi-cxxvi.

[17] Muller, "Calvin and the Calvinists, Part One", 359-75; idem, "Calvin and the Calvinists: Assessing Continuities and Discontinuities between the Reformation and Orthodoxy. Part Two," *CTJ* 31, no. 1 (1996), 125-60; idem, *Christ and the Decree : Christology and Predestination in Reformed Theology from Calvin to Perkins* (Durham, N.C.: Labyrinth Press, 1986); idem, *After Calvin: Studies in the Development of a Theological Tradition*, Oxford Studies in Historical Theology (New York: Oxford University Press, 2003); idem, *Post Reformation Reformed Dogmatics: The Rise and Development of Reformed Orthodoxy, Ca. 1520 to Ca. 1725*, 4 vols. (Grand Rapids: Baker, 2003), henceforth cited as *PRRD*; Carl R. Trueman and R. Scott Clark, eds., *Protestant Scholasticism: Essays in Reassessment* (Carlisle: Paternoster Press, 1999); W.J. van Asselt and E. Dekker, eds., *Reformation and Scholasticism : An Ecumenical Enterprise*, Texts and Studies in Reformation and Post-Reformation Thought (Grand Rapids, Mich.: Baker Academic, 2001).

[18] Carl R. Trueman, "Puritan Theology as Historical Event: A Linguistic Approach to the Ecumenical Context," in *Reformation and Scholasticism: An Ecumenical Enterprise*, ed. Willem J. van Asselt and Eef Dekker (Grand Rapids: Baker, 2001), 253-275.

[19] Trueman, *Claims of Truth*; idem, *John Owen*; Rehnman, *Divine Discourse*. Mason's work moves in the same direction methodologically but deals with Owen's doctrine of justification, union with Christ, and his *ordo salutis*. Mason, "Significance of the Systematic and Polemic Function". The work of Spence on Owen's doctrine of the

broader theological milieu in mind, the present study would be seriously impoverished if it is limited to a comparison of Owen's views with Calvin's as some studies have done.[20] Rather, it will set Owen's formulation of the atonement against the backdrop of the teachings of a range of theologians, especially those of the Reformed orthodox tradition. As far as possible, the selection of theologians and their works will be based on the auction catalogue of Owen's personal library.[21]

Secondly, Clifford's work raises the issue of the legitimacy of relying mainly on *The Death of Death* for a statement of Owen's doctrine of atonement. Trueman rightly cautions that attempts to assess the full measure of Owen's thoughts on the atonement need to bear in mind that the treatise of 1647 was that of "a comparatively young theologian with another 36 years of active theological activity in front of him."[22] As such, his later writings ought to play an important role in understanding Owen's view of the subject. It is also necessary to question the common practice of treating the treatise as merely a piece of polemical writing whose sole burden is confined to answering the question of the atonement's extent. There is certainly more to the treatise than is commonly allowed for, as will become clear below. On account of the common but unhelpful practice of representing Owen's doctrine of atonement primarily or solely on the basis of *The Death of Death*, it is necessary to delineate the approach to the selection of sources adopted in this study.

The Reformed tradition which Owen inherited understood the task of theologizing as involving the synthesis of exegesis of Scripture and doctrinal

---

incarnation is also significant in this regard, although to a lesser degree since it is concerned with the wider Western theological tradition and does not engage with the Reformed orthodox theologians. Spence, *Incarnation and Inspiration*.

[20] See Wong, "The Covenant Theology of John Owen"; Gleason, *John Calvin and John Owen on Mortification*; Bobick, "Owen's Razor"; Stover, "The Pneumatology of John Owen".

[21] Edward Millington, ed., *Bibliotheca Oweniana Sive Catalogus Librorum* (London: 1684). The editor's comments in the preface "To the Reader" gives a flavor of the vast scope of Owen's collection and no doubt the breadth of his reading: "Among the vast numbers of books he had perused, and was for several late years possessed of, I find these ensuing larger volumes preserved, and esteemed by him as the choice and curious to his death, viz. his Greek and Latin Fathers, his different editions of the Councils, his church histories, and rabbinical authors, together with great variety of the Bibles in the Oriental languages; not to mention his almost complete collection of the historians, poets, geographers, philologers, and lexicographers, in Greek, Latin, etc. All which considered together, perhaps for their number are not to be parallel'd..." This description does not include Owen's vast collection of works by authors of medieval, contemporary, and Reformed theology. Rehnman, one of the very few who has mined the catalogue for its inestimable value in historical research, estimates that it contains "almost three thousand books." Rehnman, *Divine Discourse*, 21. The catalogue is divided into two sections — *Libri Theologici* and *Divinity* — with separate paginations.

[22] Trueman, *John Owen*, 92 n96.

formulation.[23] Irrespective of its genre — confessional, catechetical, devotional, or polemical — doctrinal expositions of the Reformed orthodox were driven by the fundamental conviction that Scripture is *principium cognoscendi theologiae*.[24] As such, doctrinal expositions were founded on the results of careful exegesis of the sacred text. Even if Scriptural citations were annexed to doctrinal formulations without exegetical discussion and so appear like "proof-texting",[25] careful comparisons of the texts cited with the Biblical commentaries of the day will show that they point toward what Muller calls, "the 'assured results' of the best exegetical methods of the age."[26] What the reader finds in Reformed orthodox writings is thus "a close cooperation between the theologian and the exegete, with the theological affirmation of Scripture as final norm of theology worked out in practice as a use not merely of Biblical texts but of detailed exegesis in the original languages of Scripture as the basis for doctrinal formulations."[27] Therefore, it is necessary that the essential relationship between exegesis and doctrinal exposition be borne in mind in the choice of sources for Owen's atonement theology. This study draws upon Owen's commentary on the book of Hebrews as the major exegetical source. Doctrinal sources will include his catechisms, numerous polemical and devotional treatises, and the *Savoy Declaration* of 1658.

Scope of Study

Having surveyed the landscape of Owen research in general on the subject of atonement and established the methodology for this thesis, what follows is a consideration of the theological scope of the present study. The basic elements of Owen's atonement theology will be mapped out in order to identify the theological boundaries beyond which this study will not cross. Toward this end, a case study of *The Death of Death* will be attempted with special attention to the shape and movement of Owen's thought against the backdrop of Protestant orthodoxy, and specifically its Reformed trajectory. However, some preliminary comments are in order before the contents of *The Death of Death*

---

[23] Muller, *PRRD*, 2:502-524; cf. Henry M. Knapp, "Understanding the Mind of God: John Owen and Seventeenth Century Exegetical Methodology" (Ph.D. dissertation, Calvin Theological Seminary, 2002); idem, "John Owen's Interpretation of Hebrews 6:4-6: Eternal Perseverance of the Saints in Puritan Exegesis," *SCJ* 34, no. 1 (2003), 29-52; Thomas Jackson Tucker, "Safeguarding the Treasury: John Owen and the Analogy of Faith" (Ph.D. dissertation, Aberdeen University, 2006).

[24] Richard A. Muller, *Dictionary of Latin and Greek Theological Terms: Drawn Principally from Protestant Scholastic Theology* (Grand Rapids: Baker, 1985), 245-46, henceforth cited as *DLGTT*; idem, *PRRD*, 1:430-45.

[25] As an instance of this, cf. William Perkins, *A Golden Chaine or the Description of Theologie Containing the Order of the Causes of Salvation and Damnation, According to God's Word* (Cambridge: John Legate, 1597).

[26] Muller, *After Calvin*, 50-51; idem, *PRRD*, 2:509-13.

[27] Muller, *After Calvin*, 51.

are analysed in detail. They concern the rationale for the choice of the treatise and its general structure.

First, the thoroughness with which the atonement is dealt with in the treatise makes it an appropriate point of departure into the different aspects of his atonement theology. The following observation of it by one of Owen's biographers is to the point: "Owen does not merely touch his subject, but travels through it with the elephant's grave and solid step, if sometimes also with his ungainly motion; and more than any other writer makes you feel, when he has reached the end of his subject, that he has also exhausted it."[28] This is arguably the chief reason for its classic status, acknowledged by both protagonists and critics alike.[29]

Second, Owen's own justification for writing is of decisive importance for making clear the rationale for the choice of *The Death of Death*. Owen's treatise was the result of more than seven years of serious enquiry, written to undermine the growing influence of universal redemption in all the conceivable forms known to Owen, notably Arminian and Amyraldian.[30] The perceived threat was explicitly described in the following terms: "*a general ransom* to be paid by Christ for all; that he died to redeem all and every one, – not only for *many*, his *church*, the *elect* of God, but for everyone also of the posterity of

---

[28] Thompson, "Life of Dr Owen", in Owen, *Works*, 1:xxxviii.

[29] Jack N. MacLeod, "John Owen and the Death of Death," in *Out of Bondage* (Nottingham: The Westminster Conference, 1983; reprint, Stoke-On-Trent: Tentmaker Publications, n.d.), 52: "Owen's treatise is one of the classical works on the subject; perhaps *the* classic in the English language"; J.I. Packer, *A Quest for Godliness: The Puritan Vision of the Christian Life* (Wheaton, Illinois: Crossway Books, 1990), 125: "Some may find the very sound of Owen's thesis so shocking that they will refuse to read his book at all...but it is hoped that this classic may find itself readers of a different spirit." For the estimates of critics, see comments by John McLeod Campbell cited above. Torrance calls the treatise Owen's "classical defence of the doctrine of a limited atonement." James B. Torrance, "The Incarnation and 'Limited Atonement'," *EQ* 55 (1983), 84. Clifford maintains that with respect to limited atonement, it remains "the classic high Calvinist statement on this subject to this day." *Atonement and Justification*, 5.

[30] Owen speaks of "the daily spreading of the opinions" on universal redemption in the parts where he lived, "a greater noise concerning their prevailing in other places", and "the advantage they had obtained by some military abettors..." *Salus Electorum*, "To the Reader" (*Works*, 10:156). For details of the Arminian and Amyraldian controversies in the context of Owen's day, see Wallace, *The Life and Thought of John Owen*, 35-112, 156-72. With respect to the military, see Richard Baxter, *Reliquiae Baxterianae, or Mr Richard Baxter's Narrative of the Most Memorable Passages of His Life and Times*, ed. Matthew Sylvester (London, 1696), I.§77, where he mentions, among other things, the dangerous influence of a group of men in Cromwell's forces who "most vehemently declaimed against the Doctrine of Election, and for the power of Free-will, and all other points which are controverted between the Jesuits and Dominicans, the Arminians and Calvinists." They were later called "Levellers" who rose up against Cromwell.

Introduction 11

Adam."³¹ Specifically, he was responding to a treatise entitled, *The Universality of God's Free Grace*, written by Thomas More, and published in 1646.³² By no means was Owen the first to have responded in writing. At least three other weighty works were published as earlier polemics against it in whole or in part, two of which Owen had certainly perused.³³ Although he was generally satisfied with these responses, nevertheless, a serious weakness remained as he understood the situation. Owen observed:

> Abler pens have had, within these few years, the discussing and ventilating of some of these questions in our own language. Some have come to my hands, but none of weight…In some of these, at least, in all of them, I had rested fully satisfied, but that I observed they had all tied up themselves to some certain parts

---

³¹ Owen, *Salus Electorum*, I.i (*Works*, 10:159, cf. 149, 295).

³² Thomas More, *The Vniversallity of God's Free-Grace in Christ to Mankind. Proclaimed and Displayed from 1 Tim. 2.6. And Hebr. 2.9. According to Their Genuine Sense That All Might Be Comforted, Encouraged; Every One Confirmed and Assured of the Propitiation and Death of Christ for the Whole Race of Mankind, and So for Himself in Particular* (London: n.p., 1646). More is described by the heresiographer, Thomas Edwards, as "a great secretary and manifestarian" who "does much harm in Lincolnshire, some parts of Norfolk, Cambridgshire" and "is famous at Boston, Lynn, Holland; followed and accompanied sometimes from place to place, with many attending him…" Thomas Edwards, *The Second Part of Gangraena, or a Fresh and Further Discovery of the Errors, Heresies, Blasphemies, and Dangerous Proceedings of the Sectaries of This Time* (London, 1646), 104-105. Thomas Whitfield, at one time minister at Great Yarmouth in Norfolk, gives more details: "having often heard that many godly people at Lynn, Boston, and all that side of the country are much drawn away by the opinions of one Mr Thomas Moore (some years since a weaver in Wells near Wisbich, but of late taking on him the office of teaching, and much raised in his reputation, by the opinion which some have of his more than ordinary parts and piety…) … I was desirous to know certainly what those opinions were." Thomas Whitfield, *A Refutation of the Loose Opinions, and Licentious Tenets Wherwith Those Lay-Preachers Which Wander up and Downe the Kingdome, Labour to Seduce the Simple People or an Examination and Confutation of the Erronious Doctrines of Thomas More, Late a Weaver in Wells Neare Wisbitch, in His Book Entituled [the Universality of God's Free Grace in Christ to Mankinde* (London: Printed for John Bellamie, 1646), "To the Christian Reader".

³³ Whitfield, *A Refutation*; Samuel Rutherford, *Christ Dying and Drawing Sinners to Himselfe or a Survey of Our Saviour in His Soule-Suffering, His Lovelynesse in His Death, and the Efficacie Thereof. In Which Some Cases of Soule-Trouble in Weake Beleevers, Grounds of Submission under the Absense of Christ, with the Flowings and Heightnings of Free Grace, Are Opened* (London: Printed by J. D. for Andrew Crooke, 1647); John Stalham, *Vindicae Redemptionis, in the Fanning and Sifting of Samuel Oates, His Exposition Upon Mat. 13.44, with a Faithful Search after Our Lords Meaning in His Two Parables of the Treasure and the Pearl. Endeavoured in Severall Sermons Upon Mat. 13.44, 45* (London: Printed by A. M. for Christopher Meredith, 1647). Only the works of Stalham and Rutherford were explicitly mentioned by Owen, both of which he had undoubtedly read. *Salus Electorum*, "To the Reader" (*Works*, 10:155n5).

of the controversy, especially the removing of objections, neither compassing nor methodizing the whole; whereby I discerned that the nature of the things under debate, — namely, satisfaction, reconciliation, redemption, and the like, — was left exceedingly in the dark, and the strong foundation of the whole building not so much as once discovered.[34]

The weakness identified is the lack of theological foundation in the contemporary polemic against universal redemption. In his view, what was needed is not another "piece-meal" polemical reaction which merely tackled objections, but rather a full and constructive theological account of the atonement that "compasses" and "methodizes" the whole range of issues in question. Although a *desideratum* in the light of universal redemption's growing influence, such a work had yet to be undertaken, to the best of Owen's knowledge. Thus, *The Death of Death* was written with an eye for constructive theology in addition to the usual polemical practice of answering objections.[35] It is this constructive character of the treatise where the interconnections of various elements of the atonement in Owen's mind are explicitly demonstrated, that lends weight to its suitability as a treatise in which the contours of his atonement theology may be identified. By so doing, the theological scope of this study may then be appropriately circumscribed.

Thirdly, some knowledge of the treatise's structure will help to crystallise the general movement of thought before the details of that movement is unpacked. *The Death of Death* is divided into four books. Books I and II stand together as a Biblical and theological exposition of redemption through the death of Christ, arranged with a view to determining its intended and procured end. Book III defends the case established in Books I and II with sixteen arguments of a theological, rational, and exegetical nature, against the "general ransom" theory. In Book IV, the demolition work continues with a refutation of all the exegetical and theological arguments for universal redemption which Owen has met, with the emphasis being placed on the discussion of specific Biblical statements and terminologies. With the treatise's general structure briefly outlined, what follows is a detailed analysis of the work.

The first identifiable doctrinal locus in accordance with Owen's movement of thought is the doctrine of God, framed in terms of the works of the Trinity. Owen conceived of the triune God as the Agent of redemption, whose *ad extra* operations are "undivided and belong equally to each person, their distinct manner of subsistence and order being observed."[36] In this early axiomatic statement, Owen is drawing on Reformed orthodox expositions of the internal and external works of God.[37] Two theological principles pertaining to the

---

[34] Owen, *Salus Electorum*, "To the Reader" (*Works*, 10:155).
[35] Packer's description of *The Death of Death* as a "systematic expository treatise, not a mere episodic wrangle" fits the above assessment. Packer, *Quest for Godliness*, 135.
[36] Owen, *Salus Electorum*, I.iii (*Works*, 10:163).
[37] Muller, *PRRD*, 4:255-74; Heppe, *Reformed Dogmatics*, 115-32.

Trinity are operative and intrinsically related in his statement. The first is the undivided nature of the external works of the Trinity. The second is the principle that the external works operate according to the immanent order of subsistence. These principles will be elaborated at length in Chapter 2 within the larger context of the *opera Dei*. At this point, it is sufficient to note that Owen maintains the intrinsic relation between God's external and internal works and situates that relation soteriologically. For him, the doctrine of the Trinity and soteriology are intimately related; redemption is understood in terms of trinitarian agency.

Having asserted the undivided nature of God's external work, Owen goes on to adumbrate the peculiarities of that work relative to the persons in the Godhead. To speak of the Trinity in terms of peculiar economic distinctions is commonplace in Reformed orthodoxy. William Ames' attribution of creation to the Father, redemption to the Son, and sanctification to the Spirit is typical.[38] In Owen's case, what belonged peculiarly to the Father as an agent of redemption is his sending of the Son and his laying upon him the punishment of sin.[39] What was peculiar to the Son is his voluntary undertaking of the mediatorial office in its twofold aspect of oblation and intercession, along with the assumption of human nature.[40] What was peculiar to the Spirit is his plenary assistance and empowerment of the Son in his incarnation, oblation, and resurrection.[41] Clearly evident is Owen's thorough-going trinitarianism in which the distinction of persons with respect to God's work *ad extra* is brought to bear entirely on the soteriological front. For Owen, as for the Reformed orthodox, these external acts of the Trinity are distinguishable but indivisible. They "belong equally to each person."

However, simply to assert that all of God's external acts "belong equally to each person" is an insufficient safeguard for the unity of the Godhead. It is necessary that Owen deals with the issue of the way in which they "belong equally". This he did in passing as he summed up his case for the triune God as the agent of redemption:

> And thus have we discovered the blessed agents and undertakers in this work, their several actions and orderly concurrence unto the whole; which, though they

---

[38] William Ames, *The Marrow of Theology*, trans. John Dykstra Eusden (Grand Rapids: Baker, 1997), I.vi.31; *BO*, Libri Theologici, 288.

[39] Owen, *Salus Electorum*, I.iii (*Works*, 10:163-74). The former entails the Son's appointment to the office of Mediator, the furnishing of all the gifts and graces necessary for the fulfilment of that office, and the Father's initiation of the *pactum salutis* which ensures the success of redemption by the Son.

[40] Owen, *Salus Electorum*, I.iv (*Works*, 10:174-77).

[41] Owen, *Salus Electorum*, I.v (*Works*, 10:178-79).

may be thus distinguished, yet they are not so divided but that every one must be ascribed to the whole nature, whereof each person is 'in solidum' partaker.[42]

Owen's reference to "the whole nature" is undoubtedly pointing to the nature or essence of the Godhead.[43] His appeal to God's nature to secure the indivisibility of God's external work in redemption is significant for the reason that it also safeguards the unity of the Godhead.

Following Owen's treatment of the triune Agent in redemption, comes Christ's mediatorial office, the second identifiable doctrinal locus. It occupies the major part of Books I and II, discussed under the notion of the *means* and *end* of redemption.[44] The triune God is the Agent of redemption, Christ's work of oblation and intercession are the means, and the glory of God in the elect's salvation is the intended end.

The threefold office of prophet, priest, and king, first expressed by Calvin, is an essential component of Reformed orthodox exposition on the person and work of the Mediator.[45] Christ's twofold state of humiliation and exaltation usually follows from treatments on the threefold office. Wollebius, for instance, allocated separate chapters for the person, office, humiliation, and exaltation of Christ.[46] Where variations exist in the literature, they occur through the merging or further division of chapters in Wollebius' structure.[47]

---

[42] Owen, *Salus Electorum*, I.v (*Works*, 10:179); cf. idem, *Posthumous Sermons*, XI (*Works*, 16:497): "for though there is an order in the persons of the Trinity, there is no distinction or inequality in the nature of God. Every one who is partaker of that nature is equal in that nature, in dignity, power, and authority."

[43] Elsewhere, he employed the same language of unity for the divine nature. Owen, *Exposition of Hebrews*, Heb. 3:3, in loc. (*Works*, 19:548): "His glory as the eternal Son of God was and is personal and natural unto him, even as it is unto the Father; for each person being possessed 'in solidum' of the same nature, each of them being *God by nature*, and the *same God*, they have the same glory."

[44] Owen, *Salus Electorum*, I.vi-viii, II.i-v (*Works*, 10: 179-200, 200-236).

[45] John Calvin, *Institutes of the Christian Religion*, ed. John T. McNeill, trans. Ford Lewis Battles, 2 vols. (Philadelphia: Westminster, 1960), II.15; Heppe, *Reformed Dogmatics*, 452-58. For historical background to the threefold office, see John F. Jansen, *Calvin's Doctrine of the Work of Christ* (London: James Clarke, 1956), 26-38. On Calvin's use of it, see Stephen Edmonson, *Calvin's Christology* (Cambridge: Cambridge University Press, 2004).

[46] Johannes Wollebius, *The Abridgment of Christian Divinitie: So Exactly and Methodically Compiled, That It Leads Us, as It Were, by the Hand to the Reading of the Holy Scriptures, Ordering of Common-Places, Understanding of Controversies, Cleering of Some Cases of Conscience* (London: Printed for T. Mab and A. Coles for John Saywell, 1650), 90-132.

[47] For example, in addition to Wollebius' divisions, Ames inserts three additional chapters covering the satisfaction, death, and application of Christ. Ames, *Marrow*, I.xviii-xxiv. These additions are clearly expansions of Christ's office, humiliation, and exaltation respectively.

Owen adopted the distinction of Christ's threefold office formally in his catechetical and Christological works,[48] but focused solely on the priestly aspect in *The Death of Death*.[49] In accordance with the intratrinitarian order of subsistence, he affirmed the Father's appointment of the Son to the office of Mediator and the Son's concurrence "by a voluntary susception, or willing undertaking of the office imposed on him."[50] Unlike standard Reformed orthodox expositions, he does not unpack the contents of Christ's threefold office following their identification. Instead, he goes on to relate Christ's office as Mediator undertaken in eternity to the movement of his saving work in history. This was done through the employment of yet another threefold distinction: Christ's incarnation, oblation, and intercession. What was presupposed by Owen in relating Christ's office to this further threefold distinction is the connection between eternity and time, a connection that was foundational to his principles of theology.[51] In the immediate context, this presupposition, which relies on the connection between the divine intention and its fulfilment in history, served to prepare the ground for a key argument against the doctrine of general ransom. More will be said about Owen's key argument in the discussion on oblation and intercession below, but in adhering to the flow of his thought, it is necessary first to turn to Owen's treatment of the incarnation.

A cursory reading of *The Death of Death* will show that Owen's treatment of the incarnation is not substantial. Its most elaborate statement is confined to a single paragraph in the fourth chapter of Book I.[52] In no way does this imply an oversight on Owen's part, nor is it an indication of the incarnation's secondary status in his atonement theology. It is simply the case that the critical point of contention against the doctrine of general ransom as expressed by Thomas More did not lie in a defence of the incarnation. More himself affirmed the doctrine as it was formulated in the Church of England's Articles of Religion.[53]

---

[48] Owen, *Two Short Catechisms* (*Works*, 1:463-94, esp. 468, 480-83); idem, *Christologia* (*Works*, 1:3-272).

[49] In *The Death of Death*, the only reference to an aspect other than Christ's priestly work made by Owen is found in the appendix attached to it. There, he responded to the views of Joshua Sprigge who taught that Christ merely revealed God's love without procuring reconciliation with God. Owen repudiated Sprigge's position with twelve brief arguments. Couched rhetorically, the fourth argument queried: "Was not Jesus Christ a priest for his people, in their behalf to deal with God...as well as a prophet, to deal with them in the behalf of God? and whether the acts of his priestly office do not all of them immediately tend towards God for the procuring good things for those in whose behalf he is a priest?" Owen, *Salus Electorum*, Appendix (*Works*, 10:428).

[50] Owen, *Salus Electorum*, I.iv (*Works*, 10:174).

[51] Truman, *Claims of Truth*, 47-101.

[52] Owen, *Salus Electorum*, I.iv (*Works*, 10:174-75).

[53] Articles 6, 20, 2, 15, and 31, are cited in support of his position. More cited the following statement from Article 2, "That of the Word or Son of God, which was made Very Man": "One Christ, *very God* and *very man*, who suffered, was crucified, dead and

It is rather the inseparability of oblation and intercession that needed to be preserved. That this was Owen's perception of the central problem with universal redemption will become clear below. At this point, it is necessary that the significance of Owen's move to relate Christ's office to the incarnation be explicated despite his paucity of treatment and the uncontroversial nature of the doctrine in the context of the treatise.

Owen expressed the incarnation's significance for Christ's salvific work through the language of "means" and "end".[54] With respect to Christ's priestly work of oblation and intercession, the incarnation was, according to Owen, "a common foundation for both the others, being as it were the means in respect of them as the end, and yet in some sort partaking of the nature of a distinct action, with a goodness in itself in reference to the main end proposed to all three..."[55] In applying the means-end language in this way, the incarnation is given a soteriological orientation that echoes the patristic tradition, and indeed Calvin.[56] The end or goal of the incarnation is Christ's work of oblation and intercession for the salvation of the elect.

It needs to be noted that Owen's use of teleological language is flexible with respect to its references. As already noted in passing earlier, such language is also used to refer more broadly to Christ's oblation and intercession as the means of redemption, and the glory of God in the salvation of the elect as their intended end. With respect to the incarnation, Owen employed teleological language for the purpose of clarifying the incarnation's foundational character as it pertains to Christ's priestly acts. In Owen's movement of thought, the soteriological orientation of the incarnation allows him to transit naturally to a consideration of Christ's oblation and intercession.

The theological significance of oblation and intercession is evident from Owen's conception of how Christ's mediatorial work tied in with the whole economy of salvation:

> The means, then, used or ordained by these agents for the end proposed is that whole economy or dispensation carried along to the end, from whence our

---

buryed, to reconcile his Father to us, and to be a sacrifice, (not onely for originall guilt, but also for all actuall sinnes of men)." Parentheses added. He was citing from either the 1563 or 1571 text since the words in parentheses were post 1553 additions. Cf. Gerald Bray, ed., *Documents of the English Reformation* (Cambridge: James Clarke, 1994), 285-86. All five articles expressed, in the words of More, "the Doctrine of the Church of England...Which doctrine, had I not beleeved, I would not so have protested to main[t]aine ..." More, *Universality of God's Free Grace*, A4.

[54] See his definitions in Owen, *Salus Electorum*, I.ii (*Works*, 10:160-61).

[55] Owen, *Salus Electorum*, I.iv (*Works*, 10:174).

[56] One thinks for instance of Athanasius' *On the Incarnation of the Word*, §6-9 (*NPNF2*, 4:39-41), where he argues that the redemption of sinful humanity is dependent upon the incarnation; cf. Calvin, *Institutes*, II.12.

> Saviour Jesus Christ is called a Mediator; which may be, and are usually,... distinguished into two parts: – First, his oblation; secondly, his intercession.[57]

Christ's oblation or offering was not merely confined to his sacrificial death, but also included "his whole humiliation, or state of emptying himself, whether by yielding voluntary obedience unto the law...or by his subjection to the curse of the law."[58] By Christ's intercession, Owen was referring to Christ's heavenly intercession, along with "every act of his exaltation conducing thereunto, from his resurrection to his 'sitting down at the right hand of the Majesty on high, angels, and principalities, and powers, being made subject unto him.'"[59]

In sum, all that is commonly associated with the twofold state of Christ in Reformed orthodoxy was subsumed by Owen under the unifying heads of oblation and intercession.[60] This move is significant for understanding what is of central importance in Owen's atonement theology as well as the way in which he sought to undermine the doctrine of general ransom. In so doing, Christ's priestly office is loaded with a theological significance that is uncommon in Reformed orthodox treatments when appraised from the structural standpoint, for while it is the case that the terms "oblation" and "intercession" are commonly employed by the Reformed orthodox, yet they do not seem to have been accorded formal status in their structuring of the person and work of Christ. Turretin, for instance, divided the priesthood of Christ into two principal parts: the oblation or satisfaction given for us on the cross, and his heavenly intercession.[61] Similarly, Wollebius maintained that Christ's priestly office is "to appear for us before God, with full satisfaction, and to intercede for us: the parts whereof are, Satisfaction and Intercession."[62] However, there is no conscious attempt by both Turretin and Wollebius to integrate the whole course of the life of Christ with these priestly acts in the way Owen did. Since oblation and intercession are acts of Christ which belong exclusively to his priesthood in Reformed orthodox discussions, Owen's employment of them as unifying heads reveals the central importance of Christ's priesthood in his atonement theology.[63]

---

[57] Owen, *Salus Electorum*, I.vi (*Works*, 10:179).
[58] Owen, *Salus Electorum*, I.vi (*Works*, 10:179-80).
[59] Owen, *Salus Electorum*, I.vi (*Works*, 10:180).
[60] On Christ's state of humiliation and exaltation, see Heppe, *Reformed Dogmatics*, 488-509.
[61] Francis Turretin, *Institutes of Elenctic Theology*, ed. James T. Dennison Jr., trans. George Musgrave Giger, 4 vols. (Phillipsburg; New Jersey: P & R Publishing, 1992), XIV.viii.iv-vii, XIV.x.i.
[62] Wollebius, *Abridgment of Christian Divinitie*, 107.
[63] Cf. Wright, *John Owen's Great High Priest*, where he argues the thesis that the high-priesthood of Christ is the principal unifying theme of Owen's theology. This thesis still remains to be shown since Wright fails to relate the doctrine to the main structure of Owen's theology and demonstrate how it is the point on which the whole structure hangs. What he has undoubtedly demonstrated is the major significance of Christ's high-

Owen's use of oblation and intercession as unifying heads reveals what he was intending to establish theologically against universal redemption. It allowed him among other things, to develop a particularistic and actualistic view of the atonement against the threat of a general ransom that merely secured the universal potentiality of salvation.[64] The crux of the matter lies in the inseparability of oblation and intercession. Owen argued that both acts are united by the same subordinate end of the elect's salvation, and the ultimate end of God's praise and glory; that both acts are united by the objects for whom they are exercised, i.e. for whom Christ died, for them does he also intercede; that both acts are united by the nature of their relation since oblation is the foundation of intercession, and intercession is the continuation of oblation, so that what was procured by Christ's oblation is bestowed by virtue of his intercession.[65] Six years prior to the publication of *The Death of Death*, Owen had alluded to their inseparable nature in his earliest publication, *A Display of Arminianism* (1642): "These two acts of his priesthood are not to be separated; it belongs to the same mediator for sin to sacrifice and pray."[66] In *The Death of Death*, Owen filled in the content of that inseparable nature more fully and related the two priestly acts to the life of Christ from his incarnation to his heavenly intercession. On the grounds of the unity between the oblation and intercession of Christ, Owen summed up his case against universal redemption in the following way:

> The sum is, that the oblation and intercession of Jesus Christ are one entire means for the producing of the same effect, ...so that it cannot be affirmed that the death or offering of Christ concerned any one person or thing more, in respect of procuring any good, than his intercession doth for the collating of it: for, ...it is evident that every one for whom Christ died must actually have applied unto him all the good things purchased by his death.[67]

---

priesthood for Owen's theology and not its unifying nature. Wright works with an understanding of Christ's priesthood in the sense of his continual work in heaven, which has an apparently narrower semantic boundary than what this present study is concerned with.

[64] In Owen's own words, he speaks of "the doctrine of particular effectual redemption." *Salus Electorum*, IV.vii (*Works*, 10:410). By "actuality" is meant the procurement of salvation in terms of the rights to salvific benefits and the effecting or actualization of what is procured in the lives of those for whom salvation is procured. Owen understood the atonement to have secured these two inseparable aspects of the right to salvific benefits and its application while allowing that there was a time gap between them from the standpoint of the redeemed subject. "Actual" is preferred over the term "definite" in relation to the atonement for the reason that the latter does not capture the sense of the procurement of rights. See Owen, *Of the Death of Christ, the Price He Paid, and the Purchase He made*, X-XI (*Works*, 10:462-68); cf. the discussion in Chapter 5.

[65] Owen, *Salus Electorum*, I.vi-II.v (*Works*, 10:179-236).

[66] See *Works*, 10:91.

[67] Owen, *Salus Electorum*, I.vi (*Works*, 10:181).

Introduction

From Owen's summary, it is clear that he posits a close connection between the priestly office of Christ and the application of what is achieved through that office. The question that is begging is the theological grounds for asserting that connection. For Owen, the actuality of the atonement is driven theologically by the divine intention: what God intends, he infallibly accomplishes. Thus, he asserts: "if the *oblation* and death of Christ procured and obtained that every good thing should be bestowed upon which is actually conferred by the intervening of his *intercession*, then they have both of them the same aim, and are both means tending to one and the same end."[68] The "same aim" and "same end" of these priestly acts relate directly to the divine intention that guarantees the actual application of the procured blessings.

The relation between divine intentionality and the application of redemption is absolutely fundamental in *The Death of Death* whether Owen was discoursing on matters of theology or practical divinity. There is no room in Owen's soteriology for a view of the atonement that affirms God's universal intention in salvation on the one hand, and the particular application of that divine intention on the other. It is precisely the incongruous affirmation of divine intention and its actual outworking with respect to their objects that, in Owen's mind, poses such insurmountable difficulties for the kind of universal redemption that is espoused by the Arminians, Amyraldians, and Thomas More. In Chapter 4, their atonement theologies will be explored in greater detail to lay bare the theological commitments that underlie their common expression of the identified incongruity. It will suffice for now to note how Owen understood the implications of the perceived problem. The following statements are revealing:

> Now, unless we will blasphemously ascribe want of wisdom, power, perfection, and sufficiency in working unto the agent, or affirm that the death and intercession of Christ were not suitable and proportioned for the attaining the end proposed by it to be effected, we must grant that the end of these is one and the same. Whatsoever the blessed Trinity intended by them, that was effected; and whatsoever we find in the issue ascribed unto them, that by them the blessed Trinity intended.[69]

To affirm both universality and particularity in relation to the divine intention is tantamount to blasphemy for Owen since it implies imperfection in the triune God. Here, the doctrine of the Trinity as the Agent of redemption resurfaces, not with respect to triune agency *ad extra*, but rather its assumed ontological ground. With such a serious charge levelled against universal redemption, it is

---

[68] Owen, *Salus Electorum*, I.vii (*Works*, 10:185).
[69] Owen, *Salus Electorum*, II.i (*Works*, 10:201); cf. idem, *Salus Electorum*, IV.ii (*Works*, 10:327), where Owen appealed to this theological ground in his exegesis of the word "world" in John 3:16. Taking the term to refer to the elect, he opined: "Now if this be understood of any but believers, God fails of his aim and intention, which as yet we dare not grant."

obviously crucial that the relevant doctrinal strands at work in Owen's doctrine of God be adumbrated. However, such detailed treatments will have to wait.[70] Recognition of the necessity to do so is sufficient for the introductory purpose of this chapter.

The third doctrinal locus is a sub-division of Christ's priestly office. It deals with Christ's satisfaction for sin. While Calvin did relate satisfaction for sin to Christ's priestly office,[71] he did not load the word "satisfaction" with the kind of significance that the Reformed orthodox did, although the substance of his treatment of the priestly office and what is involved in Christ's procurement of salvation prepared the way for it.[72] In Reformed orthodox discussions, satisfaction for sin was formally identified as a vital aspect of Christ's priestly office,[73] and in some instances, was a subject that warrants separate or extended treatments in compendiums of Reformed theology.[74]

In *The Death of Death,* the subject is taken up in Book III. Of the sixteen arguments levelled against universal redemption there, the first ten are crystallizations of earlier issues covered in Books I and II, all of which tend towards a defence of the oblation/intercession conjunction. Arguments eleven to fifteen, which constitute chapters five to ten of Book III, explore the significance of five terminologies for the controversy at hand: "redemption", "reconciliation", "satisfaction", "merit", and "dying for us". Of the six chapters that cover arguments eleven to fifteen, three are devoted to "satisfaction", thus revealing its importance for Owen's case against universal redemption.[75]

Owen conceived of the term "satisfaction" as "*a full compensation of the creditor from the debtor.*"[76] It must not be mistaken that by this definition, Owen's understanding of satisfaction is construed in impersonal,

---

[70] For further treatment on the divine intention, see Chapter 2 on the *pactum salutis* and Chapter 6 on Owen's teleology.

[71] Calvin, *Institutes*, II.15.6: "The priestly office belongs to Christ alone because by the sacrifice of his death he blotted out our own guilt and made satisfaction for our sins."

[72] It is not surprising that this is the case since Calvin used the term "satisfaction" in connection with a diversity of atonement themes like God's justice, the appeasement of God's wrath, and Christ's vicarious punishment and obedience. Calvin, *Institutes*, II.15.6, II.16.1-12; cf. Robert A. Peterson Sr., *Calvin and the Atonement* (Ross-shire: Christian Focus Publications, 1999), 130-34.

[73] Perkins, *Golden Chaine*, 41: "His Priesthood, consisteth of two parts. Satisfaction, and intercession."

[74] Ames allocates a chapter to the subject. Ames, *Marrow*, I.xx. Turretin has an extended treatment of it in *Elenctic Theology*, XIV.x-xiv, covering the issues of satisfaction's necessity, truth, perfection, matter, and object. He also has an entire treatise devoted to the subject, entitled, *de Satisfactione Christi cum Indicibus* (1667), published in Geneva, a copy of which Owen owned. See *BO*, Libri Theologici, 147.

[75] Of the three chapters on satisfaction, two (chapters eight and nine) are self-acknowledged digressions from Owen's flow of thought. That these chapters are included in the treatise, their digressive nature notwithstanding, further indicates the subject's importance in the overall scheme and context of Owen's atonement theology.

[76] Owen, *Salus Electorum*, III.vii (*Works*, 10:265).

commercialistic terms. Inherent in the dynamic of satisfaction for Owen is a movement from the impersonal nature of compensation to the personal nature of the incurred debt, a movement "from things *real*...to things *personal*."[77] Personal debts are "injuries and faults; which when a man hath committed, he is liable to punishment."[78] When applied to the atonement, the referents are obvious: "...the *debtor* is man...The *debt* is sin...That which is required in lieu thereof to make satisfaction for it, is *death*...The *obligation* whereby the debtor is tied and bound is the *law*...The *creditor* that requireth this of us is *God*, considered as the party offended, severe Judge, and supreme Lord of all things...That which interveneth to the destruction of the obligation is the *ransom* paid by Christ."[79] Clearly, the dominating metaphor of the atonement is commercial at this point.[80] The prominence of the commercial metaphor was primed by the views of the Dutch jurist, Hugo Grotius (1583-1645), on the nature of sin's payment, whose views Owen went on to address at some length.[81]

However, in the wider context of Owen's thought, his understanding of satisfaction is far more comprehensive. Indeed, it entails all the concepts which he dealt with in arguments eleven to fifteen in Book III of *The Death of Death*. The clearest example of Owen's more comprehensive account of satisfaction is found in *A Brief Declaration and Vindication of the Doctrine of the Trinity* (1669). In this treatise, Owen summed up the concept of satisfaction in nine related points.[82] Points one to three rehearse the Biblical narrative of humanity's fall into sin. Points four and five highlight the necessity of sin's punishment on account of God's justice and holiness, of the veracity of his law, and consequently of humanity's liability to guilt and punishment. Points six to eight pertain to the divine response to the plight of humanity: God, out of his infinite goodness, love, and grace, sent his Son to save sinful humanity by becoming their substitute. In Owen's final point, the Son's work of redemption was explained more fully in terms of the concepts of sacrifice, ransom, sin-bearing, obedience to the law, expiation, substitution, reconciliation, and

---

[77] Owen, *Salus Electorum*, III.vii (*Works*, 10:265).
[78] Owen, *Salus Electorum*, III.vii (*Works*, 10:265).
[79] Owen, *Salus Electorum*, III.vii (*Works*, 10:266).
[80] However, the commercial metaphor is by no means the only one at work. That there is a confluence of metaphors is seen from Owen's conceptualization of the creditor in commercial, judicial, and rectoral terms. Other examples of the use of multiple metaphors abound. Cf. Owen, *Salus Electorum*, III.vii (*Works*, 10:269-70): "It was a full, valuable compensation, made to the justice of God...That God in the whole is the party offended by our sins is by all confessed. It is his law that is broken, his glory that is impaired, his honor that is abased by our sin..."
[81] Owen, *Salus Electorum*, III.vii (*Works*, 10:268-73); see Chapter 5 for more extensive discussion.
[82] Owen, *A Brief Declaration*, Of the Satisfaction of Christ (*Works*, 2:420-24).

atonement. The following protracted statement of Owen's doctrine gives an idea of his comprehensive view of satisfaction:

> For that which we intended hereby [satisfaction] is, *the voluntary obedience unto death, and the passion or suffering, of our Lord Jesus Christ, God and man, whereby and wherein he offered himself, though the eternal Spirit, for a propitiatory sacrifice, that he might fulfil the law, or answer all its universal postulata; and as our sponsor, undertaking our cause, when we were under the sentence of condemnation, underwent the punishment due to us from the justice of God, being transferred on him; whereby having made a perfect and absolute propitiation or atonement for our sins, he procured for us deliverance from death and the curse, and a right unto life everlasting.*[83]

The concept of satisfaction, then, is used by Owen in both a narrow and general sense. Arguments eleven to fifteen in Book III may be understood as dealing with the concept of satisfaction in the general sense. Throughout Owen's treatment of the subject, both the actuality and particularity of the atonement was affirmed as part of the Biblical witness on these matters.

There is no further discernible doctrinal locus of a constructive nature in *The Death of Death* after argument fifteen. Argument sixteen involves discussion on a selected number of Scriptural passages which, in Owen's estimate, are "clearly and distinctly in themselves holding out the truth of what we do affirm."[84] The remaining chapters contained in Book IV are mostly concerned with answering the objections of the universal redemptionists, not least, those of Thomas More. Having delineated Owen's treatment of Christ's satisfaction, the case study of Owen's treatise comes to a close.

Conclusion

The goal of the above study on *The Death of Death* is to map out the contours of Owen's atonement theology within the theological context of Reformed orthodoxy by explicating and analysing his movement of thought in the treatise. This task has the aim of circumscribing the theological scope of the present study. Three doctrinal loci have been identified: the triune God, the mediatorial office of Christ, and the doctrine of satisfaction for sin. The rest of this study is structured around them. Owen does not develop these loci in abstraction from the history of redemption but with a particular focus on the historical movement of Christ's redemptive work summed up in his priestly acts of oblation and intercession. As such, the organization of Owen's atonement theology is not in strict accordance with the loci method employed in, for instance, *A Brief Declaration*, where a similar movement of loci occurs, beginning with the Trinity, followed by Christology, and concluding with the

---

[83] Owen, *A Brief Declaration*, Appendix (*Works*, 2:442).
[84] Owen, *Salus Electorum*, III.xi (*Works*, 10:290).

doctrine of satisfaction.[85] Neither is it strictly in accordance with the redemptive-historical method of organization found in, for instance, *Theologoumena*.[86] Owen's atonement theology is articulated, interestingly, through a confluence of both methods but with the priesthood of Christ as the central soteriological motif. The main proposition of this study is that Owen's conception of Christ's priesthood, in terms of the united acts of oblation and intercession, performed in the twofold state of humiliation and exaltation, lies at the heart of his atonement theology. How this is so in each of the three doctrinal loci will be argued in detail in the following chapters.

Chapter 2 examines Owen's doctrine of God in the light of the work of redemption. It explores his contention that the triune God is the Agent of redemption. Chapters 3 to 5 belong together under the general heading of the "means of redemption." These chapters adumbrate Owen's view of the person and work of Christ. While Chapter 2 is concerned with the trinitarian foundation of Owen's atonement theology, Chapter 3 is concerned with its Christological foundation and focuses on the mediatorial office of Christ in general. Chapter 4 narrows the treatment to the office of Christ's priesthood, which prepares the ground for the discussion of Owen's doctrine of satisfaction in Chapter 5. By way of conclusion, Owen's conception of the end of redemption will be examined in Chapter 6.

---

[85] Owen, *A Brief Declaration* (*Works*, 10:365-454).
[86] Rehnman, *Divine Discourse*, 155-77.

CHAPTER 2

The Agent of Redemption

The doctrine of God is the first doctrinal locus to be considered in Owen's atonement theology as indicated in the case study of *The Death of Death* in the previous chapter. Specifically, the *opera Dei* is the overarching category Owen employs in working out the relationship between the intratrinitarian relations and the work of redemption. This chapter continues the examination of this relationship by giving an account of the internal and external works of God and their connection. The argument of this chapter is that Owen's understanding of the work of redemption is thoroughly trinitarian in the way he expounds its conception in eternity and its historical outworking in the life of Christ. By "trinitarian" is meant Owen's adherence to the theological principles underlying the Western, orthodox doctrine of the Trinity. An account of the *opera Dei* as it was understood in the context of Reformed orthodoxy will first be given, followed by an exposition of the key issues in God's internal and external works as they bear on the work of redemption.

Opera Dei: the Reformed Orthodox Context

A fundamental axiom asserted by Owen is that the work of redemption is the work of the triune God. Such an axiom reveals that in Owen's thought, the doctrine of the Trinity is integral for the doctrine of atonement.[1] The manner in which their connection is given expression is found in Owen's understanding of the *opera Dei*. Reformed orthodox discussions on the subject divide the *opera Dei* into personal and essential works.[2] Personal works are those which are peculiar to each person of the Trinity, while essential works are those which are common to all persons of the Trinity on account of their unity of essence.

---

[1] Owen's trinitarian orthodoxy has been amply demonstrated in the related literature. See Spence, *Incarnation and Inspiration*, 84-103, 124-37; Trueman, *Claims of Truth*, 102-50; idem, *John Owen*, 35-66; Robert Letham, "John Owen's Doctrine of the Trinity and Its Significance for Today," in *"Where Reason Fails...", the Westminster Conference 2006* (Stoke-on-Trent, U.K.: Tentmaker Publications, 2006), 7-22; Kapic, *Communion with God*, 147-205; Kay, *Trinitarian Spirituality*. The concern of this chapter is the application of Owen's doctrine of the Trinity to his work of redemption.

[2] Amandus Polanus, *The Svbstance of Christian Religion Sovndly Set Forth in Two Bookes, by Definitions and Partitions, Framed According to the Rules of a Naturall Method* trans. Thomas Wilcocks (London: Printed for Arn Hatfield for Felix Norton, 1600), 45-47; Johannes Wollebius, *Abridgment of Christian Divinitie*, 26; cf. Muller, *PRRD*, 4:255-74.

Foundational to the content of this personal/essential distinction are the principles that the divine essence is indivisible and common to the entire Godhead, and that the being of God subsists in three distinct persons. These principles are integral to the orthodox understanding of the Trinity.[3]

Fully aware that the work of God in history gives insight into the being of God in eternity, albeit in an imperfect and inadequate way,[4] some among the Reformed orthodox further divided the personal and essential works of God into *ad intra* and *ad extra*,[5] reflecting the respective correspondences with the eternal and historical economies. Others make the basic distinction to be that of God's internal and external works without formally adopting the prior distinction of personal and essential works.[6] God's work *ad intra* pertains to his actions toward himself, and his work *ad extra*, to his actions with respect to the created world. As the triune God is undivided in essence, so it is affirmed, with Augustine, that the *opera trinitatis ad extra sunt indivisa*.[7] However, as God subsists in three distinct persons, it is also affirmed that the external works may

---

[3] Muller, *PRRD*, 4:189-195.

[4] Cf. Wolfgang Musculus, *Common Places of Christian Religion, Gathered by Wolfgangus Musculus for the Vse of Such as Desire the Knovvledge of Godly Truth*, trans. Iohn Man (London: Imprinted by Henry Bynneman, 1578), 18, 19, 20: "For it is best knowen by his workes both that he is, what he is, of what qualitie he is, and how great he is. ... But when he worketh, he declareth the qualitie of his nature in his working: so that hys workes may be most assured testimonies, by which the hartes of the faithful may be persuaded of his goodnesse and will. ... the Godly man may haue some cōsideration of these matters, whereby, though he understande not the causes of al, yet he may partly obserue what is done, and make some difference of them."

[5] Polanus, *Svbstance of Christian Religion*, 47; Wollebius, *Abridgment of Christian Divitie*, 30-31.

[6] Lucas Trelcatius, *A Brief Institvtion of the Common Places of Sacred Divinitie, Wherein the Truth of Every Place Is Proved, and the Sophismes of Bellarmine Are Reprooved*, trans. Iohn Gawen (London: Imprinted by T.P. for Francis Bvrton, 1610), II.i: "The workes of God, of which wee must treate in the first part of Divinity; are of two sortes, *Inward* and *Immanent, Outward* or *Going out*; those are in the very Essence of God by an Internall and Eternall Act: these passe from (or goe out of) God into the Creatures: by an externall or temporall act."

[7] William Bucanus, *Body of Divinity, or Institutions of Christian Religion; Framed out of the Word of God, and the Writings of the Best Divines, Methodically Handled by Way of Question and Ansvver, Fit for All Such as Desire to Know and Practise the Will of God*, trans. Robert Hill (London: Printed for Daniel Pakeman, Abel Roper, and Richard Tomlins, 1659), 13; cf. Augustine, *De Trinitate*, I.v, viii (*NPNF*1, 3:21, 25): "Some persons, however, find a difficulty in this faith…especially when it is said that the Trinity works indivisibly in everything that God works, and yet that a certain voice of the Father spoke, which is not the voice of the Son…"; "Nor let any one, hearing what the apostle says, 'But when he saith all things are put under him…' think the words, that He hath put all things under the Son, to be so understood of the Father, as that He should not think that the Son Himself put all things under Him…For the working of the Father and the Son is indivisible."

be distinctly appropriated.[8] Thus, for instance, the work of creation is peculiarly ascribed to the Father, redemption to the Son, and sanctification to the Spirit, notwithstanding the concurrence of trinitarian operations in these works. Unity of essence and distinction of persons are, again, the underlying principles. It is clear, then, that the concept of *opera Dei* needs to be understood in the light of the orthodox doctrine of the Trinity. In the theological manuals of the Reformed, this is seen in the ordering of doctrinal loci. Discussions on the *opera Dei* come after and build upon the discussion on the being of God.[9]

Another important point made in the literature is that there is a significant connection between the intratrinitarian relations and the external works of the Trinity. The principle that what God does reveals something of his inner life, led to reflections of that connection in the light of the *filioque* dynamic. Just as the Father, being unbegotten is the *fons totius divinitatis* and thus the first in the order of relations, so is he first in the manner or order of external works. The Son, being begotten of the Father is second in the order of operation, and the Spirit, who proceeds from the Father and the Son, is third. In other words, the order of external operations follows the internal order of subsistence. Ames states the point clearly:

> Concerning the order, the manner of working of the Father is from himself, through the Son and Holy Spirit. Therefore, the beginning of things, or creation, is properly attributed to the Father...The manner of the working of the Son is from the Father through the Spirit. Hence the dispensation of things is properly attributed to him, especially redemption and the constitution of all church offices...The manner of working of the Spirit is from the Father and the Son through himself. Hence the consummation of all things is attributed to the Holy Spirit, such as regeneration, Titus 3:5, the bestowal of all spiritual gifts, 1 Cor 12:4, and the perfection of natural things themselves, Gen 1:2.[10]

This *filioque*-based principle of trinitarian operation has a huge impact on Owen's conception of the work of redemption as will become clear below.

---

[8] Ames, *Marrow of Theology*, I.vi.31: "As for the boundary of the action, that aspect in which one person's working or manner of working shines forth most clearly is chiefly attributed to that person."

[9] Musculus, *Common Places*, 1-16; Polanus, *Svbstance of Christian Religion*, 1-57; Wollebius, *Abridgment of Christian Divinitie*, 12-31; William Perkins, *A Golden Chaine, or the Description of Theologie, Containing the Order of the Causes of Saluation and Damnation, According to God's Word* (Cambridge: Iohn Legate, 1597), 9-19.

[10] Ames, *Marrow of Theology*, I.vi.28-30; cf. Heppe, *Reformed Dogmatics*, 118; Willem J. van Asselt, *The Federal Theology of Johannes Cocceius (1603-1669)*, Studies in the History of Christian Thought (Leiden / Boston / Koln: Brill, 2001), 183ff.

Owen and the *Opera Dei*

Owen follows the trinitarian principles and general divisions of the *opera Dei* surveyed above. In *Two Short Catechisms* (1645), discussions on the Trinity are followed immediately by adumbrations on the works of God.[11] He subdivides the *opera Dei* into internal and external works. God's internal work respects "his counsel, decrees, and purposes towards his creatures", including the decree of election and reprobation; God's external work is concerned with "his works over and about them", consisting of his works of creation and providence, performed "to the praise of his own glory."[12] This *ad intra/extra* distinction is not confined to the catechetical genre.

In an early chapter of Owen's *Pneumatologia* (1674) in which he sought to demonstrate the Spirit's deity and personality, five key principles were asserted on which the doctrine of the Spirit depends. First, all true religion and religious worship are founded upon the nature and being of God; second, the governing rule for the worship of God is his self-revelation; third, God has revealed himself as *"three in one"* and is therefore to be worshiped as "three distinct persons, subsisting in the same infinitely holy, one, undivided essence"; fourth, *"these persons are so distinct in their peculiar subsistence that distinct actings and operations are ascribed unto them"*; fifth, it thus follows that the Holy Spirit *"is in himself a distinct, living, powerful, intelligent, divine person."*[13] These principles were stated in increasing levels of specificity as to the nature of the Godhead, making clear that the ascription of distinct operations to the persons of the Godhead is due to the fact that God subsists in three persons. The *opera Dei* is thus dependent upon the tri-unity of God. Here, the ordering of principles corresponds to the ordering of doctrinal loci in his catechisms.

Further elaboration of the *opera Dei* is found in Owen's treatment of the fourth principle where he distinguishes the divine operations or works into two sorts: *ad intra* and *ad extra*. God's work *ad intra* refers to "those internal acts in one person whereof another person is the object", acts which are "natural and necessary, inseparable from the being and existence of God."[14] Owen referred to passages such as John 3:35, 5:20, 6:46, Matthew 11:27, Proverbs 8:22-31, as instances of the internal operations of divine knowledge and love between the Father and the Son. The Spirit acts towards the Father and Son as their "mutual love", "knowing them as he is known, and 'searching the deep things of God'."[15] The infinite blessedness of God consists in such *ad intra* works of mutuality.

---

[11] *Works*, 1:467, 472-475. The *Lesser Catechism* and *Greater Catechism* will subsequently be cited as LC and GC respectively.
[12] Owen, *Two Short Catechisms*, GC, IV-VI (*Works*, 1:473-76).
[13] Owen, *Pneumatologia*, I.iii (*Works*, 3:64-68).
[14] Owen, *Pneumatologia*, I.iii (*Works*, 3:66-67).
[15] Owen, *Pneumatologia*, I.iii (*Works*, 3:67).

God's work *ad extra* is divided by Owen into the acts of the persons of the Trinity "towards another", and those that are "towards the creatures."[16] As to the former, Owen was careful to qualify that the person who is the object of an external act is to be considered "with respect unto some peculiar dispensation and condescension" and not absolutely as divine.[17] This is not to deny the deity of any person of the Godhead, but simply to recognize the accommodated mode of divine operation within the historical economy. Although, for Owen, both *ad intra* and *ad extra* works consist of reciprocal acts among persons of the Trinity, nevertheless, the difference between the exercise of these acts in eternity and their exercise in time is not eradicated. Thus, the Father's act of giving, sending, and commanding of the Son is not with respect to the Son in his deity, but "as he had condescended to take our nature upon him, and to be the mediator between God and man."[18] Likewise, the act of the Father and the Son in sending the Spirit respects the Spirit "as he condescends in an especial manner to the office of being the sanctifier and comforter of the church."[19]

Besides distinguishing between the internal and external works of God, Owen also gave due consideration to their vital connection. This connection was presented in two ways. First, the unity of essence underlying Owen's discussion of God's internal work was brought to bear upon the external work with the assertion of the undivided nature of the trinitarian operations *ad extra*. Echoing Athanasius, Basil, and Ambrose, Owen insisted that each person of the Trinity is the author of every external work of God "because each person is God, and the divine nature is the same undivided principle of all divine operations; and this arises from the unity of the persons in the same essence."[20] Second, the internal distinctions, relations, and order of the persons in the Godhead were understood as regulating the external work. The Trinity works externally according to their internal order of subsistence, with the result that external works may be attributed distinctly to the persons of the Father, the Son, and the Holy Spirit. Thus, "as unto the Father are assigned *opera naturae*, the works of nature, or the old creation; to the Son, *opera gratiae procuratae*, all divine operations that belong unto the recovery of mankind by grace; and unto the Spirit, *opera gratiae applicatae*, the works of God whereby grace is made effectual unto us."[21]

From Owen's treatment of the *opera Dei*, it is clear that the orthodox doctrine of the Trinity played a crucial role in clarifying the manner in which the triune God works. Unity of triune operations is consistently grounded in the one divine essence while the distinct appropriation of divine operations to

---

[16] Owen, *Pneumatologia*, I.iii (*Works*, 3:67).
[17] Owen, *Pneumatologia*, I.iii (*Works*, 3:67).
[18] Owen, *Pneumatologia*, I.iii (*Works*, 3:67).
[19] Owen, *Pneumatologia*, I.iii (*Works*, 3:67).
[20] Owen, *Pneumatologia*, I.iv (*Works*, 3:93).
[21] Owen, *Pneumatologia*, I.iv (*Works*, 3:93).

particular persons in the Godhead is consistently grounded in the distinction of persons. This trinitarian framework is foundational to the whole of Owen's theology and surfaces early in his theological career in his treatise on the atonement. In *The Death of Death* (1647), Christ's work of redemption receives similar trinitarian grounding. Owen identified the chief agent of redemption as "the whole blessed Trinity" and immediately qualified the manner of divine operation in terms of the principles integral to his understanding of the *opera Dei*.

> The agent in, and chief author of, this great work of our redemption is the whole blessed Trinity; for all the works which outwardly are of the Deity are undivided and belong equally to each person, their distinct manner of subsistence and order being observed. ... In the several persons of the holy Trinity, the joint author of the whole work, the Scripture proposeth distinct and sundry acts or operations peculiarly assigned unto them.[22]

These axiomatic statements are introduced at the start of *The Death of Death* and functioned in a paradigmatic way for Owen's subsequent exposition of his atonement theology. For instance, the treatment that immediately follows these statements is divided according to the persons of the Godhead over the span of three chapters.[23] Although Owen was to allocate far more space to the mediatorial work of Christ relative to his exposition of trinitarian operations, nevertheless, what he went on to say of Christ's work rests upon these trinitarian moorings and often contains explicit references to what had already been said in the opening chapters of the treatise. In view of the vital importance of the *opera trinitatis* for understanding the work of redemption but the merely general nature of the *opera Dei* explicated above, the rest of this chapter will be concerned with giving an account of the significant elements in Owen's atonement theology which are located within the framework of the *opera Dei*.

The Internal Work of God in Redemption

The Divine Decrees and Counsels

Owen relates the internal work of God very closely to the divine intention. In general, God's works are "acts or doings of his power, whereby he createth, sustaineth, and governeth all things."[24] When the *ad intra* category is employed to clarify the concept of *opera Dei*, he narrows the reference to creatures and the divine intention for them. God's internal work has to do with God's "counsel, decrees, and purposes, towards his creatures."[25] The divine decrees and counsels, while intimately related, are however, not entirely synonymous. Their slightly different but complementary content expresses two sides of

---

[22] Owen, *Salus Electorum*, I.iii (*Works*, 10:163).
[23] Owen, *Salus Electorum*, I.iii-v (*Works*, 10:163-79).
[24] Owen, *Two Short Catechisms*, LC (*Works*, 1:467).
[25] Owen, *Two Short Catechisms*, GC, IV, Q.1 (*Works*, 1:473).

God's internal work espoused by Owen, following the Reformed distinction of the essential and the personal works of God.

God's decrees are defined by Owen as the "eternal, unchangeable purposes of his will, concerning the being and well-being of his creatures."[26] Divine decrees are expressed in terms of the attributes which are common to the divine persons, such as those of eternity and immutability. God's decrees, being "conformable to his nature and essence, do require eternity and immutability as their inseparable properties."[27] All the decrees of God, Owen reasoned, "as they are internal, so they are eternal acts of his will; and therefore unchangeable and irrevocable."[28] The accent, then, of the divine decrees is upon that which is common and essential to the Godhead. God's decrees of election and reprobation fall into this category of the divine intention.[29] Among the hosts of distinctions on the divine will available to Owen from medieval and Protestant theology, the distinction between the *voluntas arcana Dei* and the *voluntas revelata Dei* was the most significant to him.[30] Owen defined God's secret will as his "eternal, unchangeable purpose concerning all things which he hath made, to be brought by certain means to their appointed ends."[31] However, God's revealed will "containeth not his purpose and decree but our duty, – not what he will do according to his good pleasure, but what we should do if we will please him."[32] Predestination and reprobation belong to the *voluntas arcana*, not the *voluntas revelata*, and are therefore immutable acts of the divine will.

Owen's concept of the divine counsel, on the other hand, highlights the reciprocal relations among the persons of the Trinity. It accords with his understanding of God's internal work as involving "those internal acts in one person whereof another person is the object."[33] Whereas the reciprocal acts in the inner life of the Trinity pertain to acts of love and knowledge between the Father and the Son by the Spirit, the reciprocity of acts in the divine counsel pertains to the good of creatures in general, and of God's love for the church or elect in particular.[34] The divine intention for Owen may, therefore, be considered from two standpoints: that which accents the unity of the internal acts – the divine decrees – and that which accents the distinct nature of the acts peculiar to each person – the divine counsel. These are complementary standpoints that parallel the essence/person distinction in Owen's trinitarian

---

[26] Owen, *Two Short Catechisms*, GC, IV, Q.2 (*Works*, 1:473).
[27] Owen, *A Display of Arminianism*, II (*Works*, 10:19).
[28] Owen, *A Display of Arminianism*, II (*Works*, 10:14).
[29] Owen, *Two Short Catechisms*, GC, IV, Q.4 – Q.7 (*Works*, 1:473-74).
[30] It corresponds to the medieval distinction of the *voluntas beneplaciti* and the *voluntas signi*. See Muller, *DLGTT*, 330-34; idem, *PRRD*, 3:456-59.
[31] Owen, *A Display of Arminianism*, V (*Works*, 10:45).
[32] Owen, *A Display of Arminianism*, V (*Works*, 10:45).
[33] Owen, *Pneumatologia*, I.iii (*Works*, 3:66).
[34] Owen, *Christologia*, IV (*Works*, 1:59-60).

framework. The significance of this analysis will become clear in our treatment of the *pactum salutis* below.

Owen's considerations of the eternal counsels are strongly soteriological in orientation. They are consistently expressed in light of the understanding that the insuperable distance between eternity and time is only bridged in and by the person of Christ. As such, there is a Christological focus to his construal of the divine counsels and their execution in time. The person of Christ, he asserts, "is the foundation of all the counsels of God, as unto his own eternal glory in the vocation, sanctification and salvation of the church."[35] What this means is that the Son is the one appointed to accomplish these counsels in time and also the one without whom the constitution of divine counsels would be impossible. In this sense, all the divine counsels are said to be "laid in and with him."[36] God delights in his counsels for they are "acts of his infinite wisdom", and Christ as the "wisdom of God" (1 Cor 1:24) is "he in whom the counsels of his wisdom are to be fulfilled."[37] The Son was "fore-ordained before the foundation of the world" to be a Saviour and deliverer "by whom all the counsels of God were to be accomplished; and this by his own will, and concurrence in counsel with the Father."[38] Thus, describing the counsels as being *laid in Christ* has reference to Christ as the object of the divine election as well as the means of its execution. However, Christ is also the subject of election in that the electing decision was *laid with Christ*: that is, determined in counsel with Christ. This is evident from Owen's treatment of the *opera Dei ad intra*. The divine counsels are part of the internal work of God which involves reciprocal acts of the Trinity. The counsels between the Father and the Son are constituted by equals who act freely and voluntarily towards each other. As such, the Son is necessarily the subject of election as well as its object.[39]

In addition to the Father and the Son, the Spirit is the third integral party in the constitution and execution of the eternal counsels. Following the *filioque* dynamic of the inner trinitarian life of God, the Father and the Son act toward each other by the Spirit in the constitution of divine counsels. Adhering to the same dynamic in the execution of the divine counsels, the Spirit's operation is

---

[35] Owen, *Christologia*, IV (*Works*, 1:54).
[36] Owen, *Christologia*, IV (*Works*, 1:58).
[37] Owen, *Christologia*, IV (*Works*, 1:58).
[38] Owen, *Christologia*, IV (*Works*, 1:56); idem, *The Doctrine of Justification*, VIII (*Works*, 5:179-80): "The Lord Christ, as unto the nature which he was to assume, was hereon *predestinated* unto grace and glory...All the grace and glory of the human nature of Christ was an effect of free *divine*-preordination."
[39] Although not appealing to the *opera Dei* directly, McDonald's recent work on Owen makes the same point in the light of Owen's Western *filioque*-shaped trinitarianism. She employs Barth's idiom of Christ as the subject and object of election as an appropriate description of Owen's view of election. Suzanne McDonald, "Re-Imaging Election: The Holy Spirit and the Dynamic of Election to Representation" (Ph.D. dissertation, St Andrews University, Scotland, 2006), 20-21, esp. 21n18.

"not an original but perfecting work."[40] The Spirit is the "immediate...efficient cause of all external divine operations",[41] so that in every work of God, "the *concluding, completing, perfecting acts* are ascribed to the Holy Ghost..."[42] Just as the Spirit's work is dependent upon the Father and the Son as its originating sources, the constitution and execution of the counsels between the Father and the Son is dependent upon the Spirit as their perfecting cause. That the Spirit is the "immediate...efficient cause" of God's external works – that is, the Spirit acts directly in the created order – and not the Father or the Son, heightens the crucial role of the Spirit in the economy of salvation. Apart from the Spirit, the divine counsels will not come to fruition in time. The Spirit, then, in Owen's view of the divine counsels, is aptly described by one scholar as "the guarantor of the unity of God's determination *ad intra* and *ad extra* in the electing decree."[43]

The Eternal Compact: General Observations

Giving further clarity to the nature of the divine counsels between the Father and the Son is the covenant of redemption. It is a concept that specifies the form of these counsels to be that of a covenant. Although the concept is extremely significant for Owen and explained in great detail in his writings, he does not use terms such as *foedus redemptionis* or *pactum salutis* to express the idea of a covenant in eternity. Rather, he speaks of "the covenant of the Mediator or Redeemer", and more frequently, the "compact", "covenant", "convention", "agreement", "eternal transactions" and "eternal compact" between the Father and the Son.[44] For Owen, the means and end of redemption find their eternal ground in it; the mediatorial value of Christ's active and passive obedience, the persons to be redeemed and the historical particularities

---

[40] Owen, *Pneumatologia* (*Works*, 3:189).
[41] Owen, *Pneumatologia* (*Works*, 3:161).
[42] Owen, *Pneumatologia* (*Works*, 3:94); cf. William Perkins, *An Abridgement of the Whole Body of Divinity Extracted from the Learned Works of That Ever-Famous, and Reverend Divine, Mr. William Perkins* (London: Printed by W. B. for Will. Hope, 1654), 14: "The Holy Ghosts proper manner of working is to finish an action, Effecting it as from the Father and the Son."
[43] McDonald, "Re-imaging Election", 23.
[44] Owen, *Exposition of Hebrews*, Exercitations IV.xxviii.1 (*Works*, 18:78); idem, *Salus Electorum*, I.iii (*Works*, 10:168); idem, *The Doctrine of the Saints' Perseverance*, VII (11:299); idem, *Vindicae Evangelicae*, XXVII (*Works*, 12:496); idem, *Of Communion with God*, VI (*Works*, 2:155); idem, *Christologia*, IV, VII (*Works*, 1:55, 88). Cf. the important statement of the doctrine in *A Declaration of the Faith and Order, Owned and Practised in the Congregational Churches in England: Agreed Upon and Consented Unto by Their Elders and Messengers in Their Meeting at the Savoy, October 12 1658* (London: Printed by J. P., 1659), VIII.1, which Owen played a key role in formulating: "It pleased God, in his eternal purpose, to choose and ordain the Lord Jesus, his only begotten Son, *according to a covenant made between them both*, to be the Mediator between God and Man; ..." Emphasis added. It will subsequently be cited as *Savoy Declaration*.

of their actual salvation are all contracted in this eternal covenant. Indeed, the covenant of redemption stands in relation to Owen's atonement theology as the foundation is to a building. Apart from it, the entire edifice of his atonement theology collapses. It is, therefore, of vital importance that this subject be given extended consideration, to which the following discussion turns.

The origin of the *pactum salutis* is tied up with the development of federal theology within the Reformed tradition. Federal theologians distinguished between the antelapsarian covenant of works between God and humanity in Adam, and the postlapsarian covenant of grace between God and the elect in Christ within the *ordo temporum*.[45] Alongside this two-covenant scheme is the development of a pretemporal covenant between the Father and the Son on which the covenant of grace is grounded.[46] Herman Witsius (1636-1708), writing in the period of high orthodoxy, was cognizant of the traditional status of this eternal *pactum*. He lists Arminius, Ames, Gomarus, Essenius, and Owen, as examples of those who taught the doctrine while acknowledging that few ancient writers dealt with it explicitly.[47] Bavinck provides a helpful account of the history of the doctrine, tracing its origin to Caspar Olevianus (1536-1587), a source that predates Arminius.[48] Muller finds still earlier "hints of the concept" in Luther's 1519 Lectures on Galatians, and points to studies that identified antecedents of the doctrine in Oecolampadius, Budaeus, Calvin, and the marginal note of the Geneva Bible to Hebrews 9:15.[49]

---

[45] David A. Weir, *The Origins of the Federal Theology in Sixteenth-Century Reformation Thought* (Oxford: Clarendon Press, 1990); Heppe, *Reformed Dogmatics*, 371-409. This two-covenant scheme eventually gained confessional status. See for instance, *The Humble Advice of the Assembly of Divines, Now by Authority of Parliament Sitting at Westminster, Concerning a Confession of Faith, with the Quotations and Texts of Scripture Annexed, Presented by Them Lately to Both Houses of Parliament* (London: Printed for the Company of Stationers; Reprinted at Edinburgh by Evan Tyler, 1647), VII, subsequently cited as *Westminster Confession*; cf. *Savoy Declaration*, VII.

[46] Carol A. Williams, "The Decree of Redemption Is in Effect a Covenant: David Dickson and the Covenant of Redemption" (Ph.D. dissertation, Calvin Theological College, 2005), 23-28; Heppe, *Reformed Dogmatics*, 374-90.

[47] Herman Witsius, *The Economy of the Covenants between God and Man Comprehending a Complete Body of Divinity*, 2 vols. (Kingsburg, CA: den Dulk Christian Foundation, 1990), 1:176-77. This work was first published in Latin in 1677 as *De Oeconomia foederum Dei cum Hominibus*. Cf. J. Mark Beach, "The Doctrine of the *Pactum Salutis* in the Covenant Thought of Herman Witsius," *MAJT* 13 (2002), 101-42.

[48] Herman Bavinck, *Reformed Dogmatics: Sin and Salvation in Christ*, ed. John Bolt, trans. John Vriend, vol. 3 (Grand Rapids: Baker, 2006), 213; cf. Lyle D. Bierma, *German Calvinism in the Confessional Age: The Covenant Theology of Caspar Olevianus* (Grand Rapids: Baker, 1996), 107-12; R. Scott Clark, *Caspar Olevian and the Substance of the Covenant: The Double Benefit of Christ* (Edinburgh: Rutherford House, 2005), 177-80.

[49] Richard A. Muller, "Toward the *Pactum Salutis*: Locating the Origins of a Concept," *MAJT* 18 (2007), 12.

On the specific use of the covenant of redemption as a technical term, recent studies suggest that David Dickson (1583-1662) was the first to have employed it formally.[50] In the course of Dickson's speech against Arminianism, delivered before the General Assembly of the Kirk on 3rd December 1638, he identified the "maine errour" of the Arminians as "not knowing the Scriptures, and the power of God in the matter of the Covenant of redemption betwixt God and Christ."[51] Since the covenanting parties were specified as God and Christ, Dickson was clearly not employing the covenant of redemption as a synonym for the covenant of grace. Nor was it a synecdoche that summed up Christ's salvific work in redemptive history. There was no ambiguity in Dickson's use of the term. He clearly distinguished it from the covenant of grace or salvation with respect to the covenanting subjects, gave clear indication of its pretemporal nature, demonstrated that it was grounded in such texts as Isaiah 52 and John 6, and urged the Assembly to study the concept more thoroughly since "the whole Byble takes the denomination from this Covenant..."[52] Dickson suggested that the Arminians themselves referred to it, possibly alluding to Arminius' oration on the priesthood of Christ.[53] Had the Arminians adhered to it, he opined, "they might sein all their matter in the midst."[54] In the context of Dickson's speech, not only was the covenant of redemption introduced with clearly defined features, it was also understood to be a decisive theological concept that garrisoned the orthodox position against the Arminian onslaught.

Although Owen's earliest publication, *A Display of Arminianism* (1642), was written with the aim of addressing the fundamental tenets of Arminian theology, it contained no explicit mention of his preferred terms for the *pactum salutis* and of it being imbued with the kind of theological significance that was

---

[50] Muller, "Toward the *Pactum Salutis*", 17; Trueman, *John Owen*, 81. For development of the concept in Dickson, see Williams, "The Decree of Redemption".

[51] Alexander Peterkin, ed., *Records of the Kirk of Scotland, Containing the Acts and Proceedings of the General Assemblies, from the Year 1638 Downwards, as Authenticated by the Clerks of Assembly; with Notes and Historical Illustrations* (Edinburgh: John Sutherland, 1838), I, 158, col. 1. The whole speech is found in pages 156-59. See also, David Dickson, *Therapeutica Sacra, Shewing Briefly the Method of Healing the Diseases of the Conscience, Concerning Regeneration* (Edinburgh: Printed by Evan Tyler, 1664), 22-71.

[52] Peterkin, *Records of the Kirk*, I, 158-159, cit. 159, col.1.

[53] Peterkin, *Records of the Kirk*, I, 158, col.1; cf. Rutherford and Witsius, both of whom referred to Arminius' oration in relation to the *pactum salutis*. Samuel Rutherford, *The Covenant of Life Opened or, a Treatise of the Covenant of Grace* (Edinburgh: Printed for Andro Anderson for Robert Broun, 1654), II, 327; Witsius, *The Economy of the Covenants*, 1:176. Arminius' oration was delivered in 1603 on the occasion of his receiving the degree of Doctor of Divinity. See James Arminius, *The Works of James Arminius*, trans. James Nichols and W.R. Bagnall, 3 vols., London ed. (Grand Rapids: Baker, 1986), 1:8-40.

[54] Peterkin, *Records of the Kirk*, I, 158, col.1.

evident in Dickson's speech against the same opponent. Three years later, however, the doctrine, in its Father/Son binitarian form, was explicitly mentioned in Owen's *Greater Catechism* in the context of his discussion of Christ's priestly office.[55] In answer to the catechetical question of the means by which Christ undertook the office of eternal priest, Owen gave the following answer: "By the decree, ordination, and will of God the Father, whereunto he yielded voluntary obedience; so that concerning this there was a compact and covenant between them."[56] In Owen's answer, Christ's work of mediation is rooted in the covenant of redemption as was the case with Dickson.

The explicit relation made between the work of Christ as priest and the covenant of redemption was to take on greater prominence in Owen's subsequent writings. By 1647, the *pactum salutis* had become a vital part of Owen's atonement theology with the publication of *The Death of Death*. In this treatise, the doctrine served both to clarify the agency of the Father in sending the Son, and to anchor the mediatorial work of Christ in promises made with him by the Father in eternity.[57] The Spirit was not explicitly mentioned as a third covenanting party, but in accord with the *filioque* dynamic, was nevertheless integral to the actual outworking of the Son's covenanted work as Mediator. The Son's incarnation, mediatorial sufferings, and resurrection were all made possible and actual by the work of the Spirit.[58] Following Owen's discussion of the *pactum salutis* in the treatise, he gave an extended exposition of Christ's work as priest. Focus was placed on establishing the unity of his priestly work of oblation and intercession against the Arminian and Saumurian versions of universal redemption.[59] In unpacking the historical development of what was covenanted in eternity primarily in terms of Christ's priesthood, Owen was fleshing out in greater detail the connection made earlier in his catechism.

This connection between the covenant of redemption and Christ's priesthood was sustained along with significant elaborations in two subsequent writings: *Vindicae Evangelicae* and *Exercitations Concerning the Priesthood of Christ*,

---

[55] According to Muller, the full formulation of the doctrine occurred roughly in the years 1638 to 1645 in the writings of such Reformed orthodox theologians as Dickson, Peter Bulkeley, and Cloppenburg. Muller, "Toward the Pactum Salutis", 16-22, 64. It is plausible, on the basis of Muller's dating, that the reason the concept was only in use from 1645 in the writings of Owen and not from 1642 is that it only gained currency after its full formulation. Trueman observes that "it is not until the mid-1640s that the terminology of the covenant of redemption/*pactum salutis* starts to gain common currency both in Britain and on the continent." Trueman, *John Owen*, 82. See also Williams' survey of the concept in English writers from 1638 to 1650, in "The Decree of Redemption", 96-110.
[56] Owen, *Two Short Catechisms*, GC, XII, Q.1 (*Works*, 1:481).
[57] Owen, *Salus Electorum*, I.iii (*Works*, 10:168-71).
[58] Owen, *Salus Electorum*, I.v (*Works*, 10:178-79).
[59] Owen, *Salus Electorum*, I.vi-viii, II.iv-v (*Works*, 10:179-200, 222-36).

published in 1655 and 1674 respectively.⁶⁰ In the former, Owen argued that the *pactum salutis* is the ground of the penal and substitutionary nature of Christ's death, in response to Socinian denials of both. In addition, he supplied exegetical and theological arguments for construing the eternal transactions between the Father and Son as federal in nature. These arguments were repeated and substantiated more fully in the latter, which not only had Socinianism in view but also the exegesis of the Jewish rabbis. Contextually, then, Owen's conception of the *pactum salutis* was developed largely in the light of polemical concerns, beginning with Arminianism, and subsequently Socinianism and Judaism. Despite the varying contexts in which the *pactum salutis* was expressed, Owen was remarkably consistent in maintaining its relation with the priestly work of Christ.⁶¹ This indicates the theological and polemical importance of Christ's priesthood for Owen in his construal of God's eternal counsels concerning the work of redemption.

The Eternal Compact: Exegetical and Theological Considerations
Owen's formulation of the covenant of redemption is obtained from a synthesis of exegetical and dogmatic concerns. Two general forms of exegetical treatment are evident in his writings on the subject. The first has to do with his method of textual collation in support of the *pactum salutis*. In his *Greater Catechism*, three groups of texts are collated with respect to the eternal *pactum*, each tied to a particular phrase in his statement of the doctrine.⁶² The third group of texts, gathered in support of the phrase, "concerning this [Christ's priesthood] there was a compact and covenant between them", includes the following passages: Psalm 2:7-8; Isaiah 53:8, 10-12; Philippians 2:7, 9; Hebrews 12:2; John 17:2, 4.⁶³ The listed texts from Psalm 2 and Isaiah 53 contain explicit references to the divine decree and the divine will, but in none of the five passages does the term covenant or compact appear. This suggests that for Owen, exegetical support for the *pactum salutis* does not necessarily hang upon texts which contain explicit reference to the term covenant. Indeed, as he explained elsewhere,

> The will of the Father appointing and designing the Son to be the head, husband, deliverer, and redeemer of his elect, his church, his people, whom he did foreknow, with the will of the Son voluntarily, freely undertaking that work and

---

⁶⁰ Owen, *Vindicae Evangelicae*, XXVII (*Works*, 12:496-508); idem, *Exposition of Hebrews*, Exercitations IV.xxvii-xxviii (*Works*, 18:42-97).
⁶¹ Grounding Christ's priestly mediation on the *pactum salutis* has important implications for Owen's understanding of the necessity of Christ's priesthood. See Chapter 6.
⁶² Owen, *Two Short Catechisms*, GC, XII, Q.1 (*Works*, 1:481).
⁶³ Owen, *Two Short Catechisms*, GC, XII, Q.1 (*Works*, 1:481).

The Agent of Redemption

all that was required thereunto, is that compact (for in that form it is proposed in the Scripture) that we treat of.[64]

The qualification in parenthesis is a vital piece of information as to the rationale for the selection of textual support. If it is granted that Owen was consistent with his own qualification, then the five passages listed in his catechism would have been selected because they express the form of the covenant. The validity of such an analysis is corroborated by evidence from his detailed explanation of the covenantal form.

In *Vindicae Evangelicae*, Owen identified five aspects to the form of the covenant, all of which constitute and are necessary for the establishment of the *pactum salutis*.[65] The first aspect is his observation that the sort of covenant to which he referred involves at least two persons entering voluntarily into agreement concerning some particular design and accomplishment of a common end. This observation is applicable to the relationship between the Father and the Son since Scripture presents them "as distinct persons agreeing together in counsel for the accomplishment of the common end, — the glory of God and the salvation of the elect."[66] Listed in support of this point are Hebrews 2:9-10, 12:2; Zechariah 6:13, 13:7, Isaiah 9:6, Psalm 55:14, and Proverbs 8:22-31.

The second aspect involves one party proposing certain conditions to be fulfilled, and the other party voluntarily agreeing to fulfil them. For Owen, this aspect which concerns the covenanted conditions is found in texts that speak of what the Son is not to do in his redemptive work, as well as in texts that make positive statements of what he is to do. Negatively, the Son is not to offer up sacrifices "that had been appointed to make atonement 'suo more,' and to typify out what was by him really to be performed", or to obtain redemption by way of silver and gold, as attested in Hebrews 10:4, 5, 8, Micah 6:6-7, and 1 Peter 1:18.[67] Positively, the Son is to assume human nature, yield obedience as a servant in that nature, and suffer what according to divine justice was due to those for whom he was to obtain redemption. Owen collated three groups of texts for these three positively stated points: (a) Hebrews 2:16, 10:5, 9, Philippians 2:6-7, Galatians 4:4, Romans 8:3; (b) Isaiah 42:1, 49:5, Philippians 2:7, John 14:28, Job 33:23-24; (c) Isaiah 53:10.

In the third aspect, the party who proposes the conditions is to make promises of support and encouragement to the other who undertakes to fulfil them. Here, Owen divides the Scriptural texts into two sorts: those that contain promises for the Son himself, made out by the Father to him — such as promises of the Father's presence and assistance — and those that contain

---

[64] Owen, *Vindicae Evangelicae*, XXVII (*Works*, 12:497).
[65] Owen, *Vindicae Evangelicae*, XXVII (*Works*, 12:498-507).
[66] Owen, *Vindicae Evangelicae*, XXVII (*Works*, 12:500).
[67] Owen, *Vindicae Evangelicae*, XXVII (*Works*, 12:501).

promises with respect to the accomplishment and success of the Son's work.[68] Texts for the former include Isaiah 42:4, 6, 50:5-9, Psalms 16:10, 89:27-28, Hebrews 5:7, while texts for the latter include Isaiah 42:1-4, 53:10-11, Psalm 22:30-31, Hebrews 7:21, 28, 12:2.

In the fourth aspect, the party who receives the promises accepts the conditions proposed and voluntarily undertakes the work. In accepting and freely undertaking the work of redemption, the Son "made himself surety of the covenant, and so was to pay what he never took", voluntarily "engaged himself into this *sponsion*; but when he had so done, he was legally subject to all that attended it,— when he had put his name into the obligation, he became responsible for the whole debt."[69] Psalm 40:7-8, 16:2, Isaiah 50:5, and Philippians 2:6-8 were the supporting texts.

In the fifth and final aspect, the party who has fulfilled the conditions demands or lays claim to the promises made to him, and the party who promised approves and accepts the performance of the other, thus bringing about the intended end of both parties. In order to demonstrate that this is true of the relationship between the Father and the Son, Owen collated three groups of texts: (a) those that point to the acceptance of the Son's work by the Father: Isaiah 49:5-6, 8-9, Psalm 2:7-8, Acts 13:33, Romans 1:4; (b) those that refer to Christ's earthly and heavenly intercession: John 17:1, 4-6, 9, 12-16, Hebrews 7:25, 9:24; (c) those that indicate the accomplishment of the end of redemption: Daniel 9:24, and Job 33:24.[70]

Apart from Philippians 2:9 and John 17:2, all the other texts listed in support of the *pactum salutis* in Owen's catechism were included in his exposition of the form of the covenant. Since the aim of textual collation is not to obtain an exhaustive but representative list of texts, the absence of these passages should not be taken to undermine significantly Owen's principle for textual selection on the basis of the form of the covenant. Furthermore, Owen's use of the two texts in question on other occasions confirms his stated reason for their inclusion in his catechism. Philippians 2:9, for instance, is a supporting text for the "actual inauguration or solemn admission" of Christ into his office as Mediator, and this within the context of the Father's "authoritative imposition of the office of the Mediator, which Christ closed withal by his voluntary susception of it, willingly undergoing the office…"[71] The context makes it clear that the covenantal form is in view. This is also true for John 17:2, having been cited by Owen in support of the "end to which they [the elect] are to be brought", within the larger context of the "proper counsel and intention of God

---

[68] Owen, *Vindicae Evangelicae*, XXVII (*Works*, 12:503-505).
[69] Owen, *Vindicae Evangelicae*, XXVII (*Works*, 12:505).
[70] Owen, *Vindicae Evangelicae*, XXVII (*Works*, 12:505-507).
[71] Owen, *Salus Electorum*, I.iii (*Works*, 10:164-66).

in sending his Son into the world to die", or the end of the covenant between the Father and the Son.[72]

The second form of exegetical treatment has to do with linguistic analyses of terms associated with the concept of the eternal compact. Owen's argument for the federal nature of the transactions between the Father and the Son was not established on the basis of the terms *foedus* in Latin or *suntheke* in Greek, but *berith* in Hebrew and *diatheke* in Greek.[73] This range of terminology for the term covenant corresponds to the kinds of Scriptural texts which were available to Owen in the seventeenth-century: the Hebrew Old Testament, the Greek New Testament, the Latin Vulgate, and the Septuagint (LXX).[74] On *foedus*, Owen noted that some deduced it from the Latin *a feriendo*, or "striking", where the practice of striking or sacrificing a beast is carried out as a confirmation of the covenant being cut.[75] He was aware that this latinized understanding of covenant is found in the works of such classical writers as Cicero, Virgil, and Livy, and has some parallels in Scripture. For instance, Genesis 15:17-18, Exodus 24:5-8, and Jeremiah 34:18-20 are passages in which *berith* is translated as *foedus* in the Latin Vulgate in the context of the phenomenon just described.[76] Keenly conscious that the origin of *foedus* is "properly paganish and superstitious; and the legal use of it strict to a mutual engagement upon valuable considerations", Owen rejected the term as a point of departure for weighing the proper meaning of the *pactum salutis* despite detailed knowledge of its parallels in Scripture. As for *suntheke*, a term which denotes "a precise compact or convention" made between nations and between persons, Owen observed that it was not used to translate *berith* in the LXX. This was because *berith* "was of a larger signification, applied unto things of another nature than συνθήκη...could be extended unto."[77] Thus, like *foedus*, the term *suntheke* was of no use in determining the sense of the eternal covenant.

Having discarded *foedus* and *suntheke* from his exegetical consideration, one would expect Owen to have gone on to a decisive analysis of *berith* in relation to the *pactum salutis*. However, this was not the case. Owen was a careful

---

[72] Owen, *A Display of Arminianism*, IX (*Works*, 10:90).

[73] Owen, *Vindicae Evangelicae*, XXVII (*Works*, 12:499-500); idem, *Exposition of Hebrews*, Exercitation IV.xxviii.3-5 (*Works*, 18:78-81); idem, *Theologoumena*, III.1.155-58 (*BT*, 204-10).

[74] Owen was also aware of Syriac and Arabic translations and employed them in his exegesis. See, for instance, his exegesis of Prov 8:22, in *Exposition of Hebrews*, Exercitation IV.xxvii.9 (*Works*, 18:58-60).

[75] Owen, *Exposition of Hebrews*, Exercitation IV.xxviii.3 (*Works*, 18:78-79); idem, *Theologoumena*, III.1.155-56 (*BT*, 206-207).

[76] Other passages cited are Ps 1:5, Gen 8:20-22, 9:9-10, and Heb 9:18-20. In them, the Vulgate does not translate *berith* or *diatheke* as *foedus* but *concilium*, *pactum*, or *testamentum*. The practice of "striking" in some form or other is present in every instant. Owen, *Exposition of Hebrews*, Exercitations IV.xxviii.3 (*Works*, 18:78-79).

[77] Owen, *Exposition of Hebrews*, Exercitations IV.xxviii.4 (*Works*, 18:79-80).

exegete. He observed that the term *berith* did not have a sole referent but was used in Scripture in various ways. It was used for (a) "peace and agreement, although there was no compact or convention unto that purpose" (Job 5:23; Hos 2:18) and hence used "metonymically, and metaphorically, because peace and agreement are the end of the covenant"; (b) the law written on the two tables of stone, and hence used "synecdochically" (Exod 34:28; Deut 9:11; 1 Kgs 8:9); (c) an absolute promise (Isa 59:21; Jer 33:20).[78] From this exegetical survey, Owen drew the conclusion that "where God speaks of his covenant, we cannot conclude that whatever belongs unto a perfect, complete covenant is therein intended."[79] He further warned against the danger of reading *berith* univocally, and urged that the intended meaning of the term "must be learned from the subject-matter treated of, seeing there is no precept or promise but may be so called."[80] In other words, the meaning of *berith* is to be determined from the context in which it is used. Owen's warning for *berith* applies equally to attempts at understanding the meaning of the term *diatheke* in Scripture.[81]

For Owen, the eternal covenant is a "perfect" or "absolutely complete covenant."[82] It is a covenant that is expressed in the fullest form of what a covenant is, which form, while necessarily derived from the use of *berith* and *diatheke*, is however not sufficiently found in any one instant of their explicit use in Scripture. Nevertheless, on the basis of his exegetical work surveyed above, he was able to identify four features of this covenant. According to Owen, a complete covenant is a mutual compact that is established between distinct persons, voluntarily entered into, concerns matters which are able to be performed by the covenant partners, and is made for their mutual content and satisfaction.[83] The five aspects to the covenantal form identified earlier in *Vindicae Evangelicae* are an expansion of this more concise expression found in *Exercitation XXVIII*. Thus, for Owen, textual collation in support of the *pactum salutis* is regulated by the form of a "complete covenant", which in turn is rooted in the linguistic analyses of key Scriptural terms. Clearly, Owen's doctrine of the *pactum salutis* is, as Trueman puts it, not simply the product of

---

[78] Owen, *Exposition of Hebrews*, Exercitations IV.xxviii.5 (*Works*, 18:80-81).
[79] Owen, *Exposition of Hebrews*, Exercitations IV.xxviii.5 (*Works*, 18:81).
[80] Owen, *Exposition of Hebrews*, Exercitations IV.xxviii.5 (*Works*, 18:81).
[81] In his exegesis of Hebrews 8:6, for instance, Owen translates *diatheke* as "covenant", followed by the qualification that he was not referring to covenant "properly and strictly so called, but such a one as hath the nature of a testament also, wherein the good things of him that makes it are bequeathed unto them for whom they are designed." His reason is as follows: "Neither the word used constantly by the apostle in this argument, nor the design of his discourse, will admit of any other covenant to be understood in this place." Owen, *Exposition of Hebrews*, Heb 8.6, in loc. (*Works*, 22:61). Again, context determines the meaning of the term.
[82] Owen, *Exposition of Hebrews*, Exercitations IV.xxviii.5, 7 (*Works*, 12:81, 82).
[83] Owen, *Exposition of Hebrews*, Exercitations IV.xxviii.7 (*Works*, 18:82-83).

"some kind of apriorism or dogmatic straightjacketing."[84] His careful etymological and exegetical considerations alongside the practice of textual collation around the specific locus of the *pactum salutis,* is typical of the synthesis between exegesis and doctrinal formulation in the writings of the Reformed orthodox on the subject.[85]

Theologically, for Owen, the issue that lies at the heart of the *pactum salutis* is the integrity of the *voluntas Dei*. Since his exposition of the form of the covenant required the presence of two or more parties entering into agreement with each other, the question of the compatibility of an eternal compact between the Father and the Son with the singularity of God's will needs to be addressed. This question surfaces in the light of traditional teaching on the simplicity of God. On this doctrine, the Reformed were in agreement with the medieval doctors who identified the divine will with the divine essence, and in so doing, affirmed that what was true of God's essence — that it is simple — was also true of God's will.[86] Owen affirmed this traditional teaching in the following manner: "The essence of God, then, being a most absolute, pure, simple act or substance, his will consequently can be but simply one; whereof we ought to make neither division nor distinction."[87] However, the *pactum salutis* appears to contradict the doctrine of divine simplicity because the idea of an eternal compact requires, supposedly, some form of distinction within the will in order that the Father can be said to be the covenant proposer and not the Son, and the Son its undertaker and not the Father. While it might, exegetically, be a fairly straightforward procedure to identify texts in which God / the Father and the Son are spoken of as two distinct persons who relate to each other by way of covenant,[88] theologically, it is extremely problematic if such texts are understood to be speaking about them as distinct persons who each have their own separate will. To construe of multiple wills in God not only contravenes traditional teaching, it also promotes the construction of an *ad intra* covenantal

---

[84] Trueman, *John Owen*, 83.
[85] Cf. Patrick Gillespie, *The Ark of the Covenant Opened; or a Treatise of the Covenant of Redemption between God and Christ, as the Foundation of the Covenant of Grace* (London: Printed for Tho. Parkhurst, 1677); Rutherford, *The Covenant of Life Opened*, II, 290-315; Witsius, *The Economy of the Covenants*, 1:41-50, 165-92; Turretin, *Elenctic Theology*, XII, Q. 1, and Q. 2, xi-xv.
[86] Thomas Aquinas, *Summa Theologiae: Latin Text and English Translation, Introduction, Notes, Appendixes and Glossaries*, 61 vols. (London: Blackfriars in conjunction with Eyre & Spottiswoode, 1964-1981), Ia, Q.19, Art.1. Subsequent citations from Aquinas are from this edition. Calvin, *Institutes*, I.xviii.3; Polanus, *The Svbstance of Christian Religion*, 11; Trelcatius, *A Brief Institvtion*, I.iii; cf. Muller, *PRRD*, 3:434-35.
[87] Owen, *A Display of Arminianism*, V (*Works*, 10:44); cf. idem, *Vindicae Evangelicae, Mr Biddle's Preface Briefly Examined* (*Works*, 12:70-72); Trueman, *John Owen*, 38-39.
[88] As indeed Owen does. See *Exposition of Hebrews*, Exercitations IV.xxviii.9 (*Works*, 18:84).

relation that threatens the unity of the Trinity. Barth captures the severity of the problem aptly:

> Can we really think of the first and second persons of the triune Godhead as two divine subjects and therefore as two legal subjects who can have dealings and enter into obligations one with another? This is mythology for which there is no place in a right understanding of the doctrine of the Trinity as the doctrine of the three modes of being of the one God, which is how it was understood and presented in Reformed orthodoxy itself...The question is necessarily and seriously raised of a will of God the Father which originally and basically is different from the will of God the Son.[89]

Owen was aware of this theological conundrum. In *Exercitation XXVIII*, he cast the problem in terms of the *voluntas Dei* and its implication for trinitarian orthodoxy:

> The *will* is a natural property, and therefore in the divine essence it is but one. The Father, Son, and Spirit, have not distinct wills. They are one God, and God's will is one, as being an essential property of his nature; and therefore are there two wills in the one person of Christ, whereas there is but one will in the three persons of the Trinity. How, then, can it be said that the will of the Father and the will of the Son did concur distinctly in the making of this covenant?[90]

Concurrence of the Father's and the Son's will is a vital characteristic of the eternal compact for Owen, but it seems to presuppose either a duplicity or distinction in the divine will that is contrary to the accepted understanding of it as an essential property of God's simple nature.

Owen's proposed solution to the problem is heavily dependent upon the trinitarian framework of the *opera Dei*. In this framework, the internal and essential works of God, although pertaining to what is common to each person of the Trinity, nevertheless, consist of immanent acts which are reciprocal, such as acts of mutual love and knowledge. Reciprocity of immanent acts is possible because of the distinction of persons in the one divine essence. Likewise, in the work of God *ad extra*, divine operations may be attributed distinctly to each person of the Trinity because they subsist distinctly. Owen applied, with equal seriousness, the implications of the distinction of persons to the *voluntas Dei* as he did to the *opera Dei*. In concord with the doctrine of simplicity, he insists on the oneness of the divine will, but in view of the distinct external operations or acts of each person, the singular will of God was peculiarly applied to these distinct acts. He explained:

> And whereas all these acts and operations, whether reciprocal or external, are either with a will or from a freedom of will and choice, the will of God in each

---

[89] Barth, *Church Dogmatics*, IV/1, 65.
[90] Owen, *Exposition of Hebrews*, Exercitations IV.xxviii.13 (*Works*, 18:87).

person, as to the peculiar acts ascribed unto him, is his will therein peculiarly and eminently, though not exclusively to the other persons, by reason of their mutual *in-being*. The will of God as to the peculiar actings of the Father in this matter is the will of the Father, and the will of God with regard unto the peculiar actings of the Son is the will of the Son; not by a distinction of sundry wills, but by the distinct application of the same will unto its *distinct acts* in the persons of the Father and the Son.[91]

Owen was careful not to speak of the *appropriation* of the divine will to the divine *persons* distinctly, but of the *application* of the one will to peculiar *acts* of the persons. He seemed to have taken extreme care not to confound the divine will, an essence-appropriate category, with divine acts or operations, a person-appropriate category. Indeed, divine acts may be appropriated to distinct persons of the Trinity, but when such appropriation is done for the divine will, it can only be at the expense of the unity of the Godhead. For Owen, the divine will is to be applied to the distinct acts of each person of the Trinity, thereby deriving a form of personal eminence, not distinction, spoken in relation to the one, simple will. However, he saw it necessary, even then, to buttress the idea of personal eminence with the perichoresis or "mutual in-being" of the three persons and so guard against tritheism.[92] Evidently, Owen's solution was hammered out in a self-consciously orthodox manner that sought at every turn to do justice to the affirmation of the unity of essence and distinction of persons in the Godhead. It is on the basis of this distinct application of the divine will that the eternal transactions between the Father and the Son are understood by Owen as federal in nature.

Owen's solution led him to clarify the difference between the eternal decree and the *pactum salutis*. Divine decrees are eternal and have as their object

---

[91] Owen, *Exposition of Hebrews*, Exercitations IV.xxviii.13 (*Works*, 18:88); cf. idem, *Vindicae Evangelicae*, XXVII (*Works*, 12:497).

[92] The doctrine of perichoresis was absent from Owen's earlier statement of the solution in 1655 in which he averred: "It is true, the will of God the Father, Son, and Holy Ghost, is but one. It is a natural property, and where there is but one nature there is but one will: but in respect of their distinct personal actings, this will is appropriated to them respectively, so that the will of the Father and the will of the Son may be considered [distinctly] in this business; which though essentially one and the same, yet in their distinct personality is distinctly considered, as the will of the Father and the will of the Son." Owen, *Vindicae Evangelicae*, XXVII (*Works*, 12:497). His statement of the same point in his exercitation of 1664 as cited above clearly evidences a tighter, more careful solution to the theological problem of the divine will in the *pactum salutis*. Of course, he was not introducing anything novel in the light of the tradition on divine simplicity. John of Damascus, for instance, employed the doctrine of perichoresis as a way of safeguarding divine simplicity within his larger treatment of the Trinity and the incarnation. See Stephen R. Holmes, *Listening to the Past: The Place of Tradition in Theology* (Carlisle: Paternoster/Grand Rapids: Baker, 2002), 61-63. Owen's improvement to his solution may be understood as an attempt to appropriate the dogmatic tradition more fully.

things that do not necessarily exist. Since these characteristics are also true of the *pactum salutis*, it therefore has "the nature of the residue of God's decrees."[93] However, it is "more than a decree, and hath the proper nature of a *covenant* or compact" because of "this distinct acting of the will of the Father and the will of the Son with regard to each other."[94] It differs from a "pure decree" in that the application of the will to the distinct acts of the Father and the Son introduces "a new habitude or relation, which is not natural or necessary unto them but freely taken on them."[95] Owen's clarification provides a more nuanced account of the relationship between the *pactum salutis* and divine election than Dickson's statement of the doctrine in which the covenant of redemption is simply taken as synonymous with the eternal decree of redemption with respect to its effects.[96] This clarification has significant implications for Owen's Christology. Owen affirmed with the Reformed that Christ is Mediator according to both his human and divine natures and was therefore Mediator prior to his incarnation.[97] It is not strictly the divine decree on which this Christological point is rooted but the *pactum salutis*. Within the context of this "new habitude or relation", i.e. federal relation, the Son is appointed Mediator by the Father and voluntarily undertakes the fulfilment of that appointment. The *pactum salutis* thus provides the theological foundation for asserting the pre-incarnate mediatorship of Christ.

Owen's nuanced account of the difference between the divine decree and the *pactum salutis* also allowed him to speak of the Son's subordination to the Father in the eternal compact without compromising the consubtantiality of the Son with the Father. Unpacking in greater detail the features of a "complete covenant", he explained that the eternal compact is "an especial kind of covenant" where the end of the covenant intended by the Father and the Son is achieved solely through the personal undertakings of only one party, the Son.[98] Since it is the Father who prescribes the duties to be undertaken and who promises to give assistance and reward for its accomplishment while the Son is

---

[93] Owen, *Vindicae Evangelicae*, XXVII (*Work*, 12:497).

[94] Owen, *Vindicae Evangelicae*, XXVII (*Works*, 12:497).

[95] Owen, *Exposition of Hebrews*, Exercitation IV.xxviii.13 (*Works*, 18:88).

[96] Dickson, *Therapeutica Sacra*, 25, 33: "This covenant of *redemption*, is in effect one with the eternall decree of redemption, wherein the salvation of the elect, and the way how it shall be brought about is fixed, in the purpose of God, who worketh all things according to the counsell of His own Will, as the Apostle sets it down, *Ephes*. I. unto the 15 verse. And the decree of redemption is in effect a covenant, one God in three persons agreeing in the decree, that the second Person, God the Son, should become incarnat, and given obedience and satisfaction to divine justice for the elect: unto which piece of service the Son willingly submitted Himself, the decree becometh a reall covenant indeed…the Covenant of Redemption past between the Father and the Son is by way of an eternall decree of the Trinity, comprehending all and whatsoever belongeth to Redemption."

[97] See Chapter 3.

[98] Owen, *Exposition of Hebrews*, Exercitations IV.xxviii.8 (*Works*, 18:83).

the party who accepts these terms, there is therefore "an inequality and subordination in the covenanters as to the common ends of the covenant, however on other accounts they may be equal."[99] In such a covenant, he who prescribes, promises, and rewards, is greater than he who keeps the prescribed duties and who places trust in the promises. It follows, then, that the Son is subordinate to the Father in a qualified sense, i.e. with regard to the ends of the *pactum salutis*. However, both the Father and the Son enter into covenant freely as equals just as by an act of the divine will they freely decree or take counsel together as equals.[100]

The Eternal Compact: the Role of the Spirit

Thus far, the analyses above have demonstrated the importance of Owen's trinitarianism for his understanding of the *pactum salutis*. Since, for Owen, the parties who enter into covenant are the Father and the Son, this binitarian focus raises the inevitable question of whether Owen's treatment of the *pactum salutis* comports well with his trinitarian frame of thought. Trueman answers in the affirmative when he claims that Owen's exposition involved the Spirit in such a way as to represent an advance over the treatments of Edward Fisher and Peter Bulkeley on the doctrine.[101] Letham, however, argues that Owen's doctrine is a binitarian construction that betrays the weakness of a Western, Augustinian tradition that conceives of the Spirit in a subordinated and depersonalized way relative to the Father and the Son.[102] Having observed, with admiration, that Owen took the distinction of persons in the Godhead far more seriously than is commonly the case with theologians who stand in the tradition of the West on the Trinity, Letham expresses surprise at Owen's failure to take the Spirit into account in the *pactum salutis*. "Amazingly," he exclaimed, "the Holy Spirit receives no mention!"[103]

Letham's analysis is not entirely accurate. His analysis is based solely on Owen's *Exercitation XXVIII*, where Owen's focus was on the Father / Son dynamic. However, *Exercitation XXVIII* is the continuation of his argument in *Exercitation XXVII*, and in that exercitation, Owen argued for the existence of

---

[99] Owen, *Exposition of Hebrews*, Exercitations IV.xxviii.8 (*Works*, 18:83).

[100] Owen, *Exposition of Hebrews*, Exercitations IV.xxviii.11-12 (*Works*, 18:86-87); idem, *Vindicae Evangelicae*, VII (*Works*, 12:171): "Distinction and inequality in respect of office in Christ doth not in the least take away equality and sameness with the Father in respect of nature and essence. A son of the same nature with his father, and therein equal to him, may in office be his inferior, his subject."

[101] Trueman, *John Owen*, 86.

[102] Letham, "John Owen's Doctrine of the Trinity", 19.

[103] He does acknowledge that Owen focused on the Spirit elsewhere in his writings. This qualification, however, does not refer to treatments of the *pactum salutis* in Owen's writings where the Spirit is given more thorough treatment, but simply to the fact that Owen deals with the Spirit elsewhere. In the immediate context, Letham appears to be referring to Owen's *On Communion with God*. Letham, "John Owen's Doctrine of the Trinity", 19.

personal transactions in the Trinity, not merely of transactions between the Father and the Son. This was done through detailed exegesis of Genesis 1:26 and Proverbs 8:22-31 in critical engagement with Jewish commentators.[104] At the conclusion of his exegesis of the Genesis passage, Owen reiterated his main concern in the following way: "And that which hence we intend to prove is, that in the framing and producing the things which concern mankind, there were *peculiar, internal, personal transactions* between the Father, Son, and Spirit."[105] In his exegesis of the passage from Proverbs, Owen clarified, in a passing comment, the Spirit's role in the eternal transactions between the Father and the Son: "A personal transaction, before the creation of the world, between the Father and the Son, *acting mutually by the Spirit*, concerning the state and condition of mankind, with respect unto divine love and favour, is that which we inquire after, and which is here fully expressed."[106]

Although brief, Owen's clarification suggests that the Spirit's role in the *pactum salutis* is instrumental and thus not directly pactional. As such, the Spirit's peculiar role is not to engage in prescribing terms in the compact, nor to undertake the fulfilment of the terms proposed by the Father and thus be subordinated to the Father by voluntary submission. Owen's adherence to the principle of the unity of divine operations would further suggest that there is certainly approbation and concurrence on the part of the Spirit. However, approbation and concurrence are not expressed by entering into compact as a legal subject, but by being the willing instrument through whom the Father and the Son engage in covenantal relations. This reading of the Spirit's role is consistent with Owen's understanding of the *filioque*-based order of divine operations, where the Spirit's work is "not an original but a perfecting work."[107] Owen alluded to this order in the *pactum salutis* when he described the Father as "*the spring and fountain of that covenant* (as in all other operations of the Deity), that was between himself and his Son about the salvation and glory of the elect."[108] Accordingly, the Son, as second in order, voluntarily undertakes to fulfil the terms of the covenant proposed by the Father; the Spirit, as third in order, agrees to apply or implement the ends of the covenant. Since the *pactum salutis* is directed towards the external economy, it is not surprising that the order of operation, following the order of subsistence, is reflected in the intratrinitarian transactions whereby the Father and the Son enter into covenant agreement by the Spirit.

Owen gave far more attention, however, to developing the Spirit's role in the implementation of the eternal compact than in explicating the Spirit's role

---

[104] Owen, *Exposition of Hebrews*, IV.xxvii.1-18 (*Works*, 18:42-76).
[105] Owen, *Exposition of Hebrews*, IV.xxvii.8 (*Works*, 18:58).
[106] Owen, *Exposition of Hebrews*, IV.xxvii.13 (*Works*, 18:67). Emphasis added.
[107] Owen, *Pneumatologia*, II.v (*Works*, 3:189).
[108] Owen, *Exposition of Hebrews*, Heb 2:10, in loc. (*Works*, 19:380).

within it.[109] It is this *ad extra* dimension of the Spirit's role that is developed in *The Death of Death*, to which Trueman points, but which Letham entirely neglects. However, it is important to qualify that this applicatory role of the Spirit is an inferred conclusion and not one that is stated explicitly in Owen's treatment of the doctrine in *The Death of Death*. In that treatise, the *pactum salutis* was included as part of Owen's exposition of the peculiar work of the Father in sending the Son.[110] When Owen turned to consider the peculiar work of the Spirit, he did not expound the subject in explicit relation to the *pactum salutis*, but rather as part of the external trinitarian work in which the Spirit's acts concur with those of the Father and the Son. Since the *pactum salutis* was expounded as part of the Father's peculiar act of sending the Son, the Spirit's concurrence with the Father's act of sending would certainly be implied, leading to the inevitable implication that the role of the Spirit is the implementation of the *pactum salutis*. Structurally, then, the *opera Dei* is the more fundamental category in *The Death of Death*, not the *pactum salutis*. However, once the connection with the *pactum salutis* is grasped by inference from the wider context, it is not difficult to see why Trueman's assessment is to be preferred over Letham's.

The charge that Owen's doctrine of the covenant of redemption is binitarian simply cannot hold in the light of the evidence. Indeed, Owen's exposition of the Spirit's role in accordance with the *filioque* dynamic in which the *ad extra* dimension of the Spirit's role is emphasized, reveals the appropriation of a distinctively Western form of the doctrine of the Trinity in his conception of the *pactum salutis*. Owen's formulation of the doctrine is representative of the way in which the trinitarian structure of the doctrine developed in Reformed orthodoxy.[111]

The Prominence of Christ's Priesthood

Earlier, the connection between the *pactum salutis* and Christ's priesthood in Owen's *Two Short Catechisms* and its elaborations in subsequent writings was noted. This connection, which had remained undeveloped in previous works on Owen,[112] has been explored more fully by Trueman in *John Owen: Reformed Catholic, Renaissance Man*.[113] He points out that although the standard Reformed taxonomy of the *munus triplex* was employed by Owen in his

---

[109] Owen, *Salus Electorum*, I.v (*Works*, 10:178-79); idem, *Pneumatologia*, II.iii-v (*Works*, 3:159-206).
[110] Owen, *Salus Electorum*, I.iii (*Works*, 10:164-71).
[111] Cf. similar developments on the Spirit's role in the *pactum salutis* in Rutherford, *The Covenant of Life Opened*, II, 304-305; Gillespie, *The Ark of the Covenant Opened*, 172-74; Van Asselt, *The Federal Theology of Cocceius*, 233-36.
[112] Notably, in works on Owen's view of Christ's priesthood such as those of Wright, "John Owen's Great High Priest" and Griffith, "High Priest in Heaven", 23-62.
[113] Trueman, *John Owen*, 87-92.

elaboration of the details of Christ's work as Mediator, there was evidently a major focus on Christ's priestly office.

After unpacking Owen's treatment of the *pactum salutis* in *Vindicae Evangelicae*, Trueman made two important observations. First, he observed that for Owen, the whole of Christ's life from his incarnation to his ascension is involved in Christ's mediatorial office. This observation corresponds to his point made in an earlier monograph on Owen, that the *munus triplex* and Christ's twofold state are the two basic patterns of explicating Christ's mediatorial work which were available to Owen from the Reformed tradition.[114] Second, Trueman noted that the unity of Christ's oblation and intercession is integral to Owen's understanding of the atonement's particularity and efficacy. Undoubtedly, these are crucial observations for understanding Owen's atonement theology. However, as will be argued in the rest of this study, it is not merely the mediatorial office in general but Christ's priesthood in particular that is at the forefront of Owen's attempt to take seriously the whole of Christ's life in his mediatorial work. In other words, there is a profound relationship between Trueman's two observations about Owen's thought. At present, it will suffice to demonstrate the way in which Owen's treatment of the *pactum salutis* lays the groundwork for this relationship.

Owen's *Exercitation XXVII and XXVIII* were aimed at proving that the origin of Christ's priesthood is found in the *pactum salutis*.[115] For the whole of *Exercitation XXVII* and for most of *XXVIII*, Owen was engaged in meticulous ground-clearing work which attempted to show, from exegetical and theological considerations, that there are indeed eternal transactions among the persons in the Godhead, and that the transactions between the Father and the Son are federal in nature. His argument on the origin of Christ's priesthood was only brought home in the last three sections of *Exercitation XXVIII*. In section nineteen, he summed up the terms of the *pactum salutis* prescribed by the Father to the Son in three points. First, the Son is to assume human nature; second, he is to yield perfect obedience to the Father as servant; third, he is to make atonement in that human nature by suffering the penalty that was incurred by the elect on account of their sins.[116] The content of these three points is a description of what the Son is to do as Mediator in order to fulfil his priestly office. In addition, Owen pointed out in section eighteen that the Father's promises to the Son within the terms of the covenant entailed the success of the Son's redemptive work and his glorious exaltation to the Father's right hand where he will then intercede for the actual accomplishment of what is promised.[117] It is from these covenantal prescriptions and promises of the

---

[114] Trueman, *Claims of Truth*, 165-69.
[115] Owen, *Exposition of Hebrews*, Exercitations IV.xxvii-xxviii (*Works*, 18:42-97).
[116] Owen, *Exposition of Hebrews*, Exercitations IV.xxviii.19 (*Works*, 18:94-95).
[117] Owen, *Exposition of Hebrews*, Exercitations IV.xxviii.18 (*Works*, 18:92-94).

Father to the Son that the *pactum salutis* was identified as the "sacred spring" of Christ's priesthood.[118] Owen's exposition is thus marked by the dominance of Christ's priesthood and the importance of the whole of Christ's life on earth and in heaven in the exercise of this mediatorial office. This observation is central to the account of Owen's atonement theology given in this study. As will become clear in the course of this study, Owen's formulation of Christ's priestly office involves the integration of Christ's priestly acts of oblation and intercession with the Reformed understanding of Christ's *status humiliationis* and his *status exaltationis*. In order to understand key aspects of Owen's doctrine of atonement, it is important that this point be grasped. Evidently, the necessary contents for such integration to occur are found in Owen's exposition of the *pactum salutis*.

This connection between the *pactum salutis* and Christ's priesthood is vital for understanding three crucial concerns in Owen's view of the atonement. First, the particularity of Christ's mediation as priest arises from the particularity inherent in the *pactum salutis*.[119] In the context of this covenant, those whom the Father has given to the Son — the elect — are the ones for whom the Son undertakes the work of redemption. Christ's mediation as a public or common person is therefore restricted to the elect,[120] and the notion of a "general mediation" in the exercise of Christ's mediatorial office "as should extend itself beyond his church or chosen" is denied.[121] Exegetically, Owen's typological argument about the particularity of the Levitical sacrifices buttresses the point. Just as the sacrifices performed by the high priest in the Old Testament were offered for Israel and not the nations, so the sacrifice of Christ the great high priest is offered for the elect people of God: "It was that people, and not the whole world, that the high priest offered for; and it is the elect people alone for whom our great high priest did offer and doth intercede."[122]

Second, Owen argued that the obedience of Christ throughout his earthly life has no salvific merit for the elect apart from the *pactum salutis*. If Christ's obedience is to be meritorious, not only should there be a natural or necessary "proportion" between his obedience and the elect's salvation, but there should also be a "relation" between them in which the merit of his obedience is

---

[118] The title of section nineteen reads: "Things prescribed to the Lord Christ in this covenant reduced to three heads – The sacred spring of his priesthood discovered."
[119] Chapter 6 examines this point more fully.
[120] Owen, *Christologia*, II.viii (*Works*, 2:177); idem, *Salus Electorum*, III.iii (*Works*, 10:246-249); Trueman, *Claims of Truth*, 133-39.
[121] Owen, *Salus Electorum*, I.viii (*Works*, 10:189).
[122] Owen, *Exposition of Hebrews*, Heb 9:7, in loc. (*Works*, 22:232). Cf. idem, *Exposition of Hebrews*, Exercitation IV.xxxiii.8 (*Works*, 18:204); idem, *Salus Electorum*, III.iv (*Works*, 10:257-58); idem, *Vindicae Evangelicae*, XX (*Works*, 12:411). For Owen's use of typology in its seventeenth-century context, see Knapp, "Understanding the Mind of God", 262-334.

founded. This "relation" is not natural or necessary but arises from the eternal compact. Owen explained:

> Merit is such an adjunct of obedience as whereon a reward is reckoned of debt. [...] Suppose, then, a proportion in *distributive justice* between the obedience of Christ and the salvation of believers [...]; then add the respect and relation that they have one to another by virtue of this covenant, and in particular that our salvation is engaged by promise unto Christ; and it gives us the true nature of his merit. Such promises were given him, and do belong unto this covenant, the accomplishment whereof he pleads on the discharge of his work.[123]

Referring to the promise-trust covenantal relation, Owen asserts: "this is that which gives the nature of merit unto the obedience and suffering of Christ."[124]

Third, Owen argued that apart from the *pactum salutis*, the death of Christ has no intrinsic goodness, nor does it satisfy divine justice. The penal suffering of Christ "in itself, absolutely considered, without respect unto the ends of the covenant, would neither have been good in itself, nor have had any tendency unto the glory of God; for what excellency of the nature of God could have been demonstrated in the penal sufferings of one absolutely and in all respects innocent?"[125] However, in the light of the eternal compact, Christ's innocent sufferings were given satisfactory value, "made good", and "tend unto the glory of God."[126] This is an important point that Owen stressed in his rejection of the Grotian and Baxterian solutions to Socinus' criticism of the doctrine of atonement.[127]

Thus, the whole scope of the Son's mediatorial work as priest is encompassed in the *pactum salutis*: the Son's voluntary self-humbling in the incarnation; the meritorious nature of his perfect obedience as the Father's servant; the satisfactory value of his mediatorial sufferings and death on the cross; the promise of his exaltation; the success of his intercession by virtue of his earthly mediation and the Father's acceptance of his fulfilled work of mediation. It is reasonable, then, to conclude that Owen's doctrine of the *pactum salutis* is the eternal foundation of the entire edifice of his atonement theology.

---

[123] Owen, *Exposition of Hebrews*, Exercitations IV.xxviii.18 (*Works*, 18:94).
[124] Owen, *Exposition of Hebrews*, Exercitations IV.xxviii.18 (*Works*, 18:94).
[125] Owen, *Exposition of Hebrews*, Exercitations IV.xxviii.14 (*Works*, 18:89).
[126] Owen, *Exposition of Hebrews*, Exercitations IV.xxviii.14 (*Works*, 18:89); idem, *Of the Death of Christ*, II (*Works*, 10:441): "The death of Christ, considered absolutely and in itself, may be said to be refusable as to be made a payment, —not a refusable payment; and that not because not refusable, but because not a payment. Nothing can possibly tend to the procurement and compassing of any end, by the way of payment, with the Lord, but what is built upon some free compact, promise, or obligation of his own. But now consider it as an issue flowing from divine constitution making it a payment, and so it was no way refusable as to the compassing of the end appointed."
[127] See Chapter 5.

The External Work of God in Redemption

In accordance with the order of external operations of the Trinity, Owen's discussion of the external works of God in redemption centres on the incarnate Son. Consistent with the prominence of Christ's priesthood in the *pactum salutis*, there is a corresponding prominence of this office in Owen's discussion of God's external redemptive work. Thus, in *The Death of Death*, Owen's comparatively brief discussion of the undivided and peculiar works of each person of the Trinity is followed by an extended treatment of Christ's mediatorial office that centred specifically on his priestly mediation. These themes of Christ's person and priestly mediation will be examined at length in Chapters 3 to 5. Here, only the operations of the Father and the Spirit in the work of redemption will be noted.

Owen summed up the Father's concurrence in redemption in two ways. First, the Father sends the Son into the world to accomplish redemption.[128] Three acts of the Father were identified in this sending: the imposition of the office of Mediator upon the Son; the provision of the necessary gifts and graces for the Son in order to fulfil that office; the establishment of a covenant with the Son, or the *pactum salutis*.[129] Owen observed that there are more than twenty instances in John's Gospel where the Father is said to have sent the Son. Comparing these New Testament references with Old Testament ones such as Isaiah 19:20, 48:16, where God promises to send the Saviour, the act of sending, then, is an operation that may be suitably appropriated to the Father. On account of this promise of the Father, Scripture sometimes attributes the title of Saviour to him. In 1 Timothy 1:1, for instance, "God our Saviour" is distinguished from "Christ Jesus our hope". Owen associated the Father with "God" who is called "our Saviour". However, he was aware that in some manuscripts, the conjunction "and" is inserted between "God" and "our Saviour". Deciding in favor of this variant reading would mean that "our Saviour" no longer modifies "God" but "Christ Jesus". Owen rejected this reading by appealing to analogous passages such as Titus 1:3 and 1 Timothy 4:10 in which the title Saviour is clearly attributed to God. His preferred reading is in accord with the textual tradition underlying the translation of 1 Timothy 1:1 in the Geneva Bible of 1560 and the King James Bible of 1611.[130]

---

[128] Owen, *Salus Electorum*, I.iii (*Works*, 10:163-71).

[129] Owen, *Salus Electorum*, I.iii (*Works*, 10:164-71).

[130] Thus, these Bibles provide the following translations of the verse. *The Bible and Holy Scriptvres Conteyned in the Olde and Newe Testament* (Geneva: Printed by Roulandnald, 1560), 1 Tim 1:1, in loc.: "Paul an Apostle of Iesus Christ, by the commandment of God our Sauiour, and of our Lord Iesus Christ our hope"; *The Holy Bible, Conteyning the Old Testament, and the New: Newly Translated out of the Originall Tongues & with the Former Translations Diligently Compared and Revised by His Maiesties Speciall Comandement* (London: Robert Barker, 1611), 1 Tim 1:1, in loc. : "Paul an Apostle of Jesus Christ, by the commandement of God our Sauiour, & Lord Jesus Christ *which is* our hope."

Owen's textual decision supported his general assertion of the Father's concurrence in the work of redemption: the Father sends the Son in fulfilment of his promise; he also shares the same title of Saviour with him.

The Father's second act of concurrence is in laying the punishment of sins upon Christ. This is "everywhere ascribed to the Father", Owen claimed, referencing Zechariah 13:7, Matthew 26:31, Isaiah 53:4, 6, 10, and 2 Corinthians 5:21 as examples.[131] In this divine act, the weight of the law is exacted, tending towards the fulfilment of divine justice, while the person to be punished is changed. There is, in other words, a "relaxation of the law" as to the person suffering, but the full measure of the penalty remains unchanged.[132] Thus, instead of the sinner bearing the full penalty of sins as the law demands, it is Christ who bears it in his substitutionary and atoning death.

In this context of the nature of atonement, set against the larger issue of the Father's involvement in redemption, Owen addressed the case of universal redemption in the form of a dilemma: "God imposed his wrath due unto, and Christ underwent the pains of hell for, either all the sins of all men, or all the sins of some men, or some sins of all men."[133] The implication of the third proposition is that the death of Christ was *insufficient* to cover all sins, thus leaving all men with sins to answer for but unable to do so in the light of God's righteous judgment. This proposition essentially denies that salvation was procured for anyone. The first proposition is also untenable from Owen's standpoint. Proponents of universal redemption acknowledged that not every man will be saved since some fail to respond in faith. If, indeed, this failure is due to the sin of unbelief, it would consequently imply that Christ did not undergo punishment for the sin of unbelief and hence contradict the proposition, or that the sin of unbelief for which Christ died is still a hindrance to salvation and so deny the *efficacious* nature of Christ's death. Owen's position was, therefore, that of the second proposition.

Evidently, it is not simply the logical incoherence of universal redemption that was raised in the dilemma from Owen's perspective, but also, and more significantly, the insufficiency of Christ's death (proposition 3) and its lack of atoning efficacy (proposition 1).[134] This reading of the dilemma comports well

---

[131] Owen, *Salus Electorum*, I.iii (*Works*, 10:171-72).

[132] Owen, *Salus Electorum*, I.iii (*Works*, 10:173).

[133] Owen, *Salus Electorum*, I.iii (*Works*, 10:173).

[134] Owen deals with these issues more extensively in *Salus Electorum*, IV.i (*Works*, 10:295-301); idem, *A Display of Arminianism*, IX (*Works*, 10:89-91). The sufficiency and efficacy of Christ's death were traditional concerns. They were discussed by the medieval scholastics in their treatment of Christ's death and formed part of the wider theological context to the discussions of the Reformers and the Reformed orthodox on the atonement. See Aquinas, *Summa Theologiae*, III, Q.46, Art.5 and III, Q.48, Art.2; Calvin, *Calvin's Commentaries*, 46 vols. (Edinburgh: Calvin Translation Society, 1843-1855; reprint in 22 vols., Grand Rapids: Baker, 1996), 1 John 2:2, in loc., henceforth cited as *Commentary*; G. Michael Thomas, *The Extent of the Atonement: A Dilemma for*

with Owen's understanding of the Father's involvement in redemption. The Father's act of laying the penalty of sins upon Christ is an outworking of the *pactum salutis*, and therefore, an outworking of God's intention to save. Since God cannot fail to accomplish what he intends, an ineffectual atonement would imply the impotence of God or the contingent nature of his intention. The nature of the atonement is thus inextricably tied to its extent in Owen's thought and both are rooted in the *pactum salutis*. Failure to appreciate this theological point has led scholars such as Clifford to focus on the commercialistic expressions of the dilemma in which sin is viewed in allegedly quantitative terms, rather than noting Owen's larger theological concerns and consequently interpreting the dilemma in the light of them.[135]

Owen's treatment of the Spirit's concurrence in the work of redemption follows the basic movement of the Gospel narrative of the life of Christ. In *The Death of Death*, he divides this movement into three parts: the Spirit's work in the incarnation, oblation, and resurrection of Christ.[136] Although the heads of this division capture only the key events in the work of redemption, Owen's exposition of the events themselves reveals his concern for the Spirit's work in the entire life of Christ. Not only was Christ conceived in Mary's womb by the power of the Spirit, he was also "filled with the Spirit, and 'waxed strong' in it, Luke i.80; until having received a fullness thereof, and not by any limited measure, in the gifts and graces of it, he was thoroughly furnished and fitted for his great undertaking"; the Spirit assisted Christ "in the course of his conversation whilst he dwelt among us."[137] Referring to Christ's self-offering in Hebrews 9:14 on Christ's oblation, Owen opined that "whether it be meant the offering of himself a bloody sacrifice on the cross, or his presentation of himself continually before his Father, — it is by the eternal Spirit."[138] Again, Owen's concern for the larger context of Christ's life is evident, both his life on earth and in heaven.

Reformed Theology from Calvin to the Consensus (Carlisle: Paternoster Press, 1997), 4-6; Hans Boersma, *A Hot Pepper Corn: Richard Baxter's Doctrine of Justification in Its Seventeenth-Century Context of Controversy* (Vancouver: Regent College Publishing, 2004), 215-19. Owen did not reject the use of the sufficiency/efficacy distinction but employed it to press home his point about the infinite sufficiency of Christ's death by grounding it in the infinite dignity of Christ's person. On this, he was entirely consistent with the teachings of the Synod of Dort. Cf. *Canons of Dort*, II, Art. 3, 4. It is this particular understanding of sufficiency that formed the basis of the universal offer of salvation for Owen. The question of efficacy for him, and hence particularity, was tied to the divine intention, not to the dignity of Christ's person. In Owen's account of the distinction, affirming the particularity of the atonement does not appear to undermine the universal offer of salvation because the grounds of both are different.

[135] Clifford, *Atonement and Justification*, 111ff.
[136] Owen, *Salus Electorum*, I.v (*Works*, 10:178-79).
[137] Owen, *Salus Electorum*, I.v (*Works*, 10:178).
[138] Owen, *Salus Electorum*, I.v (*Works*, 10:178).

This threefold division of the Spirit's work was expanded by Owen into ten points in *Pneumatologia*, in which the central concern was to make clear the Spirit's peculiar acts in and upon the human nature of Christ as the head of God's new creation and of the church.[139] The following are summary statements of the content of his divisions:

1. The miraculous conception of Christ's body in Mary's womb.
2. The sanctification of Christ's human nature.
3. The growth of Christ as a man who is fully human.
4. The anointing of Christ with extraordinary powers and gifts.
5. The performance of miracles in Christ's earthly ministry.
6. The provision of guidance, direction, comfort, and support, in Christ's earthly life.
7. The self-offering of Christ in his suffering and death.
8. The preservation of Christ's body in the state of the dead.
9. The resurrection of Christ.
10. The glorification of Christ's human nature for his heavenly ministry.

There is an apparent overlap of material here with his exposition in *The Death of Death*. Points 1 to 6 correspond with his division on Christ's incarnation and earthly life, 7 to 8 with his division on Christ's oblation, and 9 and 10 with the resurrection of Christ. The order of his treatment moves in the same direction from Christ's life on earth to his life in heaven.

What is significant in Owen's expanded exposition is the consistency with which he grounds the Spirit's work in the *pactum salutis*, which in turn reveals the trinitarian structure of his thought. Two examples from Owen's exposition will suffice to demonstrate this point. The first example is the self-offering of Christ (point 7). Owen's discussion of Christ's self-offering consists of an extended exposition of Hebrews 9:14: "How much more shall the blood of Christ, who through the eternal Spirit offered himself without spot to God, purge your consciences from dead works to serve the living God?" Before unpacking what Christ's self-offering entailed, Owen noted that exegetes differed on the interpretation of the phrase "the eternal Spirit." According to Owen, some understood it to mean Christ's divine nature, while others, the Holy Spirit.[140] These exegetical options were supported by the Syriac ("the

---

[139] Owen, *Pneumatologia*, II.iii-iv (*Works*, 3:162-83); cf. the helpful treatment of these points in Trueman, *John Owen*, 92-98.

[140] Owen, *Pneumatologia*, II.iv (*Works*, 3:176): "I know that many learned men do judge that by the 'eternal Spirit' in that place, not the third person is intended, but the divine nature of the Son himself; and there is no doubt but that also may properly be called the eternal Spirit...But, on the other side, many learned persons, both of the ancient and modern divines, do judge that it is the person of the Holy Spirit that is intended."

The Agent of Redemption 55

eternal Spirit") and Vulgate ("the Holy Spirit") translations respectively, with supporting evidences from ancient manuscripts.[141]

Introducing such exegetical considerations into his exposition of the Spirit's operations was not a superfluous exercise. Owen's concern to demonstrate the Spirit's concurrence in Christ's oblation necessitated such textual considerations in the light of the translation and exegetical history of Hebrews 9:14. Three lines of interpretation may be discerned. Mainstream Reformed orthodox exegetes interpreted "the eternal Spirit" as Christ's divine nature.[142] Others, like Ambrose and Calvin, understood its referent to be the Holy Spirit.[143] A third line of interpretation accepts both interpretations as valid.[144] Owen adopted the second position in *The Death of Death* but took the third in *Pneumatologia*.[145] A possible explanation for this change in exegetical conclusion may be the different polemical situations in which Owen found himself. His earlier exposition had the Arminians chiefly in view, who were orthodox on the issue of the deity of the Son and the Spirit, but in the latter work, it was the anti-trinitarian Socinians whose views he tried to oppose. Granting validity to both exegetical conclusions would undoubtedly have lent greater weight to Owen's case against the Socinians. Thus, commenting on the Socinians, Owen observed that "both these interpretations are equally destructive to their opinions, the one concerning the person of Christ, the other the Holy Ghost..."[146]

---

[141] Owen, *Exposition of Hebrews*, Heb 9:14, in loc. (*Works*, 22:303).

[142] See William Jones, *A Commentary Vpon the Epistles of Saint Pavl to Philemon, and to the Hebrewes, Together with a Compendiovs Explication of the Second and Third Epistles of Saint John* (London: Printed by R.B. for Robert Allot, 1635), Heb 9:14, in loc.; David Dickson, *A Short Explanation of the Epistle of Paul to the Hebrevves* (Cambridge: Printed by Roger Daniel for Francis Eglesfield, 1649), Heb 9:14, in loc. Trueman lists Gouge, Diodati, Ussher, the *English Annotations*, and the *Dutch Annotations*. Trueman, *John Owen*, 97.

[143] Ambrose, *De spiritu sancto*, I.viii (*NPNF*2, 10:106): "But the Apostle also shows that the Holy Spirit is eternal, for: 'If the blood of bulls and of goats, and the sprinkling the ashes of an heifer sanctifieth to the purifying of the flesh, how much more the blood of Christ, Who through the eternal Spirit offered himself without spot to God?' Therefore the Spirit is eternal"; Calvin, *Commentary*, Heb 9:14, in loc.: "He now clearly shows how Christ's death is to be estimated, not by the external act, but by the power of the Spirit...And he calls the Spirit eternal for this reason, that we may know that the reconciliation, of which he is the worker or effecter, is eternal."

[144] George Lawson, *An Exposition of the Epistle to the Hebrewes. Wherein the Text Is Cleared; Theopolitica Improved: The Socinian Comment Examined* (London: Printed by J.S. for George Sawbridge, 1662), Heb 9:14, in loc.

[145] Paralleling this change is his defence of the second position in *Vindicae Evangelicae*, XXII (*Works*, 12:432) and the third in *Exposition of Hebrews*, Heb 9:14, in loc. (*Works*, 22:303-307).

[146] Owen, *Exposition of Hebrews*, Heb 9.14, in loc. (*Works*, 22:306); cf. his remarks on the Socinian view of the redundancy of the Spirit's work in Christ on account of Christ's divine nature. *Pneumatologia*, II.iii (*Works*, 3:160-62).

Having cleared the textual difficulty, Owen then proceeds to explicate the way in which the Spirit worked in Christ's self-offering. He especially highlighted the "actings of the grace of the Holy Spirit" in Christ which were necessary for the fulfilment of Christ's work as Mediator. These "graces of the Spirit", as Owen called them, consist of love and compassion for sinners, zeal for God's glory, submission and obedience to the Father's will, and faith in the promises of God, all of which were exercised in Christ through the operation of the Holy Spirit.[147] Owen's descriptions of these graces were based upon the content of the *pactum salutis*, which includes, for example, the Son's voluntary submission to the Father and the Father's promise of assistance, sustenance, and success for the Son's work of mediation. In light of the *pactum salutis*, the Spirit's operation in Christ's self-offering is to enable the incarnate Son to accomplish his covenant engagement with the Father. Indeed, for Owen, the Spirit's enablement is part of the Father's promise to the Son.

The second example is the Spirit's work upon Christ in "the state of the dead" (point 8).[148] By "the state of the dead", Owen was referring to the intervening period between the death and resurrection of Christ in the context of his *status humiliationis*, traditionally known as the *descensus ad inferos* in the Apostle's Creed.[149] During this period, as Owen understood it, the soul of Christ is separated from his body as is the case with a human person upon death, but the hypostatic union remains intact. In accord with the principle of the indivisibility of external divine operations, the concurring acts of the Father and the Spirit are absolutely crucial for Owen here. Drawing from Psalm 31:5 and Luke 23:46, Owen explained that the Father's role is to preserve and care for the soul of Christ, "for the Father had engaged himself in an eternal covenant to take care of him, to preserve and protect him even in death, and to show him again the 'way and path of life', Psalm 16:11."[150] The Father's act of caring and preservation, then, is rooted in the *pactum salutis*. The Spirit concurs by preserving the buried body of Christ from corruption, in fulfilment of the promise of Psalm 16:10. In the light of the covenantal context indicated by

---

[147] Owen, *Pneumatologia*, II.iv (*Works*, 3:177-79).

[148] Owen, *Pneumatologia*, II.iv (*Works*, 3:180-81).

[149] Owen's position on Christ's *descensus* is that of the Westminster Standards which advocate a non-literal understanding of the descent into hell contra the patristic and medieval interpretation of the creedal statement. His phrase, "the state of the dead", appears in the Westminster *Larger Catechism*, Q. 50: "*Wherein consisteth Christ's humiliation after his death? A.* Christ's humiliation after his death consisted in his being buried, and continuing in the state of the dead, and under the power of death till the third day; which hath been otherwise expressed in these words, he descended into hell." Christ's *descensus* was a point on which there were not only differences in interpretation between the Lutherans and Reformed orthodox, but also among the Reformed. See Muller, *DLGTT*, 89-90; Chad B. Van Dixhoorn, "Reforming the Reformation: Theological Debate at the Westminster Assembly, 1643-1652" (Ph.D. dissertation, Cambridge, 2004), vol. 7, 1:221-32.

[150] Owen, *Pneumatologia*, II.iv (*Works*, 3:180).

Owen, the Spirit's work here is to be understood as an implementation of what was contracted in the *pactum salutis*. This work of preservation is done in two ways. By the power of the Spirit, the body of Christ was "preserved in its integrity...without any of those accidents of change which attend the dead bodies of others."[151] It was also kept from "all outward force and violation" through the Spirit's use of angels, as indicated in John 20:12.[152]

Conclusion

This chapter has sought to establish the case that foundational to Owen's atonement theology is his understanding that the work of redemption is the work of the Trinity. Put in terms of divine agency, it argues the point that the Agent of redemption is the one God who is Father, Son, and Holy Spirit. This point is established within the basic framework of the *opera Dei* as Owen himself advocated. In God's work *ad intra*, the work of redemption is conceived by way of federal transactions between the Father and the Son by the Holy Spirit. For Owen, the origin of the work of redemption is found in the *pactum salutis*. His conception of the eternal *pactum* does not compromise his trinitarian principles but rests upon and stems from his vigorous adherence to them: the *filioque*-shaped dynamic of the order of subsistence and divine operations, the distinction of persons in the Godhead, and their unity of essence. Owen's trinitarianism is also evident in his discussion of God's work *ad extra* in redemption. Demonstrating the concurring operations of the Father and the Spirit upon Christ was a vital exercise for Owen that revealed his trinitarian frame of thought. This point is seen in Owen's exposition of Christ's self-offering and preservation in the state of the dead.

Something of vital significance in Owen's atonement theology has also been demonstrated in the course of the above analysis: the prominence of Christ's priesthood understood in the context of his life on earth and in heaven. This is true in Owen's understanding of the conception of the *pactum salutis* in God's work *ad intra* as shown in the above discussion. It is, therefore, to be expected that there exists a corresponding prominence of the priestly office in Owen's exposition of its execution in time. This will be explored in the following three chapters under Owen's notion of the "means of redemption."

---

[151] Owen, *Pneumatologia*, II.iv (*Works*, 3:181).
[152] Owen, *Pneumatologia*, II.iv (*Works*, 3:181).

CHAPTER 3

The Means of Redemption: Christ the Mediator

This chapter begins the examination of the second locus in Owen's atonement theology: the doctrine of Christ the Mediator. In Owen's theological framework, the person and work of Christ are not divorced or loosely coordinated but are mutually dependent. Christ as Mediator is the theological category that holds the person and work of Christ together in its proper relation. This chapter will attempt to show that the governing category of Owen's Christology is mediatorial. Not only is this category the window to a proper understanding of how the main elements of Owen's Christology hang together, it also throws light on the distinctively Reformed character of his Christology, thus paving the way for making sense of the Christological foundations of his conception of Christ's priesthood. The Christological context in which Owen found himself will first be established by highlighting the pertinent Christological concerns that arose from certain controversies in the sixteenth and seventeenth centuries. The general features of Owen's Christology will then be identified by examining his key writing on the subject, *Christologia* (1679). Finally, relying on but moving beyond *Christologia* to other relevant writings of Owen, the specific features of his Reformed Christology will be examined.

The Christological Context

Reformed Christology in the seventeenth-century is, to a great extent, the product of a prolonged theological polemic with the Lutherans. It first arose over the nature of Christ's presence at the Lord's Supper in the context of the debate between Luther and Zwingli, and as the debate progressed, became increasingly concerned with Christology as it relates to the ancient doctrine of *communicatio idiomatum*.[1] This doctrine was employed by the Lutherans to reconcile their assertion of Christ's bodily presence at the Father's right hand

---

[1] See Jaroslav Pelikan, *Reformation of Church and Dogma (1300-1700)*, The Christian Tradition: A History of the Development of Doctrine, vol. 4 (Chicago/London: University of Chicago Press, 1984), 350-59; Bruce L. McCormack, "For Us and Our Salvation: Incarnation and Atonement in the Reformed Tradition," *Studies in Reformed Theology and History* 1, no. 2 (1993), 3-16; Stephen R. Holmes, "Reformed Varieties of the Communicatio Idiomatum," in *The Person of Christ*, ed. Murray Rae and Stephen Holmes (Edinburgh: T&T Clark, 2005), 70-86; Karl-Heinz zur Muhlen, "Christology," in *The Oxford Encyclopedia of the Reformation*, ed. Hans J. Hillerbrand (New York/Oxford: Oxford University Press, 1996), 314-22; Muller, *DLGTT*, 72-75.

and their insistence on the real presence of Christ at the eucharist. According to the Lutherans, Christ's risen body was made ubiquitous by a real communication of properties in which the exalted human nature of Christ shares in the divine attribute of being everywhere present.[2] The *communicatio idiomatum* was a direct result of the *communio naturarum*, and both were possible on account of the hypostatic union.[3] In so conceiving, the Lutherans were vulnerable to the charge of espousing a Eutychian *tertium quid*, which the Reformed were quick to point out in their criticisms.[4] Against the Lutherans, the Reformed affirmed the communication of properties from nature to person, but rejected a real communication from nature to nature. They also affirmed the *communio naturarum*, but unlike the Lutherans, conceived of it as occurring indirectly through the person of the incarnate Son. Their aim was to preserve the integrity of each nature while affirming the unity of Christ's person. It comes as no surprise that the Reformed emphasis on the distinction of natures brought on the Lutheran charge of being Nestorian. The traditional character of the debate is obvious. Both sides affirmed the Chalcedonian formula, employed patristic terminologies to justify their particular account of Christology, and mapped their criticisms against the heresies which arose in patristic times. Clearly, the main Christological issue was not the constitution of the Mediator, since the Chalcedonian tradition was presupposed, but rather the consequences of adhering to it.[5]

Concerns over the implications of the hypostatic union did not merely arise from the Lutheran-Reformed debate over the issues of the Lord's Supper and Christology. They were also evident in soteriological discussions that pertained to the relations between God and humanity in which Christ is conceived as Mediator. The Stancaro controversy among the Reformed churches in Poland is a crucial instance of the growing concern in the late sixteenth-century over matters that bridged Christology and soteriology.[6] At the heart of the

---

[2] *Formula of Concord*, Epitome, VII.32-34, VIII.7, 16, Solid Declaration, VIII.9, VIII.12, VIII.27, in *The Book of Concord: The Confessions of the Evangelical Lutheran Church*, ed. Robert Kolb and Timothy J. Wengert, trans. Charles Arand et al. (Minneapolis: Fortress Press, 2000).
[3] Muller, *DLGTT*, 75; *Formula of Concord*, Solid Declaration, VIII.14-15, VIII.17-21.
[4] Pelikan, *Reformation of Church and Dogma*, 353-54.
[5] Wolfhart Pannenberg, *Jesus - God and Man*, trans. Lewis L. Wilkins and Duane A. Priebe (Philadelphia: Westminster Press, 1968), 298: "In the fifth century the discussion of the *communicatio idiomatum* involved the question of what constituted the unity in Christ. In the sixteenth and seventeenth centuries, as already in high Scholasticism, the discussion involved the consequences of this unity as unity of person for the relation between the natures."
[6] Joseph Tylenda, "Christ the Mediator: Calvin Versus Stancaro," *CTJ* 8, no. 1 (1973), 5-16; Joseph Tylenda, "The Controversy on Christ the Mediator: Calvin's Second Reply to Stancaro," *CTJ* 8, no. 1 (1973), 131-57; Stephen Edmonson, *Calvin's Christology* (Cambridge: Cambridge University Press, 2004), 14-39.

controversy is the question of the nature or natures in which Christ fulfils his office as Mediator. Francesco Stancaro (1501-1574), an Italian scholar, taught that Christ was Mediator only in respect of his humanity. In his view, mediatorial acts like prayer and intercession implied the inferior status of the Mediator in comparison to the one to whom these acts are addressed and on whom they terminate. Christ as Mediator is thus inferior to the Father and cannot be said to mediate with respect to his divinity. This teaching precipitated a crisis among the Reformed churches in Poland which was unfortunately exacerbated by the death of the Polish reformer John à Lasco (1499-1560). Without authoritative opposition to Stancaro, the Polish churches sought help from the Reformed churches of Geneva and Zurich among others, both of which responded through the writings of Calvin and Vermigli respectively.[7] Both reformers had much in common in their replies. Against Stancaro, they affirmed that Christ is Mediator according to both his divine and human natures, maintained the integrity of both natures in the hypostatic union, and nuanced their accounts through the doctrine of *communicatio idiomatum*, all of which points were argued on the basis of Scripture and the patristic tradition.[8] This controversy gives insight into the posture of Reformed Christology in the late sixteenth century, which was increasingly being defined in terms of mediation but which still moved within the bounds of orthodox Christology. By the seventeenth-century, speaking of Christ as the Mediator who fulfils his mediatorial office in his divine and human natures became the standard way of stating the person and work of Christ in Reformed orthodox writings.[9]

The necessity of stating Christology in this manner was all the more urgent in the light of Socinianism. Named after Laelius Socinus and his nephew Faustus, Socinianism originated in Poland, became influential through its printing press in Holland, and was imported into England through various tracts and personalities, chief of whom was John Biddle.[10] Although it was not a

---

[7] Calvin wrote two letters addressed to the Polish Brethren, expressing his views on this matter. They are translated into English and found in Tylenda, "Christ the Mediator", 11-16; idem, "Controversy on Christ the Mediator", 146-57. For Vermigli's response, see "A Letter to Poland", in John Patrick S.J. Donnelly, Frank A. James III, Joseph C. McLelland, ed., *The Peter Martyr Reader* (Kirksville, Missouri: Truman State University Press, 1999), 125-31.

[8] Calvin's response in particular was calculated to provide a non-speculative answer to Stancaro's position with a plethora of Scriptural citations and exegetical comments. In direct response to Stancaro's appeal to the church fathers, Calvin provided his own selections from Augustine, Cyril of Alexandria, Chrysostom, and Ambrose. Tylenda, "Controversy on Christ the Mediator", 146-57.

[9] *Westminster Confession*, VIII; Ames, *Marrow*, I.xviii-xxiv; cf. Heppe's doctrinal heads for Christology, in Heppe, *Reformed Dogmatics*, XVII: "The Mediator of the Covenant of Grace or the Person of Christ", XVIII: "The Mediatorial Office of Jesus Christ", XIX: "Christ's State of Exaninition and of Exaltation."

[10] H. John McLachlan, *Socinianism in Seventeenth Century England* (Oxford: Oxford University Press, 1951). On Biddle, see 163-217.

homogenous movement, there were nevertheless distinctive characteristics which are common to both its Polish and Anglophone expressions. McLachlan speaks of "the peculiarly dual character of Socinianism", characterized by a body of doctrine on the one hand and the principles of freedom, reason, and tolerance in religion on the other.[11] Of the former, the *Racovian Catechism* (1652) and Biddle's *Twofold Catechism* (1654) are the representative works.[12] These catechisms were the main targets of criticism in Owen's *Vindiciae Evangelicae; or the Mystery of the Gospel vindicated and Socinianisme examined*, a massive work of polemical strength, commissioned by the Council of State in 1654 and published in 1655.[13] Among the numerous controversies in which Owen was constrained to be involved, Socinianism posed the most serious threat to orthodoxy in key areas of doctrine. Christology was the crux of the debate. The extent to which the movement's antitrinitarian stance was theologically, exegetically, and rationally viable is contingent upon the extent to which orthodox Christology was shown to be untenable. Thus, three quarters of the *Racovian Catechism* and more than a third of the *Twofold Catechism* were spent on Christology.[14] The Christology of these catechisms is essentially the same. Two observations on their Christology are significant for the purpose of establishing the background to Owen's Christology.

First, with respect to the person of Christ, there is no question as to the integrity of his humanity. It was Christ's divinity that is the point of contention.

---

[11] McLachlan, *Socinianism*, 336ff.

[12] *The Racovian Catechisme; Wherein You Have the Substance of the Confession, That No Other Save the Father of Our Lord Jesus Christ Is That One God of Israel, and That the Man Jesus of Nazareth Who Was Born of the Virgin, and No Other Besides or before Him, Is the Onely Begotton Sonne of God* (Amsterledam: Printed for Brooer Janz, 1652). It was first published in Polish in 1605 and subsequently translated into Latin, German, and Dutch. Its first English translation, from which this study cites, was supposedly printed at "Amsterledam for Brooer Janz". McLachlan suggests that "Amsterledam" was a printer's blind for London, and "Broorer Janz" was none other than John Biddle. McLachlan, *Socinianism*, 36, 190ff.; John Biddle, *A Twofold Catechism: The One Simply Called a Scripture-Catechism; the Other, a Brief Scripture-Catechism for Children. Wherein the Chiefest Points of the Christian Religion, Being Question-Wise Proposed, Resolves Themselves by Pertinent Answers Taken Word for Word out of the Scripture, without Either Consequences or Comments* (London: Printed by J. Cottrel, 1654).

[13] Owen, *Vindicae Evangelicae* (*Works*, 12:1-590). The first edition consisted of 683 pages apart from the appendix entitled "Of the Death of Christ, and of Justification". In addition to the Socinian catechisms, Hugo Grotius' annotations on the Bible were also taken to task for their Socinian tendencies. Part of the sub-title reads: "The vindication of the testimonies of Scripture concerning the deity and satisfaction of Jesus Christ from the perverse expositions and interpretations of them by Hugo Grotius, in his annotations on the Bible".

[14] Of the former, 139 out of 176 pages deal with Christology. In Biddle's catechism, Christology covers nine out of a total of twenty-four chapters.

The specific form which the rejection of orthodox Christology took in the catechisms is the construal of the Chalcedonian two-natures doctrine as absurd. It is both contrary to reason and to Scripture that two natures with opposing properties can be united in one person, so the Socinian argument went.[15] The assumption is that a single person is constituted by a single nature or essence. Thus, "two Natures, each whereof is apt to constitute a severall person, cannot be huddled into one Person. For instead of one, there must of necessity arise two Persons, and consequently become two Christs..."[16] For the Socinians, the uniqueness of Christ does not lie in the hypostatic union, but in the fact of the virgin birth and the indwelling of the Spirit without measure at Christ's baptism.

Second, the work of Christ in both catechisms is constructed after the mediatorial framework.[17] Christ's threefold office is explicated on the basis of the prior conclusions arrived at with respect to his person.[18] The result is a conception of Christ's mediatorial office that is suited to his human nature alone. This is worked out structurally by placing the greatest Christological weight on the prophetic office and conceiving of the remaining two offices as post-resurrection performances. Despite Christ's exaltation to the Father's right hand and his participation in the divine prerogative of absolute dominion, both of which are acknowledged by the Socinians, he remained a mere man to them. The power of absolute dominion was not conceived as inherent to Christ but as a communicated quality from the Father. While sharing in divinity functionally, the exalted Christ remains ontologically separate from the Father according to the Socinians. The soteriological implications are not difficult to perceive. Christ is our Saviour because he has announced the way of salvation, not because he has dealt with the problem of sin as our mediating *theanthropos*. Consequently, entrance into this salvation is obtained by imitating Christ.

Thus, the Socinian controversy called into question the long standing norm of Chalcedonian Christology, but also retained and radically revised the mediatorial category of Christ's threefold office. If orthodox Christology was to

---

[15] *Racovian Catechisme*, 28ff.; Biddle's catechism does not state this explicitly but the implication is clear from the way the key questions that pertained to Christ's person are framed in terms of personal union and essence: "Qu. Could not Christ do all things of himself? And was it not an eternal Son of God that took flesh upon him, and to whom the humane nature of Christ was personally united, that wrought all his works? ... Qu. Doth the Scripture avouch Christ to be the Son of God because he was eternally begotten out of the Divine essence, or for other reasons agreeing to him onely as a man?" Biddle, *Twofold Catechism*, 28-29. Owen considered the second question as the critical one. It is, he opined, "the head...of Mr B.'s design in this chapter, and, indeed, of the greatest design that he drives in religion, namely, the denial of the eternal deity of the Son of God..." Owen, *Vindicae Evangelicae*, VII (*Works*, 12:177).
[16] *Racovian Catechisme*, 28.
[17] *Racovian Catechisme*, 74-165; Biddle, *Twofold Catechism*, 41-66.
[18] This is especially evident in the *Racovian Catechisme*. See Trueman, *Claims of Truth*, 152-54.

be defended against Socinianism, it would be necessary to reappropriate the two-natures doctrine in relation to an account of the threefold office. The crucial Christological question that needed to be addressed was not merely about the hypostatic union or the constitution of the Mediator, but also concerned the compatibility of orthodox Christology with the doctrine of the Mediator in his threefold office. Indeed, Owen does provide answers to this question in his Christology as will become clear below, but not without tapping into and drawing from the Reformed tradition that was refined in the crucible of the Lutheran-Reformed debates over the sacraments and the Reformed resolution of the kind of issue raised by the Stancaro controversy. The following section will examine Owen's main Christological treatise in order to identify the general features of his Christology, after which an account of the more specific features will be given.

Christologia (1679)

Christologia is not a polemical treatise. While Owen did engage with Catholic and Socinian theology in it, his main concern is pastoral in nature.[19] This explains the absence of any prolonged polemical engagement in it. In the Preface, Owen hints at the reason for his pastoral concern: "This, and no other is the design of the treatise...The re-enthroning of the Person, Spirit, Grace, and Authority of Christ in the hearts and consciences of men, is the only way whereby an end may be put unto these woful conflicts."[20] It is not certain if the reference to "woful conflicts" was political or doctrinal in nature.[21] The important point to note is the non-polemical nature of the treatise. The relative freedom Owen had from having to structure his treatise according to the terms

---

[19] On Catholicism, see Owen, *Christologia*, I, XII, XX (*Works*, 1:29-35, 141, 268-69); for Socinianism, see idem, *Christologia*, II, VI, VII, XI, X, XI (*Works*, 1:41, 83, 95-96, 112, 123, 136).

[20] Owen, *Christologia*, Preface (*Works*, 1:5).

[21] Spence assumes that Owen was referring to the events which followed the reversal of Puritan fortunes with the restoration of the monarchy in 1660. Spence, *Incarnation and Inspiration*, 30-31. Since there was no further elaboration by Owen, one cannot be certain if this was indeed the case. On the basis of internal evidence, it is more likely that the perceived conflict was doctrinal in nature with adverse pastoral consequences. See for instance Owen's references to Socinianism (footnote 19) and to the resurgence of Nestorianism in *Christologia*, II (*Works*, 1:40). Whether Owen saw these two as amounting to the same problem is unclear. External evidence also favours the doctrinal nature of the perceived conflict. Owen's concurrent labour on the book of Hebrews has the Socinian threat specifically in mind. The sub-title to his *Exercitations on the Epistle to the Hebrews* includes reference to "the opinions of the Socinians". Cf. references to his Hebrews commentary in *Christologia*, XI, XVII, XIX (*Works*, 1:136, 215, 251). Goold points to the rise of the antitrinitarians as confirmation of Owen's apprehensions about the increasing threat to orthodox Christology. *Christologia*, Prefatory Note (*Works*, 1:2). The doctrinal context is to the fore in Goold's observation.

set by his theological opponents allowed for a more constructive account of Christology to be given.²² His expressed intent to promote "the edification of the common sort of readers" by consciously avoiding the insertion of patristic sources in the main body of the text for fear that they might be an encumbrance to readers enhances the clarity of his account.²³ Added to these helpful features for understanding his Christology is the fact that along with his posthumous *Meditations and Discourses on the Glory of Christ* (1684), *Christologia* contains the mature thoughts of Owen on this subject. Thus, it is reasonable to expect to find crucial elements of Owen's Christology in the treatise which may have received only incidental treatment in his other writings.²⁴

The treatise consists of twenty chapters and may be divided according to Christological themes. Although Owen did not explicitly mention them, there are four discernible sections. The first introduces the whole subject and supplies the proper context to his work.²⁵ This is followed by an exposition of the person of Christ in the second section, and of Christ's office as Mediator in the third and fourth.²⁶ Section three unpacks the doctrine of the Mediator from an experiential standpoint, while section four is concerned with the theological foundations of the doctrine. The distinction between experiential and theological concerns is by no means absolute but is one of relative emphasis. An examination of the treatise in order to identify the general features of Owen's Christology will now follow.

Owen's point of departure in *Christologia* is neither the pre-existence of Christ nor the doctrine of the hypostatic union, but the person of Christ in relation to the church in history. Thus, the opening chapter locates the subject in the context of Peter's confession of Christ in Matthew 16:16, and of Jesus' response in the verses which follow.²⁷ Christ, Owen argued, is that confessed "rock" or foundation of the church against whom the "gates of Hades" will not prevail. Elaborations on satanic opposition against the church follow, illustrated in terms of the Christological heresies and aberrations in ecclesiastical history up till Owen's day.²⁸ The importance of this ecclesial context is seen in its prominence throughout the entire treatise and serves to ground Owen's Christology in both pastoral and historical concerns.

---

²² Unlike Owen's *A Display of Arminianism* (1642) or *Vindiciae Evangelicae* (1655). The former is structured after key Arminian tenets and the latter after the *Racovian Catechisme* and the *Twofold Catechism*.
²³ Owen, *Christologia*, Preface (*Works*, 1:6).
²⁴ For instance, Owen's cursory mention of the incarnation in *The Death of Death* is treated substantially in *Christologia*, XVIII (*Works*, 1:223-35).
²⁵ Owen, *Christologia*, I-II (*Works*, 1:29-44).
²⁶ Section two: *Christologia*, III-VI (*Works*, 1:44-85); section three: *Christologia*, VII-XV (*Works*, 1:85-178); section four: *Christologia*, XVI-XX (*Works*, 1:178-272).
²⁷ Owen, *Christologia*, I (*Works*, 1:29-35).
²⁸ Owen, *Christologia*, II (*Works*, 1:35-44).

Having established Christology in the context of ecclesiology, Owen went on to expound the person of Christ in the second section.[29] He argued that the person of Christ is the most ineffable effect of divine wisdom,[30] the foundation of the eternal counsels,[31] the representative of God and his will,[32] and the repository of sacred truth.[33] At the heart of these arguments is the central place that Christ occupies in the conception and accomplishment of what is necessary for the church's salvation. They are advanced in the light of a foundational principle of Owen's theology: that there exists a fundamental distinction between eternity and temporality.[34] The former, being immense and infinite is irreconcilable with the latter in its limitations and finitude. Divinity and humanity are intrinsically and ultimately poles apart: "The most glorious exaltation that a creature can have brings him not one step nearer the essence of God than a worm; for between that which is infinite and that which is not infinite there is no proportion."[35] It is in the person of Christ as the Mediator between God and humanity that these polarities are bridged. Owen's principle is assumed in the various distinctions he employed, such as the distinctions between God's essential and provisional wisdom,[36] God's essential and representative image,[37] and God's essential and declarative truth.[38] These distinctions reflect Owen's awareness of the eternal/temporal dialectic. In every case, the polarity is resolved in the person of Christ. Since the first doublet is the most prominent of the three, it will be examined at length below.

Owen's assertion that the person of Christ is the effect of divine wisdom and goodness in no way implies ontological inferiority to the Father. Neither is it to be understood that Christ obtained existence as a consequence of the exercise of the divine perfections. Owen distances himself from such heterodox views by distinguishing between the *essential* and *provisional* wisdom of God. Owen conceived of God's essential wisdom as the person of Christ considered

---

[29] Owen, *Christologia*, III-VII (*Works*, 1:44-100).
[30] Owen, *Christologia*, III (*Works*, 1:44-53).
[31] Owen, *Christologia*, VI (*Works*, 1:54-64).
[32] Owen, *Christologia*, V (*Works*, 1:65-79).
[33] Owen, *Christologia*, VI (*Works*, 1:79-85).
[34] Epistemologically, this is expressed by Owen in the distinction between *theologia archetypa* and *theologia ectypa*. Owen, *Theologoumena*, I.iii.11 (*BT*, 14-19). The extent of the distance between these two types of theology is illustrated in the *theologia unionis*, a sub-category of *theologia ectypa*. Although there is a sense in which both types of theology are applicable to Christ on account of his divine and human natures, nevertheless these types remain distinct even for the person of Christ. For a full discussion of these matters in Owen, see Rehnman, *Divine Discourse*, 57-71; cf. Muller, *PRRD*, 1:225-38.
[35] Owen, *Posthumous Sermons*, XI (*Works*, 16:495).
[36] Owen, *Christologia*, III, IV (*Works*, 1:45, 62-63).
[37] Owen, *Christologia*, V, XVII (*Works*, 1:71-72, 74, 78-79, 218-19). For Owen's doctrine of the *imago dei*, see Kapic, *Communion with God*, 38-84.
[38] Owen, *Christologia*, VI (*Works*, 1:79).

absolutely in his divinity, and God's provisional wisdom as the person of Christ considered in his incarnate state. "Thus, as all things were originally made and created by him, as he was the essential wisdom of God – so all things are renewed and recovered by him, as he is the provisional wisdom of God, in and by his incarnation."[39] According to Owen, Christ as "the effect of divine wisdom" concerned the person of Christ as God's provisional wisdom, a status that in no way negated his identity as God's essential wisdom.

> I speak not of his divine person absolutely; for his distinct personality and subsistence was by an internal and eternal act of the Divine Being in the person of the Father, or eternal generation – which is essential unto the divine essence – whereby nothing anew was outwardly wrought or did exist. He was not, he is not, in that sense, the effect of the divine wisdom and power of God, but the essential wisdom and power of God.[40]

Owen's distinction between essential and provisional wisdom relied on the Reformed orthodox conception of divine wisdom, with modifications that reflected his own peculiar concerns.[41] The concept of essential wisdom in Reformed orthodoxy is usually defined as the attribute of wisdom that is predicated of all persons of the Trinity by virtue of their common essence.[42] It is distinguished from the personal wisdom of God which conceives of wisdom in the form of the eternal Logos or Son.[43] Charnock captures this distinction succinctly: "There is an Essential and a Personal Wisdom of God. The Essential Wisdom is the Essence of God; the Personal Wisdom is the Son of God."[44] The distinguishing factor in these categories is the element of hypostatization. However, this distinguishing feature between the categories becomes the point of commonality for Owen's categories.[45] It is the person of Christ considered

---

[39] Owen, *Christologia*, IV (*Works*, 1:63).

[40] Owen, *Christologia*, III (*Works*, 1:45). On Owen's treatment of the eternal generation of the Son in the context of Socinianism, see idem, *Vindicae Evangelicae*, IX (*Works*, 12:237). For the wider Reformed orthodox context, cf. Muller, *PRRD*, 4:283-88.

[41] Muller, *PRRD*, 3:385-92.

[42] Polanus, *Svbstance of Christian Religion*, 8: "The wisdome of God is an essentiall proprietie of God, by which he certainly knoweth, and understandeth all things, truly, properly, by one eternall and unchangeable act, and that also together, most perfectly, assuredly, evidently, and distinctly, being never ignorant of anything, neither learning or knowing anything by successe, nor forgetting anything, &c."; Stephen Charnock, *Several Discourses Upon the Existence and Attributes of God* (London: Printed for D. Newman, T. Cockerill, Benj. Griffin, T. Simmons, and Benj. Alsop, 1682), 339: "The Wisdom of God is the same with the Essence of God. Wisdom in God is not a Habit added to his Essence, as it is in Man, but it is his Essence."

[43] Muller, *PRRD*, 3:386-87.

[44] Charnock, *Several Discourses*, 339.

[45] Elsewhere, Owen uses wisdom as an attribute of God. *Christologia*, IV (*Works*, 1:58): "Infinite wisdom being that property of the divine nature whereby all the actings of it are disposed and regulated, suitably unto his own glory, in all his divine excellencies – he

absolutely or in his divinity who is the essential wisdom of God, and the person of Christ as incarnate who is the provisional wisdom of God. Thus, for Owen, the person of Christ as wisdom hypostatized is the subject of both categories, with the distinguishing element being the assumption of human nature into personal union, not hypostatization. This modification of the Reformed orthodox categories is in keeping with Owen's concern against the abstraction of Christology from the economy of salvation as Scripture proposes. "This is the constant method of Scripture," he insisted: "it first proposeth unto us what the Lord Christ hath done for us, especially in the discharge of his sacerdotal office, in his oblation and intercession, with the benefits which we receive thereby. Hereby it leads us unto his person, and presseth the consideration of all other things to engage our love unto him."[46] Thus, Owen's use of the essential-provisional distinction grounds Christology in the economy of salvation, without denying the ontological equality of the person of Christ with the person of God.

Owen's essential-provisional distinction also allows him to construe of the interplay between eternity and time in a Christocentric manner. This is evident in his discussion of the enactment of God's counsels in eternity and its execution in time. The basic assertion is of Christ as the foundation of the divine counsels: "The person of Christ is the foundation of all the counsels of God, as unto his own eternal glory, in the vocation, sanctification, and salvation of the church."[47] In a later statement, he clarified this assertion by speaking of the divine counsels as being "laid in" Christ and accomplished by him:

> As God the Father did nothing in the first creation but by him—as his eternal wisdom...so he designed nothing in the new creation, or restoration of all things unto his glory, but in him—as he was to be incarnate. Wherefore in his person were laid all the foundation of the counsels of God for the sanctification and salvation of the church.[48]

For Owen, then, being the "foundation" of the divine counsels entailed Christological fulfilment and agency. The causal ground for this mediatorial vocation is the intratrinitarian *pactum salutis*, the terms of which were undertaken voluntarily by the Son.[49]

As part of his attempt to found his assertion on Scripture, Owen made much of the personification of wisdom in Proverbs 8:22-23. He equated "his ways" in

---

cannot but delight in all the acts of it"; idem, *Christologia*, III, XVI, XVII (*Works*, 1:46, 180, 222). This non-hypostatized concept of divine wisdom that has to do with the way in which events are ordered in the world is to play a pivotal role in the fourth section of the treatise. Cf. idem, *Christologia*, XVI-XX.
[46] Owen, *Christologia*, XIV (*Works*, 1:162).
[47] Owen, *Christologia*, IV (*Works*, 1:54).
[48] Owen, *Christologia*, IV (*Works*, 1:64).
[49] Owen, *Christologia*, IV (*Works*, 1:55-56).

verse 22 to God's eternal counsels, and "set him up from everlasting" to the establishment of Christ as the foundation of these counsels. What is significant is his application of the essential-provisional distinction to the exegesis of the passage. Reflecting on the phrase in verse 22, "The Lord possessed me in the beginning of his way", Owen commented:

> God possessed him eternally as his essential wisdom – as he was always, and is always, in the bosom of the Father, in the mutual ineffable love of the Father and Son, in the eternal bond of the Spirit. But he signally possessed him 'in the beginning of his way' – as his wisdom, acting in the production of all the ways and works that are outwardly of him.[50]

In this passage, the Son as wisdom hypostatized is the agent of God's external works. Reformed orthodox exegesis of the passage reflects similar concerns.[51] Poole's commentary on Proverbs 8:22-23, for instance, displays remarkable similarities with Owen's comments:

> 22. *The Lord possessed me* ° *in the beginning* ᴾ *of his way* ᑫ, *before the works of old.* ° As his Son by Eternal Generation, who was from Eternity with him... ᴾ Yea and before the beginning as it is largely expressed in the following verses. ᑫ Either 1. of his counsels or decrees. Or rather 2. of his works of Creation, as it follows...23. *I was set up* ʳ *from everlasting, from the beginning* ˢ, *or ever the earth* ᵗ *was.* ʳ Heb. *anointed,* ordained or constituted to be the Person by whom the Father resolved to do all his works, first to create and then to uphold and govern and judge, and afterwards to redeem and save the world; all which works are particularly ascribed to the Son of God. ...ˢ Before which there was nothing but a vast Eternity. ᵗ Which he mentions because this together with the Heaven, was the first of God's visible works.[52]

---

[50] Owen, *Christologia*, IV (*Works*, 1:54).

[51] Theodore Beza, *The Bible, That Is, the Holy Scripture Contained in the Old and the New Testament. Translated According to the Hebrew and Greeke, and Conferred with the Best Translations in Diuers Languages. With Most Profitable Annotations Upon All the Hard Places and Other Things of Great Importance* (London: Printed by Robert Barker, 1602), 277. Marginal notes to verse 22 reads, "He declareth hereby the divinitie and eternitie of this wisdome, which bee magnifieth and praiseth through this Booke: meaning thereby the eternall Sonne of God Jesus Christ our Savior whom Saint John calleth the Word that was in the beginning. John 1:1"; Edward Leigh, *Annotations on Five Poetical Books of the Old Testament: Job, Psalmes, Proverbs, Ecclesiastes, and Canticles* (London: Printed by A. M. for T. Pierpoint, 1657), 133; John Trapp, *A Commentary or Exposition Upon These Following Books of Holy Scripture; Proverbs of Solomon, Ecclesiastes, the Song of Songs, Isaiah, Jeremiah, Lamentations, Ezekiel & Daniel* (London: Printed by Robert White, for Nevil Simmons, 1660), 45-46, esp. comments on Prov 8:27.

[52] Matthew Poole, *Annotations Upon the Holy Bible Wherein the Sacred Text Is Inserted, and Various Readings Annex'd*, vol. 1 (London: Printed by John Richardson, 1683), Prov 8:22-23, in loc. Italics added to distinguish verses from commentary.

Poole's exegesis resembles Owen's in its concern for the divine counsels understood in the context of the trinitarian relations and divine agency *ad extra*. However, in Owen's exegesis, the application of the essential-provisional distinction to the passage grounds it more firmly in the historical economy. While Poole was not oblivious to the historical dimension of the Son's work, his emphasis is clearly on the Son's pre-existence. Hence, commenting on the phrase "in the beginning of his way" in verse 22, he writes, "Yea and before the beginning..." On verse 23, "from the beginning" receives the qualifying comment, "Before which there was nothing but a vast eternity." Owen however, understood these phrases as pointing rather to the execution of God's eternal counsels in time by the incarnate Son. As God's essential wisdom, the person of Christ is the focal point in the enactment of the eternal counsels. As God's provisional wisdom, the person of Christ is the agent through whom they are executed in time. Owen's conception of Christ as the foundation of God's counsels, supported by his Christological reading of Proverbs 8:22-23, evidences a convergence of the eternal and historical economies on the person of Christ.[53]

What was construed in section two as pertaining to God's counsels and divine wisdom is in sections three and four related to the work of salvation in mediatorial terms. It is in these sections that the mediatorial category features prominently, revolving around Christ's threefold office.[54] This prominence is apparent from the way in which the sections are structured and from the material content of Owen's discourse. Section three opens with a chapter that attempts to relate the person and office of Christ.[55] Owen maintained that the power and efficacy of the Mediator's work for the church is by virtue of the Mediator's person as divine and human. Christ's humanity made it possible for him to mediate on behalf of humanity, while Christ's divinity gave infinite worth to his person and ensured the efficacy of his mediatorial work for the church. In the elucidation of these matters, the threefold office was employed

---

[53] Owen's narrative of salvation history in his attempt to "manifest in particular how all these counsels of God were laid in the person of Christ" gives further evidence of his concern to construct his Christology in the context of the economy of salvation. Owen, *Christologia*, IV (*Works*, 1:60-62).

[54] Trueman's comment that Owen used the threefold office "as the basis for structuring his Christological discussion" in *Christologia*, and that Owen regarded it as "providing a framework for an exhaustive statement of all Christ's mediatorial dealings with the church" somewhat overstates the case. Trueman, *Claims of Truth*, 168. It is in sections three and four in particular (*Christologia*, VII-XX) that Trueman's claim holds true. Even then, the claim needs further qualification since it is only in chapters VII and XX that the threefold structure, corresponding to the threefold office, is found. This is not to deny the prominence of mediatorial concerns in sections three and four as will become clear.

[55] Owen, *Christologia*, VII (*Works*, 1:85-100).

as structural heads.[56] The remaining chapters in this section consist of discussions that pertain to way in which the power and efficacy of Christ's mediation is experienced in the life of the church.[57] Within this ecclesial context, Christ's exercise of the threefold office is assumed as the following axiomatic statement makes clear:

> It is by the exercise and discharge of the office of Christ – as the king, priest, and prophet of the church – that we are redeemed, sanctified and saved. Thereby does he immediately communicate all Gospel benefits unto us – give us an access unto God here by grace and in glory hereafter; for he saves us, as he is mediator between God and man.[58]

Section four reintroduces the concept of divine wisdom and relates it to Christ's office and work. Unlike the hypostatized form of divine wisdom, which was the preoccupation of Owen in section two, wisdom is here understood as a divine attribute. Owen defined wisdom as "the directive power or excellency of the divine nature".[59] It was mentioned alongside the attributes of goodness and power as one of the three divine attributes which are principally to be considered in the external works of God.[60] What the triune God desires to communicate in his goodness and effect through his power, divine wisdom directs. Its glory is manifested through the fittingness or "condecency" of the divinely appointed means for the accomplishment of the divinely intended redemption. This fittingness is demonstrated in the constitution of the Mediator, in the conception of his office, and in its discharge. Owen's choice of wisdom as a regulating motif keeps his exposition centred on the mediation of Christ as the means suited to divine wisdom.

In the concluding chapter, arguably the climax of the entire treatise, Owen discoursed on Christ's mediatorial work in heaven.[61] He argued that the risen and ascended Christ continues to mediate for the church on earth as high priest in heaven by representing their prayers and rendering their worship acceptable before God. But for the already prolonged reflections in *Christologia*, Owen had actually intended to impose some form of structure in accordance with the threefold office on this final chapter and unpack each aspect at some length.[62]

---

[56] Owen, *Christologia*, VII (*Works*, 1:87-96 [prophet], 96-99 [king], 99 [priest]).
[57] Owen, *Christologia*, VIII-XV (*Works*, 1:100-178).
[58] Owen, *Christologia*, VII (*Works*, 1:85).
[59] Owen, *Christologia*, XVI (*Works*, 1:180).
[60] See Chapter 6.
[61] Owen, *Christologia*, XX (*Works*, 1:252-72).
[62] That this was Owen's intention is evident from the Scriptural basis from which he draws the implication of Christ's threefold office in heaven. From John's vision of the heavenly throne in Revelation 5:6, Owen understood Christ being in the midst of the "throne" and having "seven horns" as portrayals of Christ's kingly glory. The metaphor of Christ as the slain Lamb was understood to refer to his priestly office while the

However, prior treatments of the subject and the length of the treatise constrained him to narrow his comments to the exercise of Christ's priestly office in heaven.[63] Nevertheless, it is clear from Owen's exposition that there was no privileging of the priestly over the prophetic and kingly offices, but that the heavenly work of Christ applied equally to all three. "His present state," Owen averred, "is a state of *office-power*, work, and duty. He leads not in heaven a life of mere glory, majesty and blessedness, but a life of office, love, and care also. He lives as the *Mediator* of the church; as the King, Priest, and Prophet thereof. Hereon do our present safety and our future eternal salvation depend."[64]

From the above analysis of *Christologia*, the general features of Owen's Christology are identifiable. First, the construction of Owen's Christology is done from within an ecclesial context. The treatise starts with Christ as the church's foundation and ends with the church's worship on earth made acceptable by Christ's mediation in heaven. What transpired in between is the attempt to direct the church's attention to the person of Christ as the object of faith. Second, Owen's Christology is developed within the context of the economy of salvation. From the conception of God's eternal counsels, its accomplishment in time, to Christ's continuing work in heaven, the entire movement is soteriologically oriented. Owen's conception of divine wisdom as God's "directive power" and his choice of it as a key motif facilitate the expression of this movement in the economy of salvation. Third, in Owen's Christology, the eternal-temporal dialectic finds its resolution in the person of Christ. Owen's distinction between God's essential and provisional wisdom, both of which are construed hypostatically and equated with the person of Christ, is indicative of that resolution. Fourth, the mediatorial category is the main category employed by Owen for explicating various elements of his Christology. Not only does the content of his exposition deal with mediatorial concerns, the large bulk of Owen's exposition either assumes the exercise of Christ's threefold office, or is explicitly structured after it. These general features provide the necessary framework for the more specific aspects of Owen's Christology, to which the discussion in this chapter now turns.

"seven eyes" which are the "seven spirits of God" referred to his prophetic office. Owen, *Christologia*, XX (*Works*, 1:253).

[63] Owen, *Christologia*, XX (*Works*, 1:253): "The nature of these *offices* of Christ, what belongs unto them and their discharge, as was before intimated, I have declared elsewhere. I do now no farther consider them but as they relate unto the present state and condition of the person of Christ in heaven. And because it would be too long a work to treat of them all distinctly, I shall confine myself unto the consideration of his priestly office, with what depends thereon."

[64] Owen, *Christologia*, XX (*Works*, 1:252).

Owen's Reformed Christology

Incarnation

A general feature of Owen's Christology is his conscious attempt to develop his Christology in the context of the economy of salvation as indicated above. This feature is evident in the way he relates Christ's incarnation to the problem of sin. An important aspect of Owen's argument for the necessity of the incarnation is his understanding of God as the supreme Governor and Judge who orders the universe according to his wisdom and rules in accordance with his rectoral justice.[65] Corresponding to these related views of God is Owen's view of sin as entailing disturbance in the divine ordering of the universe and the injury of God's honour. The necessity of the incarnation, for Owen, was predicated upon a twofold principle: that it is man who has to satisfy the demands of God's justice for the reparation of God's injured honour; that it is God who is able to render that satisfaction of infinite worth and efficacy. "It was necessary," Owen insisted, "that he by whom the work of reparation was to be wrought should be a man, partaker of the nature that sinned, yet free from all sin, and all the consequents of it."[66] It was also necessary that this work of reparation not simply be undertaken by a mere man, but "he must be God also" since "(t)here was no one act he was to perform, in order unto our deliverance, but did require a divine power to render it efficacious."[67] Christ the *theanthropos* was the only person fit to satisfy the demands of divine justice and render the satisfaction efficacious, and hence to bring about humanity's redemption and the restoration of order in the universe.[68] Humanity's redemption by means of the incarnation was itself a conception of divine wisdom. It is in the light of these mediatorial concerns that the incarnation's necessity is clinched.

Clearly there are significant overlaps with Anselm in Owen's account. Casting sin in terms of disorder and dishonour, the proposal of sin's solution in terms of satisfaction, and the identification of the God-man as the person in whom the solution to sin is found are unmistakable marks of the Anselmian tradition.[69] Nevertheless, there are significant differences as well. Not least among these is Owen's insistence on sin's punishment and satisfaction, unlike Anselm's presentation of them as alternatives for rectifying God's injured honour. In Owen's exposition of these themes, the Biblical narrative of redemptive history is taken seriously. The narrative of humanity's fall into sin

---

[65] Owen, *Christologia*, XVI (*Works*, 1:185-87).
[66] Owen, *Christologia*, XVI (*Works*, 1:200).
[67] Owen, *Christologia*, XVI (*Works*, 1:200).
[68] See Chapter 6 for a fuller account of Owen's narrative of redemptive history from the standpoint of God's self-glorification as the supreme end of redemption.
[69] Anselm, *Cur Deus Homo*, I.xi-xv, II.vi (*LCC* 10:118-65, 150-51); cf. Kapic, *Communion with God*, 87-90.

in Genesis 3 and the promise of redemption in the *protoevangelium* were crucial for him.[70]

Besides conceiving of the incarnation in relation to the problem of sin, the eternal basis of redemption was also an important concern for Owen.[71] The plan of salvation for fallen humanity was fully conceived in the *pactum salutis*. Thus, Owen could write of God that he was in no way taken by surprise when humanity sinned in Adam, for already in the eternal *pactum* was it established that the Son would undertake redemption's accomplishment.[72] Not only did Owen insist that the incarnation was not an afterthought in the divine mind, he also maintained that the very means of redemption by incarnation is conceived and covenanted within the inner life of the Trinity.

As to the actual event of the incarnation, Owen summed up its occurrence in the terms *assumption* and *union*. Assumption is defined by Owen as "that ineffable divine act...whereby the person of the Son of God assumed our nature, or took it into personal subsistence with himself."[73] It is "the foundation of the divine relation between the Son of God and the man Christ Jesus."[74] By union, Owen was referring to the orthodox doctrine of the hypostatic union. In his statement of the doctrine, he appealed to Scripture and tradition, cited texts such as Isaiah 7:14, John 8:58, Acts 20:28, and relied heavily on the Chalcedonian definition:

> This union the ancient church affirmed to be made ἀτρέπτως, "without any change" in the person of the Son of God, which the divine nature is not subject unto;—ἀδιαιρέτως, with a distinction of natures, but "without any division" of them by separate subsistences;—ἀσυγχύτως, "without mixture" or confusion;—ἀχωρίστως, "without separation" or distance; and οὐσιωδῶς, "substantially," because it was of two substances or essences in the same person, in opposition unto all *accidental* union, as the "fulness of the Godhead dwelt in him bodily."[75]

The first four terms are taken directly from the Chalcedonian Creed (AD 451) while the fifth is derived from that part of the creedal formula in which the Lord Jesus Christ is said to be "consubstantial with the Father according to the Godhead, and consubstantial with us according to the Manhood."[76]

Owen further qualified his statement on the hypostatic union by appealing to the anhypostatic/enhypostatic formulation. According to him, the object of

---

[70] Owen, *Christologia*, X (*Works*, 1:120ff).

[71] Trueman, *Claims of Truth*, 29-148.

[72] Owen, *Christologia*, IV (*Works*, 1:61-62).

[73] Owen, *Christologia*, XVIII (*Works*, 1:224).

[74] Owen, *Christologia*, XVIII (*Works*, 1:225).

[75] Owen, *Christologia*, VIII (*Works*, 1:226-27). The other Scriptural texts cited are Matt 1:23; Isa 9:6; John 1:14; Rom 9:5; Col 2:9; 1 John 3:16.

[76] For the Greek and English texts of the creedal definition, see Philip Schaff, ed., *The Creeds of Christendom: with a History and Critical Notes*, 3 vols. (Grand Rapids: Baker, 1993), 2:62-63.

assumption is not the man Christ Jesus but human nature. Apart from the assumption and consequent union of the human nature in the person of the Son, Christ's human nature is anhypostatic, having no independent existence of its own, but subsists in the person of the Son, that is, it is enhypostatic. Commenting on the human nature of Christ, Owen averred: "In itself it is ἀνυπόστατος,– that which hath not a subsistence of its own, which should give it individuation and distinction from the same nature in any other person. But it hath its subsistence in the person of the Son, which thereby is its own. The divine nature, as in that person, is its *suppositum*."[77]

The Reformed character of Owen's Christology is evident in his conception of the *communicatio idiomatum*.[78] This is seen, for example, in the first principle Owen gave in his elucidation of the *communio naturarum*: "*Each nature* doth preserve its own natural, essential properties, entire unto and in itself; without mixture, without composition or confusion, without such a real communication of the one unto the other, as that the one should become the subject of the properties of the other."[79] Inherent in Owen's principle is a straightforward denial of the Lutheran conception of the *communicatio idiomatum* and an assertion of the Reformed concern to preserve the integrity of each nature in the person of Christ. It is, however, in Owen's exposition of the Son's act of assumption that the full-orbed character of Owen's Reformed Christology is seen.

In one of the statements Owen made concerning the Son's act of assumption, he observed that the assumption of human nature is "the only immediate act of the divine nature on the human in the person of the Son."[80] According to Owen, what necessarily followed from the assumption is the hypostatic union. However, "all other actings of God in the *person* of the Son towards the human nature were *voluntary*, and did not necessarily ensue on the union mentioned."[81] The reason Owen gave for this observation is rooted in the basic Reformed concern to maintain the integrity of the natures of Christ by keeping them distinct: "for there was no transfusion of the properties of one nature into the other, nor real physical communication of divine essential excellencies unto the humanity."[82] To assert the voluntary nature of all actions of the Son subsequent to the assumption is, however, not the decisive move toward a Reformed Christology, although it is certainly indicative of the Reformed concern against the Eutychian heresy. The Son could, after all, still act directly upon the human nature, but voluntarily so, and in this way seriously jeopardize

---

[77] Owen, *Christologia*, XVIII (*Works*, 1:233).
[78] See Holmes, "Reformed Varieties of the *Communicatio Idiomatum*", in S.R. Holmes and M.A. Rae, eds., *Person of Christ*, 78-81.
[79] Owen, *Christologia*, XVIII (*Works*, 1:234).
[80] Owen, *Christologia*, XVIII (*Works*, 1:225).
[81] Owen, *Pneumatologia*, II.iii (*Works*, 3:161).
[82] Owen, *Pneumatologia*, II.iii (*Works*, 3:161).

the integrity of that nature. Owen's decisive move lay in his understanding of pneumatology in its relation to Christology. "The Holy Spirit is the Spirit of the Son, no less than the Spirit of the Father. He proceedeth from the Son, as from the Father."[83] According to this immanent order of subsistence, the Spirit is thus "the immediate operator of all divine acts of the Son himself, even on his own human nature."[84] Subsequent to the act of assumption, the Son acts indirectly upon the human nature by means of the Spirit. This, then, rules out the possibility of a direct communication of properties from the Son's divine to his human nature. Owen's pneumatological Christology thus provided a robust safeguard against the confusion or mixture of the natures. It also has far reaching implications for Owen's conception of the mediatorial life of Christ on earth. In concert with his pneumatological understanding of the incarnation, Owen argued that it was by the power of the Spirit that the incarnate Son performed miracles, was "*guided, directed, comforted, supported*, in the whole course of his ministry, temptations, obedience, and sufferings", and offered himself as a sacrifice for sin.[85]

Although not explicitly stated, the doctrine of appropriation was operative in Owen's understanding of the incarnation, for he maintained that it was the Son in particular who was the subject of that divine act of assumption and not the Father or the Spirit. The Father, he insisted, "did not assume human nature, he was not incarnate; neither did the Holy Spirit do so; but this was the peculiar act and work of the Son."[86] However, Owen also maintained the patristic rule that *opera trinitatis ad extra sunt indivisa*. Thus, he insisted: "There is no such division in the external operations of God that anyone of them should be the act of one person, without the concurrence of the others; and the reason of it is, because the nature of God, which is the principle of all divine operations, is one and the same, undivided in them all."[87] In asserting the indivisibility of trinitarian operations alongside the appropriation of the act of assumption to the Son, Owen does appear to entertain two incompatible positions as Spence has observed.[88] How is the rule of indivisible operations to be maintained if there is no concurrence of the Father or Spirit in the act of assumption? This problem is heightened by Owen's contention that in the operations of the Spirit *ad extra*, performed in the context of the Spirit's office in the economy of salvation, "the others [the Father and the Son] have no concurrence but by approbation and consent."[89]

---

[83] Owen, *Pneumatologia*, II.iii (*Works*, 3:162).
[84] Owen, *Pneumatologia*, II.iii (*Works*, 3:162).
[85] Owen, *Pneumatologia*, II.iv (*Works*, 3:174, 177).
[86] Owen, *Pneumatologia*, II.iii (*Works*, 3:160).
[87] Owen, *Pneumatologia*, II.iii (*Works*, 3:160).
[88] Alan J. Spence, "John Owen and Trinitarian Agency," *SJT* 43 (1990), 162-67; Spence, *Incarnation and Inspiration*, 128-31.
[89] Owen, *Pneumatologia*, I.iv (*Works*, 3:94).

Owen's resolution of the problem indicated above is found in his concessions of approbation and consent. These concessions were introduced by John of Damascus with respect to the incarnation of the Son, a patristic antecedent of which Owen was clearly aware and from which he borrowed. Thus, on the Son's assumption of human nature, Owen appealed to John in the assertion that "the Father and the Spirit had no interest nor concurrence, εἰ μὴ κατ' εὐδοκίαν καὶ βούλησιν, 'but by approbation and consent,' as Damascen speaks."[90] These concessions suggest that Owen understood the indivisibility of trinitarian operations in a qualified manner. This qualification receives further clarity in Owen's contention of a twofold operation of the Trinity: "The first hereof is absolute in all divine works whatever; the other respects the economy of the operations of God in our salvation."[91] It is in the former that "the working and the work do in common and undividedly belong unto and proceed from each person."[92] When divine operations are considered in relation to the acting subject as divine, they are "the effects of the essential properties of the divine nature" and therefore indivisible.[93] When divine operations are of the sort where "the Father, Son, and Holy Spirit do graciously condescend" in the economy of salvation, they may be considered distinctly by way of their appropriation to distinct persons of the Trinity.[94] Owen's resolution thus reflects both his sensitivity to the eternity/time dialectic and the distinction between essence and person in the orthodox doctrine of the Trinity. With the necessary concessions and qualification in place, Owen described the concurrence of trinitarian operations in the *"framing, forming, and miraculous conception of the body of Christ in the womb of the blessed Virgin"* as follows:

> This work, I acknowledge, in respect of *designation*, and the authoritative disposal of things, is ascribed unto the Father...As to *voluntary assumption*, it is ascribed to the Son himself...But the immediate divine *efficiency* in this matter was the peculiar work of the Holy Ghost.[95]

Mediator According to Two Natures

Following certain portions of Augustine's writings, medieval Christology related Christ's work of mediation to his human nature.[96] Although the divinity

---

[90] Owen, *Pneumatologia*, II.iii (*Works*, 3:160); John of Damascus, *De Fide Orthodoxa*, X (*NPNF2*, 9:12-13).
[91] Owen, *Pneumatologia*, II.v (*Works*, 3:198).
[92] Owen, *Pneumatologia*, II.v (*Works*, 3:198); Spence, *Incarnation and Inspiration*, 132-33.
[93] Owen, *Pneumatologia*, II.v (*Works*, 3:198).
[94] Owen, *Pneumatologia*, II.v (*Works*, 3:198-99).
[95] Owen, *Pneumatologia*, II.iii (*Works*, 3:162-163); idem, *Christologia*, XVIII (*Works*, 1:225).
[96] Augustine, *A Treatise on the Grace of Christ and on Original Sin*, II.33 (*NPNF1* 5:248): "Now to all who find death in Adam, Christ is of this avail, that He is the Mediator for life. He is, however, not a Mediator, because He is equal with the Father;

of Christ was maintained in accordance with orthodox Christology, it was however not brought into vital relation with the office of the Mediator. Christ as *medius* or mid-point between God and man was acknowledged, but the recognition of Christ's divinity as a fundamental condition for the office of *mediator* was perceived to be problematic. Thomas, for instance, spoke of the function of a mediator as the bringing together of those "between whom he acts as mediator", for the reason that "extremities are united in the middle-point."[97] He distinguished between an intermediary and the work of mediation, taking both to be elements of what constitutes a mediator.[98] When applied to Christ, Thomas restricted the realization of these elements to Christ's human nature and explicitly denied the participation of his divine nature in the exercise of the mediatorial office: "Neither of these elements is realized in Christ in so far as he is God, but exclusively in so far as he is man. For as God he is not distinct in nature and lordship from the Father and the Holy Spirit; nor do the Father and Holy Spirit possess anything which the Son does not possess and which, as belonging to them and not to himself, he might bear to others."[99]

From the standpoint of Owen's Christology, the medieval tradition on the doctrine of the Mediator would be inadequate for achieving the end of Christ's mediation as Owen understood the issue. While it is necessary for Christ to be man for mediation to be possible, yet it would be ineffectual if it was undertaken by Christ merely as man. "There was yet more required thereunto, or to render his offices effectual unto their proper ends. Not one of them could have been so, had he been no more than a man – had he had no nature but ours."[100] For Owen, the nature of work inherent in the threefold office required no less than divinity for its successful performance and consequent effect upon the church.[101] He asserts:

> This is the sum of what we plead for: we can have no due consideration of the offices of Christ, can receive no benefit by them, nor perform any act of duty with

---

for in this respect He is Himself as far distant from us as the Father; and how can there be any medium where the distance is the very same? ... He is the Mediator, then, in that He is man, - inferior to the Father, by so much as He is nearer to ourselves, and superior to us, by so much as He is nearer to the Father"; idem, *The City of God*, XI.2 (*NPNF1* 2:206); idem, *Confessions*, X.43 (*NPNF1* 1:162); Aquinas, *Summa Theologiae*, III, Q.26, Art.1-2.

[97] Aquinas, *Summa Theologiae*, III, Q.26, Art.1.
[98] Aquinas, *Summa Theologiae*, III, Q.26, Art.2.
[99] He goes on to assert in *Summa Theologiae*, III, Q.26, Art.2: "But both elements are realized in Christ as man. For as man he is set apart from God in nature and from men in the eminence of his grace and glory. Likewise as man his office is to unite men with God, which he does by setting before men the divine commandments and gifts and by atoning and interceding for men with God. It is, therefore, as man that he is, in the truest sense of the word, mediator."
[100] Owen, *Christologia*, VII (*Works*, 1:87).
[101] Owen, *Christologia*, VII (*Works*, 1:87-100).

respect unto them, or any of them, unless faith in his *divine person* be actually exercised as the foundation of the whole. For that is it whence all their glory, power, and efficacy are derived. Whatever, therefore, we do with respect unto his rule, whatever we receive by the communication of his Spirit and grace, whatever we learn from his Word by the teachings of his Spirit, whatever benefit we believe, expect, and receive by his sacrifice and intercession on our behalf; our faith in them all, and concerning them all, is terminated on his *divine person*. The church is saved by his offices because they are his.[102]

In relating Christ's divinity to his office, Owen departs from the medieval tradition that confined Christ's mediation to his human nature. He stands with the Reformers and the Protestant orthodox who taught that Christ is both *medius* and *mediator* according to his divine and human natures.[103] Here, there is a vital connection between the person and work of Christ integrated around the mediatorial category. The prophetic, priestly, and kingly offices obtain their validity by virtue of Christ's humanity, and their efficacy upon the church by virtue of Christ's divinity.

A related argument that Owen propounded as grounds for maintaining that Christ's mediation involves his divine nature is the argument that Christ is already Mediator prior to his incarnation. According to Owen, the Son was appointed Mediator in eternity. As indicated in Chapter 2, this Christological point is a crucial aspect of Owen's doctrine of the *pactum salutis*. In addition, Owen also affirmed the exercise of the Son's mediatorial office prior to his assumption of human nature. In the context of elucidating the prophetic office, Owen argued that the care of the church in the provision of divine instruction has always been borne peculiarly by the second person of the Trinity since the giving of the first promise.[104] Owen provided four kinds of Old Testament evidences for the Son's pre-incarnate work as Mediator. It was seen in the Christophanies; in angelic activity under the charge of and dependent upon the Son; in the ministry of the prophets through the Spirit who was sent by the Son; and in the ministry of "holy men" for the inscripturation of divine revelation

---

[102] Owen, *Christologia*, VII (*Works*, 1:99). Emphasis added.

[103] See "mediator" and "medius" in Muller, *DLGTT*, 188, 189; idem, *Christ and the Decree*, 33, also 33n128. Calvin, *Institutes*, II.xiv.3: "Let this, then, be our key to right understanding: those things which apply to the office of the Mediator are not spoken simply either of the divine nature or of the human"; Thomas Goodwin, *The Works of Thomas Goodwin*, 12 vols. (Eureka: Tanski Publications, 1996), 5:48-50; Ames, *Marrow*, I.xviii.23. Owen lists seven characteristics of the office of the Mediator in his exposition of the term μεσίτης (mediator), in which the concepts of *medius* and *mediator* are expressed. Owen, *Exposition of Hebrews*, Heb. 8:6, in loc. (*Works*, 22:55-58); cf. idem, *Posthumous Sermons*, XI (*Works* 16:493): "A mediator must be a middle person, and God in his divine nature is one: 'A mediator is not of one'."

[104] Owen, *Christologia*, VII (*Works*, 1:88). This argument is advanced on the basis of texts like Micah 5:2, Zechariah 2:8-9, and John 8:58.

through the Spirit.[105] Although it was primarily the prophetic office that was in view, Owen's argument embraced the Son's office in general. Thus, to the specific question, "If any shall now inquire how the Lord Christ could be the prophet of the church before he took our nature upon him and dwelt among us", Owen answered by appeal to the ministry of the Spirit, which led to the following general comment: "To confine the offices of Christ, as unto their virtue, power and efficacy, unto the times of the Gospel only, is utterly to evacuate the first promise, with the covenant of grace founded thereon."[106] To argue that the Son is Mediator before his incarnation is no novelty. Owen was merely echoing Calvin and Vermigli, both of whom had argued in similar fashion against Stancaro.[107]

For the purpose of this present study, it is important to note that Owen's doctrine of the Mediator is not merely a restatement of orthodox Christology on the hypostatic union, a position which medieval Christology also acknowledged. What distinguishes his view from the medieval tradition is the theological relation he makes between the office of the Mediator and the active participation of the Mediator's divine and human natures in its accomplishment. Owen's view of the atonement rests upon this theological relation. He could speak, for instance, of the vicarious nature of Christ's obedience and satisfaction for sin as contingent upon the participation of both natures.[108] Equally important is the caveat that in the discharge of Christ's office, mediatorial acts are not to be attributed to his natures *in abstracto* apart from his person. The significance of this qualification lies in Owen's conscious attempt to preserve the unity of Christ's person while distinguishing his natures, a qualification which was necessary in light of the neo-Nestorian views of his day.[109] Side-stepping Christ's person in the attribution of mediatorial acts to his natures has a precariously Nestorian orientation. In Owen's thought on the hypostatic union, "the whole Christ was one person, and all his mediatorial acts were the acts of that one person, of him who was both God and man..."[110] Thus, in concord with the Reformed tendency to speak of Christ *in concreto*, all mediatorial acts of Christ are predicated of the one divine-human person of the

---

[105] Owen, *Christologia*, VII (*Works*, 1:89-90).

[106] Owen, *Christologia*, VII (*Works*, 1:90).

[107] Tylenda, "Christ the Mediator", 12; Tylenda, "Controversy on Christ the Mediator", 147; Vermigli, "A Letter to Poland", in *The Peter Martyr Reader*, 128-29.

[108] Owen, *Christologia*, XVI (*Works*, 1:200ff.).

[109] Commenting on the "pernicious imagination" of the Nestorian heresy, Owen opined: "This seems to be the opinion of some amongst us, at this day, about the person of Christ, and they allow in the like manner the verity of his human nature, or own that man Christ Jesus. Only they say, that the eternal Word was in him and with him, in the same kind as it is with other believers, but in a supreme degree of manifestation and power." To Owen, this is "to put a new color and appearance on old imaginations." *Christologia*, II (*Works*, 1:40).

[110] Owen, *Christologia*, II (*Works*, 1:40).

Mediator. "Whatever acts are ascribed unto him," Owen averred, "however immediately performed, in or by the human nature, or in and by his divine nature, they are all the acts of that one person, in whom are both these natures."[111] On this, Owen is echoing the Reformed confessional understanding of the doctrine of the Mediator.[112]

One Common Work, Two Principles of Operation

In Protestant scholastic parlance, the participation of Christ's natures in his mediatorial work is encapsulated in the terms *communicatio apotelesmatum* or *communicatio operationum*. These terms refer to "*the communication of mediatorial operations in and for the sake of the work of salvation*; terms used by the Reformed to indicate the common work of the two natures of Christ, each doing what is proper to it according to its own attributes."[113] Lutheran scholastics distinguished the communication of properties into three genus of which the *communicatio apotelesmatum* is the second.[114] Their account of the concept arose directly from the attempt to develop the doctrine of the communication of properties in relation to Christ's work as Mediator. In the Mediator's work, both natures operate according to their own properties to produce one common work of mediation. The Lutherans argued further, that it was not merely properties peculiar to the human nature of Christ which were exercised but also divine properties which were imparted to it. Chemnitz explained: "Christ's human nature has received from the hypostatic union supernatural qualities and qualities which are contrary to nature, so that in these works of Christ the Saviour the human nature can cooperate even beyond and above its own natural properties."[115] This is consistent with the Lutheran view of the *communicatio idiomatum*. In agreement with the Lutherans, the Reformed affirmed the one common work of the Mediator and the operations of Christ's natures according to their own properties. However, unlike the Lutherans, they did not construe of the *communicatio apotelesmatum* as part of their exposition of the communication of properties. Rather, the hypostatic

---

[111] Owen, *A Brief Declaration, Of the Person of Christ* (*Works* 2:415).

[112] *Westminster Confession*, VIII.7: "Christ, in the work of Mediation, acteth according to both Natures, by each Nature doing that which is proper to it self: yet, by reason of the unity of the Person, that which is proper to one Nature, is sometimes in Scripture attributed to the Person denominated by the other Nature."

[113] Muller, *DLGTT*, 74; cf. Karl Barth, *Church Dogmatics: The Doctrine of Reconciliation*, ed. T.F. Torrance G.W. Bromiley, vol. IV.2 (London/New York: T & T Clark International, 2004), 104-105.

[114] The first and third being the *idiomatic* and the *majestatic genus*. Heinrich Schmid, *The Doctrinal Theology of the Evangelical Lutheran Church, Verified from the Original Sources*, ed. Charles A. Hay and Henry E. Jacobs (Philadelphia: Lutheran Publication Society, 1889), 319-23; for arguably the most extensive treatment of all three genus to date, see Martin Chemnitz, *The Two Natures in Christ*, trans. J.A.O. Preus (St Louis, Missouri: Concordia Publishing House, 1971), 171-246.

[115] Chemnitz, *Two Natures in Christ*, 218.

union was their immediate point of reference from which the content of the scholastic terminology was a direct consequence.[116]

Although the scholastic terminology was not employed by Owen, there is however evidence to suggest that he was very much aware of its use and chose to adopt the Reformed version of it in various settings. In his treatise, *Of Communion with God the Father, Son, and Holy Ghost* (1657), he observed three necessary consequences of the hypostatic union, all of which are indicative of the "*personal excellency* and grace of the Lord Jesus Christ."[117] In the third, which is concerned with the discharge of Christ's office as Mediator, Owen delineated four aspects for consideration:

> The *execution* of his office of mediation in his single person, in respect of both natures: wherein is considerable, ὁ ἐνεργῶν,—the agent, Christ himself, God and man. He is the *principium quo*, ἐνεργητικὸν,—the principle that gives life and efficacy to the whole work; and then, 2*dly*, The *principium quod*,—that which operates, which is both natures distinctly considered. 3*dly*. The ἐνέργεια, or δραστικὴ τῆς φύσεως κίνησις,—the effectual working itself of each nature. And, *lastly*, the ἐνέργημα, or ἀποτέλεσμα,—the effect produced, which ariseth from all, and relates to them all: so resolving the excellency I speak of into his personal union.[118]

The *communicatio apotelesmatum* is clearly evident in the fourfold distinction.[119] Owen affirmed one common effect of mediation, which is the *apotelesma*, produced by the exercise of Christ's natures according to their distinct principles of operation. Unlike the Lutherans, the *communicatio idiomatum* is conspicuously absent. In the immediate context, the concept has a hermeneutical and pastoral function. It is introduced by Owen as part of the attempt to make sense of the opening words of Paul's benediction in 2 Corinthians 13:14 and to aid readers of his treatise in their contemplation of the

---

[116] Heppe, *Reformed Dogmatics*, 445-46.
[117] Owen, *Of Communion with God*, II.ii (*Works*, 2:50-51).
[118] Owen, *Of Communion with God*, II.ii (*Works*, 2:51); cf. Peter van Mastricht, *Theoretico-Practica Theologia*, V.iv.13, cited in Heppe, *Reformed Dogmatics*, 446: "(1) The producing cause, the *theanthrōpos* person *energōn* (2) The two principles *energētika* of the producing cause, the two natures in the mediator. (3) The twofold efficacy of the divine and human natures, answering to the number of the two principles, or the twofold *energeia*. Finally (4) the one work, the *energoumenon* or *apotelesma theandrikon*, which the one mediator produces for the two natures through the efficacy peculiar to each."
[119] That this is so has not been acknowledged in Owen scholarship even in instances where the above fourfold distinctions or the terms *apotelesma* and *apotelesmata* are present in citations from Owen's writings. See Spence, *Incarnation and Inspiration*, 107-109; Trueman, *Claims of Truth*, 222; Daniels, *Christology of John Owen*, 346; Kapic, *Communion with God*, 197.

person of Christ. Other uses of the concept are found in contexts where Owen engaged in polemics against Socinian views on the priestly office of Christ.

In *Vindicae Evangelicae* (1655), the concept appears in Owen's answer to a Socinian objection concerning the value of Christ's sacrifice. "If only the human nature of Christ was offered," it was asked, "how could it be a sacrifice of such infinite value as to [satisfy] the justice of God for all the sins of all the elect, whereunto it was appointed?"[120] Two issues needed to be addressed in the question – the grounds upon which the infinite value of Christ's sacrifice is asserted, and the effect which results from it. Owen answered: "Though the thing sacrificed was but finite, yet the person sacrificing was infinite, and the ἀποτέλεσμα of the action follows the agent, that is, our mediator, Θεάνθρωπος,—whence the sacrifice was of infinite value."[121] Assuming the theandric constitution of Christ, Owen's answer to the first issue hinges on the infinite worth of the person of Christ. Since Christ is of infinite worth, it follows that his sacrifice is of infinite value. As to the second issue, which pertains to the effect of Christ's sacrifice, there is an unstated implication in Owen's answer, namely the positive relation that exists between the infinite value of Christ's sacrifice and the *apotelesma* that arises from it. That the relation is implicit is due to Owen's expressed intention to treat only of the sacrificial character of Christ's death at this juncture, and not of its effect.[122] Owen simply takes it for granted that the infinite value of Christ's sacrifice obtains the corresponding *apotelesma* in which God's justice is satisfied with respect to the sins of all the elect.

Another instance of its use is found in *A Brief Declaration and Vindication of the Doctrine of the Trinity* (1669).[123] Again, the Socinian objection to Christ's satisfaction for sin is the motivation for Owen's employment of the concept.[124] Citing one of the objections, Owen remarked: "It is yet further objected, '*That if Christ made satisfaction for sin, then he did it either as God or as man, or as God and man.*'"[125] Owen replied to this objection in four points. In the first, he affirmed that Christ made satisfaction for sin as God and

---

[120] Cited in Owen, *Vindicae Evangelicae*, XXII (*Works*, 12:431).

[121] Owen, *Vindicae Evangelicae*, XXII (*Works*, 12:431).

[122] Owen, *Vindicae Evangelicae*, XXII (*Works*, 12:432): "And this is the second consideration of the death of Christ,—it was a sacrifice. What is the peculiar influence of his death as a sacrifice into the satisfaction he hath made shall be declared afterward."

[123] Owen, *Works*, 2:365-454.

[124] Although Owen does not mention any Socinians or Socinianism in the main body of the text, nevertheless, he does so in the preface to the work. Comments that relate to Owen's section on satisfaction for sin include a citation from Socinus in which the need for satisfaction and for Christ's involvement in it was rejected. Socinus was cited in order to clarify "the true state of the question". Thus, objections to Christ's satisfaction for sin raised in the treatise have an unmistakably Socinian context. See Owen, *A Brief Declaration*, "To the Reader" (*Works* 2:367-69).

[125] Owen, *A Brief Declaration*, Of the Satisfaction of Christ (*Works*, 2:432).

man. In the second, he affirmed the mediatorial acts of Christ as acts of one person, who is both God and man. In the third, the *communciatio apotelesmatum* was employed to expose the nature of the Socinian objection:

> There is yet another mistake in this inquiry; for satisfaction is in it looked on as a real act or operation of one or the other nature in Christ, when it is the *apotelesma* or effect of the actings, the doing and suffering of Christ – the dignity of what he did in reference unto the end for which he did it. For the two natures are so united in Christ as not to have a third compound principle of physical acts and operations thence arising; but each nature acts distinctly, according to its own being and properties, yet so as what is the immediate act of either nature is the act of him who is one in both; from whence it hath its dignity.[126]

Here, Owen attempts to demonstrate that the Socinian objection is wrong-headed in the very way the objection is framed. He points out that the objection contains a fundamental error: that it confuses satisfaction as a mediatorial effect with satisfaction as a mediatorial operation. Satisfaction is, in Owen's understanding, the effect that is obtained from the exercise of the natures according to their own distinct principles of operation and not part of the operations themselves. Once this confusion is acknowledged, it becomes immediately apparent that inherent in the Socinian objection is the implication that there are three principles of mediatorial operation: "*as God or as man, or as God and man*". To then say that Christ made satisfaction for sin as God and man as to speak of "a third compound principle of physical acts and operations" involves a "blending of the natures into one common principle of operation, as the compounding of mediums unto one end."[127] To Owen, this is a ridiculous notion. Owen rejected such an erroneous construal of the principles of operation, and went on to reassert in his fourth point the distinction between the operations of natures from their one common effect or *apotelesma*, a distinction that is maintained in the concept of the *communcatio apotelesmatum*:

> The sum is, that in all the mediatory actions of Christ we are to consider, —(1.) The agent; and that is the person of Christ. (2.) The immediate principle by which and from which the agent worketh; and that is the natures in the person. (3.) The actions; which are the effectual operations of either nature. (4.) The effect or work with respect to God and us; and this relates unto the person of the agent, the Lord Christ, God and man.[128]

The fourth and final instance is found in *The Doctrine of Justification by Faith* (1677). It is a polemical treatise aimed chiefly at the writings of Socinus and

---

[126] Owen, *A Brief Declaration*, Of the Satisfaction of Christ (*Works*, 2:433).
[127] Owen, *A Brief Declaration*, Of the Satisfaction of Christ (*Works*, 2:433).
[128] Owen, *A Brief Declaration*, Of the Satisfaction of Christ (*Works*, 2:433). This fourfold distinction is a condensed version of the fourfold distinction cited earlier from *Of Communion with God*.

the Catholic theologian, Bellarmine. The context in which the scholastic concept was employed treats only of Socinus' view of justification. Socinus had denied that Christ's obedience is in any way meritorious for others. His argument rests on the view that as a man, the merit of Christ's obedience pertained only to Christ and was obtained for himself. Since vicarious obedience was impossible for any man, Socinus rejected the imputation of the merits of Christ's obedience, a view which was essential to Owen's doctrine of justification. Owen's defence turned on his assertion that the obedience of Christ is the obedience of his person. As the Son of God, the person of Christ is unable to be wholly subjected under the law, "for the divine nature cannot be subjected unto an outward work of its own, such as the law is, nor can it have an authoritative, commanding power over it, as it must have if it were made ὑπὸ νόμον,—'under the law.'"[129] According to Owen, it was Christ's human nature that was subjected under the law, but it is the person of the incarnate Son of whom the act of obedience was to be predicated and not his human nature. This point would, of course, neutralize the potency of Socinus' criticism, but it begs the question of the basis on which the obedience of Christ is to be predicated of his person and not his human nature. The following passage gives insight to Owen's basis for doing so:

> As in the person of a man, some of his acts, as to the immediate principle of operation, are acts of the body, and some are so of the soul; yet in their performance and accomplishment, are they the acts of the person: so the acts of Christ in his mediation, as to their ἐνεργήματα, or immediate operation, were the actings of his distinct natures,—some of the divine and some of the human immediately; but as unto their ἀποτελέσματα, and the perfecting efficacy of them, they were the acts of his whole person...Wherefore, the obedience of Christ, which we plead to have been for us, was the obedience of the Son of God.[130]

It is clear from Owen's explanation that the basis for speaking of Christ's obedience as the obedience of his person is the distinction between the ἐνεργήματα and the ἀποτελέσματα of Christ's mediatorial acts. This distinction is crucial to the doctrine of the *communicatio apotelesmatum*. Mediatorial effects, or what Owen terms as "perfecting efficacy", while depending on the operations of the divine and human natures of Christ, are nevertheless obtained through the communication of mediatorial operations to the person of Christ. The obedience of Christ concerns mediatorial effects, which assumes the communication of mediatorial operations to Christ's person, and is thus to be predicated of Christ's person and not of his human nature in the abstract.

To consolidate the evidence gathered above on Owen's use of the *communicatio apotelesmatum*, several observations are in order. First, Owen was clearly aware of the concept and used it in different contexts for different

---

[129] Owen, *The Doctrine of Justification*, XII (*Works*, 5:256).
[130] Owen, *The Doctrine of Justification*, XII (*Works*, 5:255).

purposes. In *Of Communion with God*, the concept has pastoral and hermeneutical functions, where Owen's main concern in its employment was exposition of Scripture and the edification of his readers. In *Vindicae Evangelicae*, *A Brief Declaration*, and *The Doctrine of Justification*, it was employed apologetically in defence of Christ's atonement for sin and justification against Socinian criticisms of these doctrines. Second, in all four instances, the concept was not a derivative form of the *communicatio idiomatum*, but took its immediate point of departure from the hypostatic union. Neither is there any hint of predication across the natures. The natures of Christ are consistently kept distinct, along with the resultant and corresponding distinction of mediatorial operations. On these points, Owen clearly follows the Reformed. Third, while the distinction of natures and their operations are strictly maintained, there is a conscious attempt to place the emphasis on the person acting. In Owen's own words, "the immediate act of either nature is the act of him who is one in both."[131] The work of mediation "relates unto the person of the agent, the Lord Christ, God and man," from whom it derives its dignity and worth.[132] The *apotelesmata* arising from the operation of Christ's natures "were the acts of his whole person,—his acts who was that person, and whose power of operation was a property of his person."[133] Owen's consistent attempt to predicate mediatorial acts concretely of the person of Christ and not abstractly of his natures is again characteristic of the Reformed.

Conclusion

The overarching argument of this chapter is that the governing category of Owen's Christology is that of Christ the Mediator. This argument has been demonstrated in three ways, corresponding to the three main sections of this chapter. First, Owen's context reveals the crucial importance of the doctrine of Christ the Mediator. This is especially so in the light of Socinianism's Christological scheme which was structured after the threefold office of Christ. Second, the prominence of the mediatorial category for Owen is evident in *Christologia*, his key writing on Christology. Not only do mediatorial concerns pervade the entire treatise as indicated by the general features of his Christology, certain chapters were explicitly structured according to the threefold office. Third, these general features provide the framework in which the more specific features of his Christology are comprehended. On the incarnation, the catholicity of Owen's Christology is apparent in his appeal to the formulations of orthodox Christology and the principles of trinitarian operations. The strong pneumatological character of his Christology reflects his

---

[131] Owen, *Of Communion with God*, II.ii (*Works*, 2:51).
[132] Owen, *A Brief Declaration*, Of the Satisfaction of Christ (*Works*, 2:433).
[133] Owen, *The Doctrine of Justification*, XII (*Works*, 5:255).

Reformed concern to preserve the integrity of the natures of Christ. Owen's Reformed Christology is also seen in his treatment of the mediatorial operations of Christ. His use of the *communicatio apotelesmatum* reveals him to be conversant with Reformed orthodox theology, and that he draws from the tradition to vindicate orthodox Christology against the Socinians in particular. All these have far reaching implications for Owen's doctrine of atonement. Of crucial importance here is the fact that the theological grid through which the doctrine of atonement is adumbrated and defended is the mediatorial office of Christ. In view of the emphasis that Owen placed on Christ's priestly office, Christ's work as priest will be the concern of the next chapter.

CHAPTER 4

The Means of Redemption: Christ's Priestly Office

In the introduction, it was proposed that Owen's conception of Christ's priestly office in his twofold state of humiliation and exaltation lies at the heart of his atonement theology. Chapter 2 supported this claim by demonstrating that this understanding of Christ's priesthood dominates Owen's conception of the eternal compact. Chapter 3 established the Christological foundation of Owen's atonement theology by showing that Christ as Mediator in his threefold office is the main category of his Christology. In view of the crucial significance of Christ's priesthood for Owen, this chapter examines the subject directly from three vantage points: Owen's own statement of the polemical significance of Christ's priesthood in his case against universal redemption; the views of Owen's universalist opponents, namely, the Arminians, Saumurians, and Thomas More; Owen's formulation of Christ's priestly office in both his early and late writings. Since the fullest, clearest statement of the central contention in this study is found in *The Death of Death*, as will become clear below, the following discussion will take Owen's treatment of the above matters in the treatise as the main point of reference but will not be confined to it.[1]

The Polemical Significance of Christ's Priesthood

Trueman makes the important observation that Christ's priesthood, "while not dominating Owen's theology, appears to have been something of a preoccupation with him."[2] He provides two reasons to substantiate his claim. First, Owen's concern for Christ's priesthood was an echo of the central soteriological concern of Reformed orthodoxy for dealing with the objective problem of sin. This is facilitated by the Augustinian understanding of sin and anthropology on the one hand, and the "Anselmic roots of orthodox Christological patterns" that makes sense of Christ's person from his work on the other.[3] Second, the polemical context of Owen's day explains his

---

[1] Although the most extensive treatment of Christ's priesthood is found in Owen's writings on the book of Hebrews, nevertheless, the structure of his commentary is not doctrinally but textually based. Thus, from the standpoint of positive theological construction, *The Death of Death* has priority over his commentary.
[2] Trueman, *Claims of Truth*, 187.
[3] Trueman, *Claims of Truth*, 188; cf. Trueman's earlier statement: "Whereas the Anselmic approach, which was of great importance in the development of Reformed Christology, facilitated the construction of a doctrine of Christ's person as an inference

preoccupation with this subject.[4] Three groups are identified by Trueman, all of whose understanding of the subject contain significant differences from those of the Reformed orthodox: the Arminians, Socinians, and Catholics. Presumably, they were identified from the title of an early but unpublished work of Owen to which Trueman referred: *Tractatu de Sacerdotio Christi, contra Armin. Socin. et Papistas, nondum editio*.[5]

There is a third reason, not mentioned by Trueman, that reveals much of what was at the heart of Owen's concern over Christ's priesthood: the perceived misconception and misapplication of Christ's priestly acts of oblation and intercession. In Owen's estimate, this was the theological hub around which much of the debate over universal redemption turned. It is by no means independent of the reasons Trueman gave but a more precise statement of the *status controversiae* with his universalist opponents. For Owen, to concede the validity of his opponents' construction of Christ's priestly acts of oblation and intercession would result in destructive consequences for Reformed orthodoxy.

In Book II of *The Death of Death*, the title given to Chapter IV provides the leading evidence: "Of the distinction of impetration and application – The use and abuse thereof; with the opinion of the adversaries upon the whole matter in controversy unfolded; and the question on both sides stated."[6] By the time Owen came to treat of the contents of this chapter, he had already constructed most of the theological structures of his atonement theology in *The Death of Death*. In Book I, he established the trinitarian authorship of the work of redemption, gave substantial consideration to the Son's appointment and work as Mediator, and elaborated on the need to hold the two priestly acts of oblation and intercession together with respect to their eternally conceived intention and their historical outworking. In Chapter IV of Book II, Owen took aim at the theological nerve centre of his opponents: the distinction between impetration and application. That the case against universal redemption hangs upon this distinction is seen in his concluding words to the chapter. Having stated the proper sense in which the distinction was to be maintained and contrasted this with his opponents' construction of it, he concluded in the following manner:

---

from the nature of the work he was to do, the *Racovian Catechism* implicitly rejects such an approach" (152).

[4] Trueman, *Claims of Truth*, 188.

[5] Owen referred to this tract in *The Duty of Pastors and People Distinguished*, II (*Works*, 13:18), which is absent from the catalogue of his personal library, *BO*. See *Claims of Truth*, 189n118. In the "Prefatory Note" to Owen's *The Duty of Pastors and People Distinguished* (1643), the editor indicated that the tract seemed never to have been published (*Works* 13:2). It was further suggested by the editor that its materials may have been incorporated into Owen's preliminary discussions to his commentary on Hebrews, probably in Part IV of *Exercitations on the Epistle to the Hebrews*, entitled "Concerning the Sacerdotal Office of Christ" (*Works*, 18:3-259).

[6] Owen, *Salus Electorum*, II.iv (*Works*, 10:222).

But because the whole strength thereof lieth in, and the weight of all lieth on, that one distinction we before spoke of, by our adversaries diversely expressed and held out, we will a little farther consider that, and then come to our arguments, and so to the answering of the opposed objections.[7]

One chapter was insufficient to deal the death-blow to what Owen perceived to be the critical problem. Owen continued to deal with the subject in Chapter V of Book II with a brief summary of the previous chapter, reiterating the crucial importance of the distinction in his opening comment: "Now, seeing that this is the πρῶτον ψεῦδος of the opposite opinion, understood in the sense and according to the use they make of it, I shall give it one blow more, and leave it, I hope a-dying."[8] Prior to this statement involving the term *prōton pseudos*, Owen had already dealt with the arguments of his opponents in passing and, more substantially, those of Thomas More.[9] Therefore, it is unlikely that he was using *prōton* in the chronological sense. It is more likely that Owen was using the term in the sense of *priority* or *degree*, with the implication that he considered his opponents' form of the distinction to be the "foremost deception" or "highest deception" rather than it being the "first deception" of many in a series.[10] The significance of this reading lies in its association with oblation and intercession as will become clear.

Owen defined impetration as "the meritorious purchase of all good things made by Christ for us with and of his Father", and application as "the actual enjoyment of those good things upon our believing."[11] Impetration and application are not his preferred terms but were adopted out of necessity in order to delineate their proper uses in contrast to the way his opponents

---

[7] Owen, *Salus Electorum*, II.iv (*Works*, 10:232).
[8] Owen, *Salus Electorum*, II.iv (*Works*, 10:232).
[9] Owen, *Salus Electorum*, I.viii, II.iii (*Works*, 10:187-200, 215-21).
[10] Wright understands Owen's use of the term *prōton pseudos* differently. He relates it to Owen's view of the implications for faith that arise from adhering to universal redemption. Owen had pointed out that with the denial of faith as part of what was procured by Christ's death by adherents of universal redemption, two implications necessarily followed: faith would be an act of the human will apart from divine grace, and the human agent would be the ultimate cause of salvation. Owen, *Salus Electorum*, III.iv (*Works*, 10:255). Wright suggests that for Owen, "this is both the heart and worst feature of Arminianism, and its πρῶτον ψεῦδος (first lie) as he had said earlier." Wright, "John Owen's Great High Priest", 112. However, this is an incorrect interpretation of how the term was used by Owen. Wright's interpretation disregards the context in which the term is found in *The Death of Death*. The only occurrence of *prōton pseudos* in *The Death of Death* is found in Book II Chapter IV, where Owen's concern is to get at the heart of the controversy with universal redemption over the impetration/application distinction. Thus, Owen used the term in relation to the distinction's abuse. Wright was oblivious to this context. Instead, he applied it to Owen's comment on the Arminian understanding of human free will and salvation's ultimate cause.
[11] Owen, *Salus Electorum*, II.iv (*Works*, 10:223).

employed them. According to Owen, four caveats need to be observed if the terms are to be properly applied. First, the distinction between impetration and application exists in so far as it is considered from the standpoint of the salvific benefits procured by Christ. When considered from the standpoint of Christ's intention in the atonement, however, they are one.[12] Second, the will of God in the atonement is not to be conceived as conditional, "as though he gave Christ to obtain peace, reconciliation, and forgiveness of sins, upon condition that we do believe"; "There is a condition in the things, but none in the will of God; that is absolute that such things should be procured and bestowed."[13] Impetration and application, considered in relation to God's will, are absolute, non-contingent realities. Third, not all things procured by Christ are bestowed on condition. For those things which are indeed so, the condition itself is obtained and given on account of Christ's atoning work.[14] Faith, for instance, is a condition for sin's remission, but it is a condition that is purchased by Christ and bestowed by virtue of that purchase. Fourth, both impetration and application are equal in scope and terminate upon the same object: "the one is not extended to some to whom the other doth not reach."[15]

Owen's account of impetration and application bears close resemblance to his treatment of oblation and intercession.[16] Although the language is different, a careful reading of the relevant sections on Christ's oblation and intercession in *The Death of Death* reveals similar comments made in relation to impetration and application. These similarities are evident when the impetration/application and oblation/intercession terminologies are compared in three areas. The first area of comparison is between Owen's reasons for the inseparability of Christ's oblation and intercession and his strictures for ensuring the proper uses of impetration and application. Owen acknowledged that oblation and intercession are "distinct acts in themselves, and have distinct immediate products and issues assigned ofttimes unto them", but was nevertheless careful to warn against their division or separation.[17] At the head of Owen's list of reasons for this caution against division is the oneness of God's intention in the exercise of both priestly acts: "they are both alike intended for the obtaining and accomplishing the same entire and complete end proposed..."[18] His next reason for their unity is their concurrence in the scope of their exercise: "what persons soever the one respecteth, in the good things it obtaineth, the same, all, and none else, doth the other respect, in applying the good things so obtained."[19] In addition, Owen argued that "the *oblation* of

---

[12] Owen, *Salus Electorum*, II.iv (*Works*, 10:223).
[13] Owen, *Salus Electorum*, II.iv (*Works*, 10:223).
[14] Owen, *Salus Electorum*, II.iv (*Works*, 10:223).
[15] Owen, *Salus Electorum*, II.iv (*Works*, 10:224).
[16] Cf. Owen, *Salus Electorum*, I.vi-vii (*Works*, 10:179-87).
[17] Owen, *Salus Electorum*, I.vi (*Works*, 10:181).
[18] Owen, *Salus Electorum*, I.vi (*Works*, 10:181).
[19] Owen, *Salus Electorum*, I.vi (*Works*, 10:181).

Christ is, as it were, the foundation of his intercession, inasmuch as by the oblation was procured everything that, by virtue of his intercession, is bestowed; and that because the sole end of why Christ procured any thing by his death was that it might be applied to them for whom it was so procured."[20] Owen's insistence on the unity of Christ's oblation and intercession is founded upon similar grounds as his insistence on the proper uses of impetration and application: unity of the divine intention or will, and unity of scope.

The second point of comparison is Owen's use of similar terms to elucidate the oblation/intercession and impetration/application terminologies. In arguing for the unity of the former, Owen described Christ's oblation in terms of "the good things obtained" and Christ's intercession in terms of the application of these things.[21] Oblation is said to "procure" what is "bestowed" by intercession.[22] Thus, Owen described impetration and application in exactly the same way as oblation and intercession, employing similar terms of description such as "obtain", "procure", "bestow" and "apply" for both sets of terminologies.

A third point of comparison is Owen's use of similar Scriptural passages. Isaiah 53:5, 11 and Romans 4:25, 8:32-34, were common texts cited in Owen's exposition of the oblation / intercession and impetration / application distinctions.[23] It is worth citing Owen himself to demonstrate the point. He interpreted the passages from Isaiah in the following way for Christ's oblation and intercession:

> 'By his knowledge shall my righteous servant justify many, for he shall bear their iniquities,' Isa liii. 11. The actual justification of sinners, the immediate fruit of his intercession, certainly follows his bearing of their iniquities. And in the next verse they are of God so put together that surely none ought to presume to put them asunder: 'He bare the sin of many' (behold his *oblation*!), 'and made intercession for the transgressors;' even for those many transgressors whose sin he bears. And there is one expression in that chapter, verse 5, which makes it evident that the utmost application of all good things for which he intercedes is the immediate effect of his passion: 'With his stripes we are healed.' Our total healing is the fruit and procurement of his stripes, or the oblation consummated thereby.[24]

Verses 5 and 11 of Isaiah 53 were explained in similar fashion for impetration and application:

> Isa. liii. 11, "By his knowledge shall my righteous servant justify many,' – there is the application of all good things; 'for he shall bear their iniquities', – there is the

---

[20] Owen, *Salus Electorum*, I.vi (*Works*, 10:181).
[21] Owen, *Salus Electorum*, I.vi (*Works*, 10:181).
[22] Owen, *Salus Electorum*, I.vi (*Works*, 10:181).
[23] Owen, *Salus Electorum*, I.vii, II.iv (*Works*, 10:182-83, 225-26).
[24] Owen, *Salus Electorum*, I.vii (*Works*, 10:182).

impetration. He justifieth all whose iniquities he bore. As also verse 5 of that chapter, 'But he was wounded for our transgressions, he was bruised for our iniquities: the chastisement of our peace was upon him; and by his stripes we are healed.' His wounding and our healing, impetration and application, his chastisement and our peace, are inseparably associated.[25]

While it might legitimately be argued that similarities in exposition do not of necessity imply that the oblation/intercession and impetration/application distinctions are synonymous, nevertheless, the substantial semantic overlap does indicate something more than mere superficial comparability. In the context of *The Death of Death*, impetration and application are features of the more theologically encompassing distinction between oblation and intercession. The implication of this is important. In locating the theological nerve centre of his opponents in the distinction between impetration and application, Owen was but identifying the crux of his debate with them as centring on the priestly office of Christ.[26] Griffith's observation that the unity of oblation and intercession is "only a small part of Owen's case against universal atonement in *The Death of Death*" is surely incorrect.[27] On the contrary, their unity is of key importance and plays a major role in Owen's articulation of his atonement theology. Owen's reading of the central problem with universal redemption requires some contextual basis and it is to this matter that the following discussion now turns.

Arminians, Saumurians, and Thomas More

Owen's summary of part four of *The Death of Death* in the sub-title of his treatise indicates that Arminianism was his chief opponent although not the only one. He averred that it was his purpose to answer "all considerable objections as yet brought to light, either by the Arminians or others (their late followers as to this point), in the behalf of universal redemption."[28] "Others" include Thomas More and the theologians of Saumur. More and the Saumurians were said to be "their late followers as to this point", that is, followers of the Arminians as to universal redemption.[29]

Arminius' position on Christ's priestly office has to do with the attempt to relate various points of doctrine in a way that is consonant with his doctrine of

---

[25] Owen, *Salus Electorum*, II.iv (*Works*, 10:225).
[26] Cf. the following statement where the language of priesthood and the distinctions under consideration are spoken in connection with each another. Owen, *Salus Electorum*, III.iii (*Works*, 10:249): "Now, to a priest it belongs, as was declared before, to sacrifice and intercede, to procure good things, and to apply them to those for whom they are procured."
[27] Griffith, "High Priest in Heaven", 33.
[28] Owen, *Salus Electorum*, Title Page (*Works*, 10:139).
[29] Owen, *Salus Electorum*, II.iv (*Works*, 10:222).

predestination.[30] The nature of Christ's priestly work was an issue for which Arminius was taken to task by his critics in light of his predestinarian scheme. In 1608, amid increasing harassment after his rejection of Theodore Beza's supralapsarian views, Arminius was charged with doctrinal novelty in a document published probably by Sibrandus Lubbertus.[31] It consists of thirty-one theological propositions, partly attributed to Arminius and partly to Adrian Borrius, with the intention of imputing heresy to these authors. Arminius subsequently repudiated false attributions and caricatures which included accusations on his view of the extent of Christ's death. Article XII attributed to him the proposition that "Christ has died for all men and for every individual."[32] In defence, Arminius interpreted the statement in two ways and made plain which interpretation he endorsed. He observed that the statement, "Christ has died for all men and for every individual", could either mean "the price of the death of Christ was given for all and for every one", or that "the redemption, which was obtained by means of that price, is applied and communicated to all men and to every one."[33] He rejected the second interpretation and aligned himself with the first.

Despite Arminius' clarification of Article XII, ambiguity remained.[34] His approved interpretation of Article XII did not indicate if it referred to the universal offer or the universal meriting of salvation. Nor was there any mention of the end of Christ's death which would provide further specification of what was procured by Christ through his death. In all likelihood, this ambiguity was deliberate on Arminius' part. His subsequent catena of

---

[30] For the broader theological context behind his doctrine of predestination, see Richard A. Muller, *God, Creation, and Providence in the Thought of Jacobus Arminius: Sources and Directions of Scholastic Protestantism in the Era of Early Orthodoxy* (Grand Rapids: Baker, 1991).

[31] Carl Bangs, *Arminius: A Study in the Dutch Reformation* (Nashville: Abingdon Press, 1971), 300-301; A.W. Harrison, *The Beginnings of Arminianism to the Synod of Dort* (London: University of London Press, 1926), 113-15.

[32] Arminius, *Apology*, XII, in James Arminius, *The Works of James Arminius*, 3 vols. (Grand Rapids: Baker, 1986; reprint, London edition of 1825, 1828, 1875), 2:9.

[33] Arminius, *Apology*, XII, in *Works of Arminius*, 2:9.

[34] Arminius was not entirely innocent of adding to the confusion he tried to clear. His response to the charge found in Article XXVIII did not clearly distinguish between the application of Christ's atoning death and the universal offer of salvation. He was alleged to have taught the following: "The grace sufficient for salvation is conferred on the Elect, and on the Non-elect; that, if they will, they may believe or not believe, may be saved or not saved." In his response, two different senses of election were distinguished, on the bases of which he then approved of the asymmetrical affirmations that "Sufficient Grace is *conferred on*, or rather is *offered* to, the Elect and the Non-elect", and that "Sufficient Grace is not *offered* to any except the Elect." Arminius, *Apology*, XXVIII, in *Works of Arminius*, 2:53. Emphases added. The lack of clarity here between grace conferred and grace offered mitigates his rejection of the universal application of Christ's procured redemption.

Scriptural references and appeal to the testimony of Prosper of Aquitaine indicate that he was treading carefully on what was undoubtedly a highly charged issue.[35] His citation of Scriptural references without any attempt at exegesis reflects his dependence on the Reformation principle of Scripture's perspicuity, while appeal to Aquitaine demonstrates his attempt to deflect accusations of novelty.[36]

By 1610, Arminius' statement on the extent of Christ's atoning death was developed with greater precision by his followers in the context of what has come to be known as the quinquarticular controversy within the Reformed churches in the Netherlands. Under the leadership of Uytenbogaert, the Arminian party presented their "Remonstrance" before the States of Holland. It included a summary of the supralapsarian scheme of predestination in the form of five articles which they rejected,[37] and five additional articles in which their position on the controverted points of doctrine was stated.[38] The first article advocates the infralapsarian view of predestination. The second asserts:

> Jesus Christ, the Saviour of the world, died for all men and for every man, so that he has obtained for them all, by his death on the cross, redemption and the forgiveness of sins; yet that no one actually enjoys this forgiveness of sins except the believer...[39]

This article was to receive still further elaboration in the Arminian "Opinions" presented to the Synod of Dort in 1618 in four points. The first, third, and fourth are particularly pertinent in the light of Owen's concern:

> 1. The price of the redemption of Christ offered to God the Father is not only in itself and by itself sufficient for the redemption of the whole human race but has also been paid for all men and for every man, according to the decree, will, and grace of God the Father; therefore no-one is absolutely excluded from participation in the fruits of Christ's death by an absolute and antecedent decree of God.
>
> 3. Though Christ has merited reconciliation with God and remission of sins for all men and for every man, yet no one, according to the pact of the new and gracious covenant, becomes a true partaker of the benefits obtained by the death of Christ in any other way than by faith; nor are sins forgiven to sinning men before they actually and truly believe in Christ.
>
> 4. Only those are obliged to believe that Christ died for them for whom Christ has died. The reprobates, however, as they are called, for whom Christ has not died,

---

[35] Arminius, *Apology*, XII, in *Works of Arminius*, 2:9-10.
[36] For his views on Scripture and tradition, cf. Arminius, *Public Disputations*, I-III, in *Works of Arminius*, 2:80-111.
[37] Schaff, *Creeds of Christendom*, 1:517.
[38] Schaff, *Creeds of Christendom*, 3:545-49.
[39] Schaff, *Creeds of Christendom*, 3:546.

are not obligated to such faith, nor can they be justly condemned on account of the contrary refusal to believe this. In fact, if there should be such reprobates, they would be obliged to believe that Christ has not died for them.[40]

Not only was the extent of the atonement unequivocal as to its universality, the actuality and end of the atonement are likewise evident above. The objects for whom Christ died are "all men" and "every man"; Christ's death is said to have merited reconciliation and remission of sins for them. By grounding the universal extent of Christ's atoning death in the decree and will of God, the universality of God's intention is assumed.[41] When it is also insisted that the actualization of salvific benefits is confined to believers, the implication of a narrower intention than what is asserted for Christ's death is unavoidable. This asymmetry in the divine intention becomes glaringly conspicuous in the fourth point in which those "for whom Christ has died" are distinguished from the reprobates "for whom Christ has not died." In the light of such assertions, the charge of dividing impetration and application which Owen levels at the Arminians seems reasonable.

The second group of Owen's opponents is associated with the Academy at Saumur and the controversy surrounding it within the French Reformed churches during the first half of the seventeenth-century.[42] Owen did not single out Moïses Amyraut as the representative of the theology of Saumur, which is often the case,[43] but rather the Scottish theologian, John Cameron (1579-1625), who was a formative influence upon Amyraut.[44] Owen spoke of "Camero and

---

[40] "The Opinions of the Remonstrants", in Peter Y. De Jong, ed., *Crisis in the Reformed Churches: Essays in Commemoration of the Great Synod of Dort, 1618-1619* (Grand Rapids: Reformed Fellowship, Inc., 1968), Appendix H (224-25). The translation is that of Anthony A. Hoekema.

[41] Schaff's own summary of the second Remonstrance article includes the following comments in terms of God's universal intention: "His atoning sacrifice is in and of itself sufficient for the redemption of the whole world, and is intended for all by God the Father." *Creeds of Christendom*, 1:518.

[42] See F.P. van Stam, *The Controversy over the Theology of Saumur, 1635-1650: Disrupting Debates among the Huguenots in Complicated Circumstances* (Amsterdam/Maarssen: APA-Holland University Press, 1988); Brian G. Armstrong, *Calvinism and the Amyraut Heresy: Protestant Scholasticism and Humanism in Seventeenth-Century France* (Madison/Milwaukee/London: University of Wisconsin Press, 1969).

[43] Thus, Clifford criticises Owen for failing to consider the claim of Amyraut in *Defence de la doctrine de Calvin* (1644) to be the heir of Calvin's theology contra the seventeenth-century high orthodox theologians who departed from Calvin's teachings. Clifford, *Atonement and Justification*, 11. He fails to consider the fact that it was Cameron, not Amyraut, whom Owen sought to engage on the issue of the atonement.

[44] For Cameron's life and theology, see Armstrong, *Calvinism and the Amyraut Heresy*, 42-70; G. Michael Thomas, *The Extent of the Atonement: A Dilemma for Reformed Theology from Calvin to the Consensus* (Carlisle: Paternoster Press, 1997), 162-86. Owen owned Cameron's *Opera Omnia Theologica. BO, Libri Theologici in Folio,* 66.

the divines of France, which follows a new method by him devised."[45] Although he did not state what this "new method" was, it is possible to offer a reasonable postulation of the subject to which it referred. Pierre du Moulin, a persistent and outspoken critic of Amyraut's teaching provides an important lead in this regard.

In a letter to the Synod of Alençon held in 1637, du Moulin warned against the teachings of Amyraut and Paul Testard found in certain of their treatises.[46] He also complained of the outcry of these divines over his letter to *Monsieur de la Militierre*, in which he described them as endeavoring to make "a new Religion, a Hotch-potch of Popery and Cameronianism."[47] He spoke positively of the memory of Cameron, but expressed regret over Cameron's failure to consider the consequences of his own teaching, which du Moulin claimed had "over-turned the Order of Decrees" expressed by the Synod of Dort. "For this new Method of his," he charged, "is that very Foundation upon which the Arminians have built all their Doctrines."[48] Again, there is no elaboration of what the "new method" entailed, but it is clear that it had to do with the *ordo decretorum Dei*.[49]

According to Cameron, the decree of God is essentially one. However, because of human weaknesses, God has accommodated himself and revealed his decree in a fourfold manner:

> The first decree has to do with the restoration of the image of God in the creature, but so as to be consistent with God's justice; the second with the sending of the Son who saves each and every one who believes in Him. …; the third with rendering men capable of believing; the fourth is to save those who believe. The first two decrees are general, the last two are particular.[50]

In Cameron's scheme, the decree to save any particular individual is posterior to the decree to send the Son for the work of redemption. This inverts the *ordo decretorum* underlying the *Canons of the Synod of Dort* (1619) where the decree to save the elect is logically prior to the decree to send Christ as the

---

[45] Owen, *Salus Electorum*, II.iv (*Works*, 10:222).
[46] John Quick, *Synodicon in Gallia Reformata or the Acts, Decisions, Decrees, and Canons of Those Famous National Councils of the Reformed Churches in France* (London: Printed for T. Parkhurst and J. Robinson 1692), XXX, 408-11. Quick's work is divided according to various Synods with new chapters and paginations for each of them. The present chapter and page references are those of "The Synod of Alanson" or Alençon.
[47] Quick, *Synodicon*, XXX, 410.
[48] Quick, *Synodicon*, XXX, 410.
[49] Van Stam equates the new method with Cameron's decretal order. See *Controversy*, 106-107; Muller, *DLGTT*, 215.
[50] Cited in Armstrong, *Calvinism and the Amyraut Heresy*, 58; Thomas heightens the particularity of the third decree in his summary of it: "to render *some* people able to believe." Thomas, *Extent of Atonement*, 165. Emphasis added.

means of executing that decree.[51] Without the work of Christ being regulated in some way by a particularistic decree as is the case with Dort,[52] Christ's atoning death is consequently generalized to embrace "each and every one" for Cameron. A closely related concept to the divine decrees is Cameron's twofold view of God's love. Drawing on a scholastic distinction that was usually employed in relation to God's will, he applied it to God's attribute of love, thus distinguishing between God's antecedent and consequent love. This twofold distinction of divine love was employed in his covenant theology as its eternal ground,[53] and in his view of the atonement's extent.[54]

In a letter to Louis Cappel on the atonement, Cameron wrote of two degrees of God's antecedent love. The first is universal, relating to the giving of Christ for both Jews and Gentiles with the condition of faith annexed. For this degree of antecedent love, "God is said to have given Christ for the life of the world, to will the salvation of all, inasmuch as He truly calls all to repentance, either by the law of Nature, by the written Law, or by the preaching of the Gospel."[55] The second degree of antecedent love is particular to the elect. It concerns the giving of faith where Christ is said to be "given for the elect only, and that He wills to save them only."[56] Thus, God's will in the giving of Christ is both universal and particular for Cameron. This comports well with his *ordo decretorum* where Christ is sent to save "each and every one" who believes on the one hand, yet faith is given only to those who believe. Such asymmetrical conception of the divine will with regard to the atonement's extent and efficacy found a ready following at Saumur. Amyraut and Testard were two to whom Owen referred.[57]

---

[51] See *Canons of Dort*, "Of Divine Predestination", Article VII, and "Of the Death of Christ, and the Redemption of Men thereby", Article VIII-IX, in Schaff, *Creeds of Christendom*, 3:582-83, 587.

[52] To say that the decree to save the elect has a regulative influence upon Christ's work does not necessarily require adherence to the view that Christ died only for the elect. The universalistic positions of the English and German (Bremen and Hesse) delegates to the Synod of Dort certainly did not prevent them from subscribing to the *Canons of Dort*. See Stephen Strehle, "The Extent of the Atonement and the Synod of Dort," *WTJ* 51 (1989), 1-23.

[53] John Cameron, *Certain Theses or Positions of the Learned John Cameron Concerning the Threefold Covenant of God with Man*, III, in Samuel Bolton, *The True Bounds of Christian Freedom, Whereunto Is Annexed a Discourse of the Learned John Camerons, Touching the Three-Fold Covenant of God with Man* (London: Printed for P.S., 1656), 354.

[54] Armstrong, *Calvinism and the Amyraut Heresy*, 57-58; Thomas, *Extent of the Atonement*, 174-78.

[55] Cited in Armstrong, *Calvinism and the Amyraut Heresy*, 58.

[56] Armstrong, *Calvinism and the Amyraut Heresy*, 58.

[57] Thomas, *Extent of the Atonement*, 192-94; van Stam, *Controversy*, 39-46; Owen, *Salus Electorum*, II.iv (*Works*, 10:222n1): "Camero, Testardus, and Amyraldus."

On Cameron's particularistic understanding of God's will, it is necessary to note his qualification that faith is a divine gift. Indeed, he states without hesitation that the bestowal of faith and perseverance to the elect is promised in God's absolute covenant in which "there cannot be conceived any *condition* to be annexed, which is not *comprehended* in the promise it self."[58] Nevertheless, the force of this statement is reduced in the light of another aspect of his covenant theology. His categorization of the covenant of grace as a conditional rather than an absolute covenant tended towards the dependence of salvific efficacy upon the response of faith.[59] Not surprisingly, Cameron's subsequent elucidation of the covenant of grace in comparison with the covenant of nature was framed in general terms whenever the covenanting subjects were mentioned.[60] Both covenants "agree in the persons Covenanting, who are God and man", and differ "in the Quality, and manner of the Persons covenanting; for in the Covenant of Nature, God the Creator does require his due, or right, of man pure and perfect; but in the Covenant of Grace, God as a mercifull Father, doth offer himselfe to a sinner, wounded with the conscience of sinne."[61] Framers of the *Formula Consensus Helvetica* (1675) were well aware of what was at stake over the issue of the covenants and addressed it in Canons XXIII to XXV.[62] In defence of the Canons of Dort against the theology of Saumur, Cameron's threefold scheme of the covenant was rejected,[63] and a twofold covenant of works and grace was maintained with the assertion that the latter was "made with only the elect in Christ."[64]

Cameron's view of God's love and will, his *ordo decretorum* and covenant theology, were all foundational to the theology of his followers. Like the Arminians, the Saumurian conception of the divine decrees is composed of

---

[58] Cameron, *Theses*, I (Bolton, *True Bounds*, 353). By "absolute covenant" he meant an unconditional covenant where "there is nothing in the creature that doth impell God either to promise, or to performe what he hath promised." *Theses*, IV (Bolton, *True Bounds*, 355).

[59] Cameron, *Theses*, VI-VII (Bolton, *True Bounds*, 356). On this, Armstrong went so far as to state that Cameron "runs the risk of making God dependent on man." *Calvinism and the Amyraut Heresy*, 68. Thomas recognizes that there is an unexplained difficulty in Cameron of asserting that faith is not meritorious and that faith is also a condition. Thomas, *Extent of the Atonement*, 178.

[60] Cameron adhered to a threefold covenant scheme: the covenant of nature, covenant of grace, and the old or subservient covenant which is sometimes known as the legal covenant. *Theses*, VII (Bolton, *True Bounds*, 356). For a Reformed orthodox defence of the twofold covenant of works and grace against Cameron's threefold covenant, see Turretin, *Elenctic Theology*, XII.12.

[61] Cameron, *Theses*, VIII-IX (Bolton, *True Bounds*, 357-58).

[62] *Formula Consensus Helvetica*, in John H. Leith, ed., *Creeds of the Churches: A Reader in Christian Doctrine from the Bible to the Present* (Atlanta: John Knox Press, 1982), 320-22.

[63] *Formula Consensus Helvetica*, XXV (Leith, *Creeds*, 321-22).

[64] *Formula Consensus Helvetica*, XXIII (Leith, *Creeds*, 320).

both universalistic and particularistic elements, which implied a twofold view of the divine intention, differing in the objects on whom the decrees terminate. Owen would have understood such lack of singularity in the divine intention as evidence of a divided will. The tendency to highlight federal conditions only made the separation of impetration and application more pronounced. Owen's summary of Saumurian soteriology is therefore a reasonable one:

> Christ died for all indeed, but *conditionally* for some, if they do believe, or will so do (which he knows they cannot of themselves); and *absolutely* for his own, even them on whom he purposeth to bestow faith and grace, so as actually to be made possessors of the good things by him purchased.[65]

The third opponent to be considered is Thomas More. More's views on the atonement are found in his treatise, *The Universality of God's Free Grace*, which was published in 1646, a year before the publication of Owen's *The Death of Death*.[66] One key difference between More's approach to the atonement and those of the Arminians and Saumurians is the relative absence of broader doctrinal issues which bear upon the subject apart from their cursory and incidental occurrences in the preface.[67] More does not begin with the *ordo decretorum* or provide any nuanced account of God's love in relation to the eternal decrees, nor does he propound any developed form of covenant theology that provides the framework for what he would subsequently claim with respect to issues within the historical economy of salvation. His point of departure is the salvation that Christ obtains and effects through the Spirit, set within the context of the divine-human dynamic. It is the distinctions he employed to elucidate this starting point and their implications that resemble the Arminian and Saumurian positions on the atonement.

One fundamental distinction lay at the heart of More's entire treatise for which Scriptural warrant was claimed. It is summarized in the heading of the opening chapter: "Of the distinction between the Redemption, reconciliation, and Salvation which Jesus Christ effected in his owne body with God for men, And of that hee effecteth by his Spirit in men to God, and of which here meant."[68] More's emphasis fell on the parallel between the salvation obtained *in Christ's body with God for men*, and that effected *in men to God*. The former entailed the incarnation of the Son, his penal substitutionary work on the cross and his resurrection from the dead, all of which were said to be in accordance

---

[65] Owen, *Salus Electorum*, II.iv (*Works*, 10:222).

[66] See Chapter 1, 10n32, for full reference and historical details of More's life.

[67] The following are some distinctions More accepted as validated by Scripture: "And God his love of Compassion, and his love of delight. And Election to Sonship, and Predestination to the Adoption of Sonnes, And Secret Election in God, and Actuall Election, of and by God." More, *Universality*, "To the Christian Reader."

[68] More, *Universality*, 2.

with the will of the Father.[69] In sum, it was Christ's "Oblation and Sacrifice of himself to God" which was in view.[70] More had no hesitation in stating the first half of the distinction in universalistic terms. According to More, the incarnate Christ stood as a public person "in the Nature, and room of all Mankind"; "All the sinne and punishment, The whole debt of mankind, by order of Justice, became his"; "God was pleased to challenge the whole debt of him, and to impute all the sinnes the Law could charge mankind withall unto him, and to arrest, and call him to account, and enter into judgment with him for all."[71]

The salvation *effected in men to God* entailed the Spirit's salvific involvement on account of Christ's exaltation to the Father's right hand, and Christ's act of intercession. More distinguished between Christ's general and particular intercession. The former is universal in extent and the latter particular. On the one hand, Christ was said to have appeared before God "in some sort Interceding, or putting in for Transgressours, even the sonnes of men, yet in, and of the world."[72] On the other hand, "in more Speciall manner doth he enterceede, being the Advocate for his chosen ones, that by the heavenly Call, are brought in to him, and doe through his grace, submit to him, and beleeve on him."[73]

Thus far, More's distinctions have been clearly expressed. The salvation "obtained in Christ's body with God for men" pertained to Christ's oblation, while that which is "effected in men to God" pertained to Christ's intercession and the Spirit's application of salvation. However, his construction becomes increasingly confused as his argument develops. In addition to the distinctions already made, More distinguished between a common and special salvation:

> First, there is a common Salvation, which by vertue of his death and Resurrection, and Sacrifice, and the acceptableness, and the effectualness thereof, with the Father, he hath obtained, and worketh for all men…Secondly, there is a speciall and eternall Salvation, which Jesus Christ by vertue of his death and resurrection, doth in his spirituall application thereof, to the hearers and consciences of men, worke in men to God.[74]

Following this, More applied the common/special distinction to the phrases "with God for men" and "in men to God." He explained: "Now between those two Salvations, that with God for men, and that in men to God, The Common and the Speciall; The Scripture doth often and many ways distinguish, and that very clearly…"[75] More clarified that common salvation "is affirmed in

---

[69] More, *Universality*, 2-5.
[70] More, *Universality*, 4.
[71] More, *Universality*, 3-4.
[72] More, *Universality*, 7.
[73] More, *Universality*, 7.
[74] More, *Universality*, 9, 11.
[75] More, *Universality*, 14.

Scripture to be for all men" but special salvation "is only for and to beleevers."[76] This explanation introduces confusion into his argument since More would then be offering two different versions of Christ's intercession. The first version is that of Christ's general and particular intercession which he recounted earlier. The second version is that of Christ's intercession that is "only for and to beleevers", implied under the rubric of special salvation effected "in men to God." This implication arises because "in men to God" was a phrase used by More in relation to Christ's intercession. More's scholastic methodology seemed to have clouded rather than clarified his argument.

Readers of More would be hard pressed to find answers as to whether Christ's intercession is both universal and particular, or whether it is strictly particular in scope. Whichever the case, Owen's perception that the crux of the problem was a division of the priestly office is valid. If Christ's intercession is both universal and particular, this would imply a twofold oblation by virtue of the unity of Christ's priestly office. Together, these priestly acts would then be indicative of a general and particular mediation of Christ and thus of a twofold divine intention that is asymmetrical in its scope, both of which Owen rejects.[77] If Christ's intercession is strictly particular and his oblation universal in extent, then the acts of oblation and intercession do not concur on similar objects. There would then be division in the priestly office and derivatively in the divine intention. Furthermore, More claimed that Christ "makes all saveable, so as there is a possibleness in & through him, and possibility with him, for all men to come in to him, to beleeve on him, and in beleeving, to be eternally saved."[78] The end of Christ's oblation and intercession is not the actual redemption of the elect but a universal, salvific potentiality. Such a non-actualistic view of the atonement was rejected by Owen.

What the above analyses of the Arminian, Saumurian, and More's positions demonstrate is the legitimacy of Owen's concern for the unity of Christ's priestly office. Owen's perception of the crux of the controversy with his universalist opponents as the division between Christ's oblation and intercession is not without historical justification.[79] Arguing for the unity of Christ's priestly office was not confined to *The Death of Death* for Owen but

---

[76] More, *Universality*, 15.
[77] Owen, *Salus Electorum*, I.viii (*Works* 10:188-89, 192-94).
[78] More, *Universality*, 11.
[79] Cf. William Cunningham, *Historical Theology: A Review of the Principal Doctrinal Discussions in the Christian Church since the Apostolic Age*, Reprint ed., 2 vols. (St Edmonton, Canada: Still Waters Revival Books, 1991), 2:327: "Indeed, one of the principal uses to which the Arminians commonly apply the distinction between impetration and application, as they explain it, is this,–that they interpret the scriptural statements which seem to speak of all men as comprehended in the objects of Christ's death, of the impetration of pardon and reconciliation for them; and interpret those passages which seem to indicate some limitation in the objects of His dying, of the application of those blessings to men individually."

was a persistent preoccupation in both his early and late writings. This point will become evident as developments in Owen's formulation of Christ's priestly office are traced below.

Owen's Formulation of Christ's Priestly Office

While it is not impossible to examine every instance of Christ's priestly office in Owen's writings, it would be more expedient to examine only the writings that reveal developments of a formal nature.[80] A helpful way to achieve this aim is to examine those writings in which key distinctions are made on the issue.[81] In order to highlight significant developments, these writings will be examined chronologically.[82] *A Display of Arminianism* (1642), *Two Short Catechisms* (1645), and *The Death of Death* (1647), will be taken as works that represent Owen's early formulation. *Exercitations Concerning the Sacerdotal Office of Christ* (1674) will represent his mature writing on the subject.

A Display of Arminianism (1642)

In Owen's first publication, *A Display of Arminianism*, the priestly office of Christ was not made to bear the polemical and theological weight that is evident in *The Death of Death* despite the identification of Arminianism as a common opponent in both treatises. This is due in large measure to the different questions Owen was facing and addressing. Universal redemption is not his chief concern in *A Display of Arminianism* but the foundational principles of the Arminian system of thought deduced from the perceived ends of that system. These perceived ends are two according to Owen: exemption from God's supreme dominion and jurisdiction by insisting on the independence of the human will, and the vindication of humanity from the imputation of sin and inability to do good.[83] From these foundational principles, Owen derived and discussed a range of doctrinal issues, most of which are similar to those raised in the controversy involving Arminius and the Dutch Remonstrants.[84] Owen's

---

[80] That is, developments in the structure of Christ's priestly office in Owen's formulation. For this reason, *The Doctrine of the Saint's Perseverance* (1654) and *Vindicae Evangelicae* (1655) are excluded in the following survey although Christ's priesthood is a key concern in both treatises. They do not reveal developments of a structural kind but merely provide the material contents of an already established soteriological structure.

[81] On the Reformed orthodox use of distinctions, see Willem J. van Asselt, "The Theologian's Toolkit: Johannes Maccovius (1588-1644) and the Development of Reformed Theological Distinctions," *WTJ* 68 (2006), 23-40.

[82] For a chronological listing of Owen's writings, see Toon, *God's Statesman*, 179-81.

[83] Owen, *A Display of Arminianism*, I (*Works*, 10:11-14).

[84] See, for instance, his treatment of predestination, the extent of Christ's death, and the response of faith, found respectively in *A Display of Armimianism*, II-VI, IX, X-XI (*Works*, 10:14-68, 87-100, 100-114). Cf. also his numerous citations from the works of Arminius and the Remonstrants (*Works*, 10:21-22, 29-30, 43, 52, 67, 81-82, 87, 99-100,

primary intention in the treatise is the exposure and overthrow of the principles that underlie the Remonstrant controversy: "I have endeavored to lay open to the view of all some of their foundation-errors, not usually discussed, on which the whole inconsistent superstructure is erected..."[85]

Since Christ's priestly office was not a central issue for Owen in this, his treatment of the subject in *A Display of Arminianism* was understandably brief.[86] However, brevity has the advantage of narrowing content selection to what is essential, sieving out matters of secondary importance. Thus, it is all the more striking to observe that of the many aspects of Christ's priestly office that could have been discussed,[87] Owen chose to include the unity of Christ's oblation and intercession not only as an argument, but as a recurring one. Owen discussed this subject in the chapter entitled "Of the death of Christ, and of the efficacy of his merits."[88] He identified the Arminian case as having to do with both the objects of Christ's death and the efficacy of the merits of his death. According to Owen, the Arminians universalized the former and advanced a provisional rather than an actualistic understanding of the latter. Introducing the unity of Christ's priestly office as a riposte to the Arminian case, Owen argued:

> His intercession in heaven is nothing but a continued oblation of Himself. So that whatsoever Christ impetrated, merited, or obtained by his death and passion, must be infallibly applied unto and bestowed upon them for whom he intended to obtain it; or else his intercession is vain, he is not heard in the prayers of his mediatorship. An actual reconciliation with God, and communication of grace and glory, must needs betide all them that have any such interest in the righteousness of Christ as to have it accepted for their good.[89]

Like his later account of the priestly office in *The Death of Death*, Christ's intercession is a continuation of his oblation; impetration and application are employed as explanatory concepts for these priestly acts; the divine intention supplies the ground on which these acts are united in their objects. In speaking of intercession as Christ's continued oblation, the unity of Christ's priestly office is assumed. Owen's assertion of an "actual reconciliation" obtained by Christ rests upon this unity although the unity itself was not made explicit. However, as he summed up his case against Arminianism, the unity of Christ's

---

107-108, 113-14, 129). Not all the issues raised by the Arminian controversy were addressed, as Owen himself confessed (*Works*, 10:8-9).

[85] Owen, *A Display of Arminianism*, "To the Christian Reader" (*Works*, 10:8).

[86] Issues of predestination and human free-will take up seven of the fourteen chapters (Chapters II-VI, XII-XIII), but the death of Christ is covered in only one (Chapter IX).

[87] See, for example, the range of issues in "Concerning the Sacerdotal Office of Christ." Owen, *Exercitations on the Epistle to the Hebrews*, IV.xxv-xxxiv (*Works*, 18:3-259).

[88] Owen, *A Display of Arminianism,* IX (*Works*, 10:87-100).

[89] Owen, *A Display of Arminianism*, IX (*Works*, 10:90).

priestly office was clearly expressed, along with assertions of the atonement's particularity. Referring to Christ's oblation and intercession, Owen argued:

> These two acts of the priesthood are not to be separated; it belongs to the same mediator for sin to sacrifice and pray...But Christ doth not intercede and pray for all, as himself often witnesseth...He is not a mediator of them that perish, no more than an advocate of them that fail in their suits; and therefore the benefit of his death also must be restrained to them who are finally partakers of both...And, therefore, seeing he doth not intercede for every one, he did not die for every one.[90]

At this earliest stage of Owen's writings on the atonement, the formulation of Christ's priestly office in terms of oblation and intercession is already apparent. That it is not merely incidental, but has the definite theological purpose of demonstrating their unity which would secure the atonement's actuality and particularity against the Arminian threat, is indicative of a developed understanding of the priestly office prior to its first articulation in 1642. Since *A Display of Arminianism* is the earliest extant writing of Owen, there is no way of tracing his prior thoughts on the subject. Nevertheless, it is significant that the key distinction employed in conceptualizing Christ's priestly office is already present at the outset of Owen's theological career. Notwithstanding supplementation and an increasingly nuanced account in Owen's later writings, the distinction is to remain unchanged in form throughout the rest of Owen's writings.

Two Short Catechisms (1645)

Owen's catechetical writings, composed in 1645 for his congregation at Fordham in Essex, indicated further developments of his early formulation.[91] The *Lesser Catechism* consists of thirty-three questions and answers composed for the instruction of children.[92] It is closely tied to Owen's *Greater Catechism* in the range of doctrinal topics and the order in which they were handled. Owen's *Greater Catechism*, written for adults, expands on the respective topics in his *Lesser Catechism* over twenty-seven chapters with the inclusion of the relevant Scriptural texts.[93] Consistent with Owen's Christology, the mediatorial framework governed his composition of the catechetical materials which are related to the person and work of Christ. Christ was said to be "God and man united in one person, to be a Mediator between God and man."[94] This is

---

[90] Owen, *A Display of Arminianism*, IX (*Works*, 10:91-92). This is the third of six points Owen proposed in his case against Arminianism on the atoning death of Christ.
[91] Owen, *Two Short Catechisms* (*Works*, 1:463-94).
[92] Owen, *Two Short Catechisms*, LC (*Works*, 1:467-69).
[93] Owen, *Two Short Catechisms*, GC (*Works*, 1:470-94).
[94] Owen, *Two Short Catechisms*, LC (*Works*, 1:468); cf. GC, X (*Works* 1:478-79).

followed by the conception of that mediatorial relation in terms of the threefold office of prophet, priest, and king.[95]

In Owen's elucidation of the threefold office, two significant developments are apparent. First, there was a conscious attempt to relate Christ's mediatorial office to his twofold state of humiliation and exaltation, an attempt that was absent in *A Display of Arminianism*. This can be seen in his *Lesser Catechism*, where the question, "In what condition doth Jesus Christ exercise these offices?" received the answer, "He did in a low estate of humiliation on earth, but now in a glorious estate of exaltation in heaven."[96] Owen unpacked the nature of Christ's states in his *Greater Catechism* as follows:

> Q.2. Wherein consisteth the state of Christ's humiliation?
> A. In three things; first, in his incarnation, or being born of woman; secondly, his obedience, or fulfilling the whole law, moral and ceremonial; thirdly, in his passion, or enduring all sorts of miseries, even death itself...
>
> Q.3. Wherein consists his exaltation?
> A. In, first, his resurrection; secondly, ascension; thirdly, sitting at the right hand of God;—by all which he was declared to be the Son of God with power...[97]

In this catechetical entry, there is an emphasis on the movement from Christ's incarnation to his heavenly session. This emphasis comports well with Owen's emphasis on the economy of salvation in his Christology.[98] What gave rise to the introduction of this movement is the apparent need to clarify the context in which Christ exercised his threefold office.

The second significant development is the broadening conception of Christ's oblation. Owen's earlier description of oblation in *A Display of Arminianism* was narrowly focused on Christ's "death", "sacrifice", and "passion", all of which were presumably encapsulated in the heading of the relevant chapter coined in terms of Christ's death and the efficacy of its merits. In his *Lesser Catechism*, oblation has a wider reference, indicated by his inclusion of the adjective "chiefly" in the following item:

> Q. In what doth the exercise of his priestly office chiefly consist?
> A. In offering up himself an acceptable sacrifice on the cross, so satisfying the justice of God for our sins, removing his curse from our persons, and bringing us unto him.[99]

---

[95] Owen, *Two Short Catechisms*, LC: "Q. What is he unto us? A. A King, a Priest, and a Prophet" (*Works*, 1:468); cf. GC, XI-XIII (*Works*, 1:480-83).
[96] Owen, *Two Short Catechisms,* LC (*Works*, 1:468); cf. GC, XIV, Q.1 (*Works*, 1:483): "In what estate or condition doth Christ exercise these offices? A. In a two-fold estate; first of humiliation or abasement; secondly, of exaltation or glory. – Phil. ii. 8-10."
[97] Owen, *Two Short Catechisms*, GC, XIV (*Works*, 1:484).
[98] See Chapter 3 above.
[99] Owen, *Two Short Catechisms*, LC (*Works*, 1:468).

In other words, Christ's sacrificial death was conceived by Owen to be the main event of his oblative performance as priest but certainly not the only one.[100] Owen understood that there is more to oblation than simply Christ's death on the cross. However, no further clarification was provided in Owen's elaboration of the subject in his *Greater Catechism* where he simply defined oblation as the "offering up of himself upon the altar of the cross, an holy propitiatory sacrifice for the sins of all the elect throughout the world; as also the presentation of himself for us in heaven, sprinkled with the blood of the covenant."[101] Christ's intercession or "presentation of himself" is again presented as integral to his oblation, but there is no further evidence of what the broadening conception of Christ's oblation might entail in addition to Christ's sacrificial death. Owen concluded his catechetical discussion on Christ's priestly office with a succinct definition of Christ's intercession as his "continual soliciting on our behalf, begun here in fervent prayers, continued in heaven by appearing as our advocate at the throne of grace."[102] No attempt was made to widen the conception of Christ's intercession in the way oblation was.

The Death of Death (1647)

The developments in Owen's catechisms outlined above converged in a remarkable way in *The Death of Death*. What was not previously clarified in the broadening conception of Christ's oblation received unequivocal statement with Owen's explicit relation of oblation to the entire state of Christ's humiliation.

> By his oblation we do not design only the particular offering of himself upon the cross an offering to his Father, as the Lamb of God without spot or blemish, when he bare our sins or carried them up with him in his own body on the tree, which was the sum and complement of his oblation and that wherein it did chiefly consist; but also his whole humiliation, or state of emptying himself, whether by yielding voluntary obedience unto the law, as being made under it, that he might be the end thereof to them that believe, Romans 10:4, or by his subjection to the curse of the law, in the antecedent misery and suffering of life, as well as by submitting to death, the death of the cross...[103]

In the above statement, Owen does not speak of an integration of Christ's threefold office with his state of humiliation as the developments identified in his catechisms would have led one to expect. Rather, it is specifically Christ's priestly oblation into which his state of humiliation is subsumed. Along with

---

[100] Cf. the following comments from Owen, *Exercitation,* IV.xxxiii.2 (Owen, *Works,* 18:195): "The time and place when and wherein Christ, as our high priest, thus offered himself a sacrifice unto God, was in the days of his flesh, whilst he was yet in this world, by his suffering in the garden, *but especially on the cross.*" Emphasis added.
[101] Owen, *Two Short Catechisms,* LC, XII (*Works*, 1:481).
[102] Owen, *Two Short Catechisms,* LC, XII (*Works*, 1:483).
[103] Owen, *Salus Electorum,* I.vi (*Works* 10:179-80).

this is the corresponding integration of Christ's state of exaltation with his priestly intercession.

> Neither by his intercession do I understand only that heavenly appearance of his in the most holy place for the applying unto us all good things purchased and procured by his oblation; but also every act of his exaltation conducing thereunto, from his resurrection to his 'sitting down at the right hand of the Majesty on high, angels, and principalities, and powers, being made subject unto him'. Of all which his resurrection, being the basis, as it were, and the foundation of the rest…, is especially to be considered, as that to which a great part of the effect is often ascribed.[104]

Clearly, it was to the entire state of Christ's exaltation and not merely his heavenly appearance that Owen referred, which for him consisted of the movement from Christ's resurrection to his ascension, heavenly appearance before the Father, and heavenly session. For Owen, then, the priestly office of Christ, considered in terms of the acts of oblation and intercession, is a soteriological category into which the entire span of the economy of salvation centring on Christ is integrated. This formulation is, arguably, the most theologically weighty of Owen's statements on Christ's priestly office in his entire corpus. Such a construction not only buttressed Owen's argument for the unity of Christ's priestly acts, it simultaneously raised the stakes in his controversy with proponents of universal redemption. On the basis of Owen's developed formulation of Christ's priestly office, severing oblation from intercession, as the Arminians, Saumurians, and Thomas More did, would not only be injurious to the singularity of divine intention, it would also lead to a disjunction of all that is entailed in the humiliation of Christ from all that is entailed in his exaltation. Thus, for instance, on the terms of universal redemption, Christ being "delivered for our offenses" would have to be divided from his being "raised again for our justification", a position that was incompatible with their conjunction in Romans 4:25 as Owen understood it. Christ's resurrection is brought into the sacerdotal equation since intercession has now to do with Christ's state of exaltation of which resurrection is a part. According to Owen, the resurrection of Christ in Scripture is not to be thought of simply as a single historical event in the life of Christ, but "the whole following dispensation and the perpetual intercession of Christ for us in heaven is intended."[105] Such a construction of the priestly office in which Christ's priestly acts are integrated with his twofold state means that Owen took the entire life of Christ seriously in his understanding of the atonement. This is an

---

[104] Owen, *Salus Electorum*, I.vi (*Works*, 10:180).
[105] Owen, *Salus Electorum*, I.vi (*Works*, 10:180). "Rom iv.25;—where, and in such other places, by his resurrection, the whole following dispensation and the perpetual intercession of Christ for us in heaven is intended."

important characteristic of Owen's atonement theology that will be explored further in the next chapter.

Exercitations Concerning the Priesthood of Christ (1674)

Thus far, Owen's formulation of Christ's priestly office in his early writings has been established by tracing its formal developments. Did his formulation reach a stable form in *The Death of Death* or were there further developments in his mature writings? For answers to this question, it is necessary to examine Owen's *Exercitations Concerning the Priesthood of Christ*. Being the lengthiest of his writings on Christ's priesthood, published within a decade to his death, the *Exercitations* encapsulate Owen's mature thoughts on the subject.[106] In *Exercitations*, Owen's opponents were not the Arminians but the Socinians. The Socinians rejected orthodox Christology and maintained that Christ was devoid of the divine nature.[107] This rejection has obvious implications, indeed serious ones, for the Socinian view of Christ's priesthood. What is important to note about Socinianism at this juncture is not an elaborate discussion of its position on the priesthood of Christ, but rather Owen's response to some of its significant characteristics.

Like his analyses of the Arminian and Saumurian positions, Owen assessed the Socinian stance on Christ's priestly office against the framework of Christ's priestly acts. Characteristically, these acts were distinguished by Owen into oblation and intercession.[108] Owen defined oblation as follows:

> The oblation of Christ is that act or duty of his sacerdotal office whereby he offered himself, his soul and body, or his whole human nature, an expiatory sacrifice to God in his death and blood-shedding, to make atonement for the sins of mankind, and to purchase for them eternal redemption.[109]

The above definition captures the narrower conception of oblation, one that has Christ's death as the main reference point. This is followed by further elaborations on the nature, efficacy, and historical context of Christ's oblation:

---

[106] Owen, *Exercitations on the Epistle to the Hebrews Concerning the Priesthood of Christ* (London: Printed by John Darby, 1674). The entire project was originally published in four folio volumes in the years 1668, 1674, 1680, and 1684 respectively. For the history surrounding their publication, see Owen, *Works*, 17:2-24, and the editor's "General Preface"; cf. also "Appendix I" in Toon, *God's Statesman*, 179-81. The second volume referred to above is massive and is divided in the 1854-55 Goold edition of *The Works of John Owen* into three separate volumes (vols. 19, 20, 21). These are reprinted as volumes 18, 19, and 20 in the Banner of Truth reprint. The chapter divisions in the original 1674 publication are different from those in the Goold edition (vol. 19) and Banner reprint (vol. 18). Unfortunately, there is no existing account of this change. Subsequent citations follow the chapter divisions found in the Banner reprint.

[107] *Racovian Catechisme*, 28ff.

[108] Owen, *Exposition of Hebrews*, Exercitations IV.xxxiii.1 (*Works*, 18:194-95).

[109] Owen, *Exposition of Hebrews*, Exercitations IV.xxxiii.2 (*Works*, 18:195).

(1) The nature of the oblation of Christ consisted in a bloody expiatory sacrifice, making atonement for sin by bearing the punishment due thereunto. And, (2) As to the efficacy of it, it hath procured for us pardon of sin, freedom from the curse, and eternal redemption. (3) The time and place when and wherein Christ, as our high priest, thus offered himself a sacrifice unto God, was in the days of his flesh, whilst he was yet in this world, by his suffering in the garden, but especially on the cross.[110]

The above elaborations give insight into what Owen perceived to be the areas of contention with the Socinians. Point (3) was fundamental to (1) and (2). For the Socinians, Christ is not a priest in his earthly life but only became a priest in heaven.[111] The Socinians considered the priestly acts of oblation and intercession as post-ascension performances. Christ's sacrifice of atonement is not a historical but heavenly reality. The sacrificial language that is applied to Christ in the New Testament was not interpreted literally by the Socinians but figuratively as the "manner of assisting" that the ascended Christ provided for believers: "The Priestly Office of Christ therefore consisteth herein, that as by his Kingly Office, he is able to assists us in all our necessities, so by his Priestly Office he is willing to doe so, and consequently assisteth us. And this manner of assisting, or giving aid to us, is called his Sacrifice."[112] Consequently, on the issue of the efficacy of Christ's death, the Socinians denied that Christ's oblation procured anything. Thus, the main problem posed by Socinianism is not the separation of Christ's oblation from his intercession, but the historical and temporal reality of Christ's oblation. Problems with the nature and efficacy of Christ's oblation turn largely on the Socinian denial of the historical reality of Christ's priesthood. In Owen's words, it was an "imaginary oblation" that the Socinians contested for.[113]

Given the figurative conception of Christ's death as sacrifice by the Socinians, it is not surprising to find Owen defending the real nature and

---

[110] Owen, *Exposition of Hebrews*, Exercitations IV.xxxiii.2 (*Works*, 18:195).

[111] *Racovian Catechisme*, 163: "Q. What? Was he not a priest until he entered into the heaven? Not when he hung upon the cross? A. At no hand; for, as you heard even now, the Divine Author to the Hebrews, chap. 8.4 expressly saith, that if Christ were upon the Earth, hee would not be a Priest. Besides, for as much as the same Author, chap. 2.17, testifieth, that Christ ought in all things to be made like unto his Brethren, that he might become a mercifull and faithfull High-Priest to God ward, it is evident, that until he be made like unto his brethren in all things, that is, in afflictions and death, he was not our mercifull and faithfull High-Priest. Whereby it cometh to pass, that his afflictions, and death were not his very Sacrifice, but a preparation thereunto."

[112] *Racovian Catechisme*, 160.

[113] Owen, *Exposition of Hebrews*, Exercitations IV.xxxiii.2 (*Works*, 18:196). Cf. idem, *Exposition of Hebrews*, Exercitations IV.xxv.4 (*Works*, 18:6): "This they have attempted with much subtilty and diligence, introducing a metaphorical or imaginary priesthood and sacrifice in their room; so, robbing the church of its principal treasure, they pretend to supply the end of it with their own fancies. They are the Socinians whom I intend."

efficacy of Christ's priesthood in his discussion on the historical context of Christ's work as priest. This was argued in terms of the time and place in which Christ exercised his priesthood.[114] Conceiving of Christ's suffering as part of his oblation, Owen stressed that it was "especially on the cross" that Jesus suffered as priest.[115] This would have been sufficient in Owen's definition of oblation to distinguish his conception from that of the Socinians. However, Owen made it clear that Christ's oblation had a wider reference when he affirmed that it was "in the days of his flesh, whilst he was yet in this world" that the priestly act of oblation was performed.[116] Owen's understanding of the phrase "in the days of his flesh" includes not only the event of the cross, but also Christ's "suffering in the garden" and events in the period when Christ was "in this world, even as he was also the king and prophet of the church."[117] Clearly evident in Owen's exposition is the integration between Christ's oblation and his state of humiliation.

With regard to the act of Christ's intercession, its important connection with Christ's oblation was again expressed by Owen. He insisted that Christ's intercession is integral to the application of what is procured by Christ's oblation. The language Owen employed to assert this is akin to that of the author to the Hebrews. For Christ's oblation to be efficacious, Owen argued, "it was necessary that, as our high priest, he should enter into the holy place, or the presence of God in the heavens, there to represent himself as having done the will of God and finished the work committed to him; whereon the actual efficacy of his oblation...doth depend."[118] Thus, for Owen, Christ's heavenly intercession depends upon his oblation as application is upon the procurement of salvific benefits.

On the nature of Christ's intercession itself, Owen employed the scholastic method of making distinctions in order to clarify the issue under investigation. This is seen in the course of his attempt to distinguish between two types of intercession performed by Christ. The first was termed by Owen as "formal" and "oral":

> There is a *formal*, oral intercession, when, any one, by words, arguments, supplications, with humble earnestness in their use, prevails with another for any good thing that is in his power to be bestowed on himself or others. Of this nature was the intercession of Christ whilst he was on earth.[119]

---

[114] Owen, *Exposition of Hebrews*, Exercitations IV.xxxiii.5-12 (*Works*, 18:198-216).
[115] Owen, *Exposition of Hebrews*, Exercitations IV.xxxiii.2 (*Works*, 18:195).
[116] Owen, *Exposition of Hebrews*, Exercitations IV.xxxiii.2 (*Works*, 18:195).
[117] Owen, *Exposition of Hebrews*, Exercitations IV.xxxiii.2, 5 (*Works*, 18:195, 199).
[118] Owen, *Exposition of Hebrews*, Exercitations IV.xxxiii.2 (*Works*, 18:195). Cf. Heb 9:24: "For Christ is not entered into the holy places made with hands, which are the figures of the true; but into heaven itself, now to appear in the presence of God for us."
[119] Owen, *Exposition of Hebrews*, Exercitations IV.xxxiii.3 (*Works*, 18:196-97).

The second type of intercession was termed "virtual" or "real". It is distinguished from formal intercession in the following manner:

> *Virtual* or real intercession differs not in the substance or nature of it from that which is oral and formal, but only in the outward manner of its performance with respect unto the reasons of it as now accomplished.[120]

After distinguishing formal from virtual intercession, Owen clarified the grounds for conceptualizing intercession in a twofold manner. The crucial factor that necessitated such a distinction was, for Owen, the state or condition of the intercessor. Whether Christ is in his earthly or heavenly state is of paramount importance for understanding the nature of his intercession. Owen explained:

> When Christ was upon the earth, his state and condition rendered it necessary that his intercession should be by way of formal supplications; and that, as to the argument of it, it should respect that which was for to come, his oblation…being not yet completed. But now, in heaven, the state and condition of Christ admitting of no oral or formal supplications, and the ground, reason, or argument of his intercession, being finished and past, his intercession, as the means of the actual impetration of grace and glory, consists in the real presentation of his offering and sacrifice for the procuring of the actual communication of the fruits thereof unto them for whom he so offered himself.[121]

Thus, application of the scholastic method allowed Owen to clarify the grounds of Christ's intercession to be that of Christ's twofold state. This throws light on the kind of formulation concerning Christ's priestly office that Owen was working with. Like his formulation in *The Death of Death*, it is one in which Christ's priestly office and twofold state are integrated. Such a formulation of Christ's intercession bore no resemblance to the Socinian version of it apart from the use of common terminologies like "priesthood", "sacrifice", "oblation", and "intercession". In correlating Christ's intercession with his earthly state, Owen assumed the historical reality of Christ's earthly priesthood which the Socinians denied. For the Socinians, Christ's intercession was not "the real presentation of his offering and sacrifice" which ensured the application of salvific benefits, as Owen had argued. Instead, it was a request made to God to reveal "the care which Christ takes of our salvation", and served rather to safeguard "the Prerogative, and eminency of the Father above Christ…"[122] According to the Socinians, it was the authority which God conferred on the ascended Christ that was instrumental in the communication of

---

[120] Owen, *Exposition of Hebrews*, Exercitations IV.xxxiii.3 (*Works*, 18:197).
[121] Owen, *Exposition of Hebrews*, Exercitations IV.xxxiii.3 (*Works*, 18:197).
[122] *Racovian Catechisme*, 165.

salvation to believers, not the intercession of Christ.[123] So radically different were the Socinian versions of Christ's oblation and intercession from Owen's that he perceived the *status controversiae* to be over the very existence of Christ's priestly office itself.[124]

There is no doubt that Christ's priestly office remained an issue of great concern in Owen's mature writing. Although the battle was no longer over universal redemption, nevertheless, analysis of the Socinian problem on Christ's priesthood was still framed in terms of the oblation / intercession distinction, as was the case with his earlier writings against the Arminians. The integration of Christ's priestly acts with his twofold state continues to be a prominent characteristic in his late formulation. Owen's distinction between formal and virtual intercession served to clarify the way in which Christ's twofold state is brought into his consideration of Christ's priesthood. It did not add to his formulation of Christ's priestly office in any formal way but was simply a further detail within the space of an existing and stable soteriological structure. It can reasonably be concluded that from the writing of *The Death of Death* in 1647 to his *Exercitations Concerning Christ's Priesthood* in 1674, Owen's formulation of Christ's priestly office remained consistent.

Conclusion

This chapter has argued the significance of Christ's priestly office in Owen's atonement theology from three vantage points. First, Christ's priestly office provides the basic framework for Owen's analysis of the key problem with universal redemption, which is that of dividing Christ's oblation from his intercession. Second, the various accounts of Christ's priesthood, by the Arminians, Saumurians, and Thomas More, show that Owen's assessment of the key problem with universal redemption is justified. This means that Christ's priestly office is contextually significant for Owen. Third, in Owen's formulation, Christ's priestly office is a category into which Christ's twofold state is integrated. This formulation is evident in Owen's early and mature

---

[123] *Racivian Catechisme*, 165: "Quest. *What is the meaning of that place, Heb. 1.3. Christ having made a purgation of our sinnes, sate down at the right hand of the majesty on high?* Answ. That the manner of expiating and purging our sinnes, is, since Christ, being raised from the dead, entred into Heaven, and offered himself to God for us, I say, is perfect and compleat; that is, all is now finished whereby we may be moved to embrace the remission of sinnes, which God hath offered to us; and Christ hath obtained authority to conferre that remission upon us. Whence afterwards perpetually issueth the cleansing from sinnes, and true freedom from the penalties of them."

[124] Owen, *Exposition of Hebrews*, Exercitations IV.xxxiii.10 (*Works*, 18:209-10): "Hence, therefore, it is evident what is the true state of the controversy between these men and us about the priesthood of Christ. It is not, indeed, about the nature of that office, nor about the time and place of its exercise, though they needlessly compel us to treat about them also; but the sole question is, whether Christ *have any such office or no*."

writings, which indicate not only the consistency of his thought, but also the persistent importance of the subject throughout his theological career.

CHAPTER 5

The Means of Redemption: Christ's Satisfaction for Sin

In the previous chapter, it was explicitly shown that Owen's formulation of Christ's priestly office entailed Christ's twofold state of humiliation and exaltation. This chapter explores the extent to which Owen's formulation is applicable to his doctrine of satisfaction. It argues the thesis that Owen's conception of Christ's priesthood played a crucial role in his view of satisfaction with respect to key points of the doctrine. In particular, it will be shown that Owen's high esteem for Christ's priesthood is seen in his decision for the satisfactory value of Christ's whole obedience, and in his explication of the nature and fruits of Christ's death. The seventeenth-century debate over the imputation of Christ's obedience provides the backdrop against which the former is explored, while the latter will be examined within the context of Owen's controversy with Baxter.

Satisfaction and the Whole Obedience of Christ

The Matter of Satisfaction: Seventeenth-Century Background

In Protestant orthodoxy, the doctrine of satisfaction was not a theological locus in which the details of the doctrine had obtained unanimous agreement. This is particularly true with respect to the seventeenth-century debates over the extent to which the whole of Christ's life had direct bearing upon satisfaction for sin. Turretin states the issue in his *Elenctic Theology* as one that concerns "The Matter of the Satisfaction": "Is the satisfaction of Christ to be restricted to the sufferings and punishments which he endured for us? Or is it to be extended also to the active obedience by which he perfectly fulfilled the law in his whole life?"[1]

Differing answers to these questions were present in both Lutheran and Reformed orthodoxy. Answers were commonly coined in terms of Christ's *obedientia passiva* alone or as including his *obedientia activa*.[2] On the Lutheran side, some theologians of the *Augsburg Confession* spoke of being

---

[1] Turretin, *Elenctic Theology*, XIV.xiii.
[2] See "iustificatio" in Muller, *DLGTT*, 162-63. These terms are synonymous with Christ's active and passive righteousness but should not be confused with active and passive justification. Alister E. McGrath, *Iustitia Dei: A History of the Christian Doctrine of Justification*, 3rd ed. (Cambridge/New York/Melbourne: Cambridge University Press, 2005), 271-72.

saved by Christ's "perfect obedience" and of being "accepted as children of God for the sake of Christ's obedience alone, which is reckoned as righteousness through faith alone, out of sheer grace, to all who truly believe."[3] This perfect obedience of Christ is understood by some Lutherans as his rendering of "passive satisfaction to the punitive justice of God" and "active satisfaction to the demands of the law for a perfectly righteous life."[4] Others, like George Kargius and John Gerhard, restricted it to Christ's passive obedience.[5]

Diversity of positions was also evident on the Reformed front. On the continent, Johannes Piscator (1546-1625), who was professor of divinity at Herborn, had published a treatise on justification with an English translation in 1594 entitled, *A Learned and Profitable Treatise of Mans Iustification.*[6] It was written in response to Conrad Vorstius' request for Piscator's opinions on the views of a leading Jesuit theologian, Robert Bellarmine, on justification.[7] In the treatise, Piscator sought to defend justification as the "imputing of iustice" against the Catholic concept of justification as the "infusing of iustice."[8] A key argument he advanced is that justification consists of the forgiveness of sins.[9] For Piscator, the imputation of justice is synonymous with sin's pardon or forgiveness and did not include a man's inherent righteousness.[10]

---

[3] *Formula of Concord*, Solid Declaration, III.4.

[4] Pelikan, *Reformation of Church and Dogma*, 152; cf. J.A. Quenstedt, *Theologica Didactico-Polemica*, III, 525, in Heinrich Schmid, *The Doctrinal Theology of the Evangelical Lutheran Church, Verified from the Original Sources*, ed. Charles A. Hay and Henry E. Jacobs (Philadelphia: Lutheran Publication Society, 1889), 440: "The righteousness of Christ, or his obedience, active and passive, which is imputed to us, is most true and real, for it corresponds entirely to the mind and will of God expressed in the law."

[5] Gulielmum Forbesius, *Considerationes Modestae Et Pacificae Controversiarum De Justificatione, Purgatorio, Invocatione Sanctorum, Christo Mediatore, Et Eucharista Una Cum Versione Anglica*, 2 vols. (Oxonii: Apud J.H. Parker, 1850-1856), 1:102-105. Kargius was a pastor of Anspach in 1570; John Gerhard was an influential theologian who held a professorship at Jena from 1616 until his death in 1637.

[6] Johannes Piscator, *A Learned and Profitable Treatise of Mans Iustification, Two Bookes, Opposed to the Sophismes of Robert Bellarmine, Iesuite* (London: Thomas Creede for Robert Dexter, 1599).

[7] Piscator, *A Learned and Profitable Treatise*, Preface.

[8] Piscator, *A Learned and Profitable Treatise*, I.2.

[9] Piscator, *A Learned and Profitable Treatise*, I.1.

[10] Piscator, *A Learned and Profitable Treatise*, II.4: "Now forgiueness of sinne, and imputing of iustice, differ onely in name, indeed they are the same: as appeareth by the Apostles words Rom. 4.6.7. as we haue declared elswhere." He connects justification with sin's forgiveness so tightly and exclusively that actual obedience to the law is taken for granted without positing its actual fulfillment: "For remission of sinnes does not onely deliuer from paine, to wit, eternall death; but also bringeth glory or eternall life. The reason for which thing is this, that remission of sinnes, wherein mans iustification consisteth, is remission of all sinnes: and therefore not onely of sinnes committing, but

Notwithstanding the force of his argument against the Catholic concept of infused righteousness, Piscator's argument however opened the door to serious criticisms from Protestant divines who conceived of justification as entailing both the forgiveness of sins and the imputation of Christ's obedience to the law. Since for Piscator, it is Christ's death only which secured the forgiveness of sins, his argument effectively restricted imputation to Christ's passive obedience.[11] Thus, Piscator's view was controversial. It raised serious concerns within the French Reformed churches and was deemed sufficiently grave to warrant a statement at the Synod of Gap in 1603.[12] The Synod declared Piscator's view as erroneous, asserted the "Imputation of Christ's Active and Passive obedience (by which he hath perfectly fulfilled the whole Law) unto us for Righteousness", warned ministers of deposition if the other view was persistently held, and purposed to convey their decision to the Universities in England, Scotland, Leiden, Geneva, Heidelberg, Basle, and Herborn.[13] This matter was reiterated at the Synod of Privas in 1612 and the Synod of Tonneins in 1614, indicating the severity of the matter.[14]

In England, ecclesiastical resolution of the issue within Reformed orthodoxy was not monolithic. Confessional documents revealed ambivalence about the satisfactory value of Christ's whole obedience on the one hand, and strict adherence to it on the other. As will become clear, the former is seen in the *Westminster Confession* and the latter in the *Savoy Declaration* of the Congregational churches in England. When the Thirty-Nine Articles of the Church of England were formulated, Article XI, "Of the Justification of Man", had not dealt with Christ's obedience or the imputation of Christ's righteousness. It was concerned to establish a distinctly Protestant doctrine of justification with an emphasis on "fayth onely."[15] Given the diversity of views among the Reformed orthodox on the question and the lack of treatment in Article XI, the subject of Christ's obedience was, unsurprisingly, a hotly contested issue when revisions to the article were debated in the Westminster

---

also of sinnes omitting: whereby it cometh, that he to whome God forgiueth sinnes, is so accounted of, as if he had not only committed nothing which God hath forbidden in his law: but also omitted nothing of that which he hath commanded: and therefore, as if he had perfectly fulfilled the law of God."

[11] McGrath suggests that Piscator's understanding of the satisfactory value of Christ's active obedience is indirect, not non-existent. McGrath, *Iustitia Dei*, 272 n218.

[12] Quick, *Synodicon*, 226-27.

[13] Quick, *Synodicon*, 227.

[14] Quick, *Synodicon*, 348, 401.

[15] Schaff, *Creeds of Christendom*, 3:494: "We are accompted righteous before God, onely for the merite of our Lord and sauior Jesus Christe, by faith, and not for our owne workes or deseruynges. Wherefore, that we are iustified by fayth onely, is a most wholesome doctrine, and very full of comfort, as more largely is expressed in the Homilie of iustification" (1571 English Edition).

Assembly.[16] Among the members of the Assembly who had made two or more speeches during the debates on the article, twenty-one argued for the imputation of Christ's active obedience,[17] six were against it,[18] and the position of six others cannot be determined with certainty.[19] The review committee's recommendation to insert the phrase, "whole obedience", was not taken up by the Assembly in the final form of the *Westminster Confession*. It was stated in Chapter VIII, on Christ the Mediator, that the Father's justice is fully satisfied on account of Christ's "perfect obedience, and sacrifice of himself."[20] Chapter XI, on justification, spoke of the imputation of "the obedience and satisfaction of Christ", the vicarious nature of Christ's "obedience and satisfaction", and Christ's "obedience and death" that "did fully discharge the debt of all those that are thus justified, and did make a proper, real, and full satisfaction to his Father's justice in their behalf."[21] Evidently, there was room to interpret Christ's "perfect obedience"/"obedience" and "satisfaction"/"death" as pointing to the same event of the cross but from different vantage points and so support a passive-obedience-only position. It was equally possible to interpret the phrases in the light of Christ's whole obedience.

The *Westminster Confession* was, most likely, a consensual document. This is seen in the Independent party's subscription to it despite their dissatisfaction with its accommodating stance.[22] This dissatisfaction was obvious in their revision of the *Westminster Confession* at Savoy in 1658, in which the ambiguity on Christ's obedience was removed by aligning themselves with the confessional majority. Chapter XI of the *Savoy Declaration* states:

> Those whom God effectually calleth, he also freely justifieth...by imputing Christ's active obedience unto the whole Law, and passive obedience in his death for their whole and sole righteousness, they receiving and resting on him and his

---

[16] Van Dixhoorn, "Reforming the Reformation", 1:292-323. For the broader context of the subject in seventeenth-century England and New England, see Michael P. Winship, "Contesting Control of Orthodoxy among the Godly: William Pynchon Reexamined," *WMQ* 54, no. 4 (1997), 795-822.

[17] Joshua Hoyle, George Walker, Herbert Palmer, Thomas Goodwin, Lazarus Seaman, William Gouge, Peter Smith, Theodore Bathurst, Thomas Coleman, Henry Wilkinson Sr, Thomas Case, Charles Herle, Daniel Featley, Thomas Wilson, Samuel Gibson, John Leigh, William Price, Cornelius Burges, Thomas Carter, William Carter, Anthony Tuckney. The information in footnotes 17 to 19 is based on Table 5.1 in Van Dixhoorn, "Reforming the Reformation", 1:332-34.

[18] Thomas Gataker, Richard Vines, Thomas Temple, Francis Woodcock, Francis Taylor, William Raynor.

[19] Thomas Bayly, William Twisse, Stanley Gower, Richard Herrick, Thomas Hill, Thomas Hodges.

[20] *Westminster Confession*, VIII.5.

[21] *Westminster Confession*, XI.1, 3.

[22] Van Dixhoorn, "Reforming the Reformation", 1:330.

righteousness by Faith; which Faith have they not of themselves, it is the gift of God.[23]

As a key drafter of the *Savoy Declaration*, Owen's own stance would have been reflected in the above article.[24] This is confirmed in his 1677 treatise on justification where the imputation of Christ's active and passive righteousness was given exegetical, theological, and polemical expression.[25] Being extremely well versed in the relevant literature, Owen was fully aware of the kind of objections that were being levelled against the imputation of Christ's whole obedience. Acceding to the Council of State's request in March 1654 to respond to the Socinian catechisms of John Biddle and Valentinus Smalcius, he wrote a substantial treatise that addressed, among other things, the Socinian objections to the doctrine.[26] Personally, he was involved in a prolonged debate with Richard Baxter that touched on related matters against the background of seventeenth-century antinomianism.[27] He was familiar with the writings of Bellarmine,[28] cited him in various works, and sought to refute his views on the question of Christ's obedience in justification.[29] More significantly, Owen was acutely aware of the orthodoxy of those divines who repudiated Socinianism, antinomianism, and Catholicism, but who nevertheless held to the passive-

---

[23] *Savoy Declaration*, VIII.1.

[24] Baxter identified Owen and Philip Nye as the "Dividers of *England*" whose divisive policies won the day at Savoy. Richard Baxter, *Reliquiae Baxterianae, or Mr Richard Baxter's Narrative of the Most Memorable Passages of His Life and Times* (London: Printed for T. Parkhurst, F. Robinson, F. Lawrence, and F. Dunton 1696), I, §147. Relying on the opinions of "some yet living", presumably participants of the Savoy conference, Owen was singled out by Baxter as the chief influence on the question of justification. Richard Baxter, *Catholick Communion Defended against Both Extreames: And Unnecessary Division Confuted, by Reasons against Both the Active and Passive Ways of Seperation: Occasioned by the Racks and Reproaches of One Sort, and the Impatience and Censoriousness of the Other; and the Erroneous, Tho Confident Writings of Both. And Written in Compassion, of a Distracted, Self-Tearing People, Tho with Little Hope of Any Great Success. In Five Parts.* (London: Printed for Tho. Parkhurst, 1684), V:8; cf. A.G. Matthews, ed., *The Savoy Declaration of Faith and Order 1658, with an Additional Notice by Daniel T. Jenkins* (London: Independent Press, 1959), 9-50.

[25] Owen, *The Doctrine of Justification by Faith, through the Imputation of the Righteousness of Christ; Explained, Confirmed, and Vindicated* (1677) (*Works*, 5:1-400).

[26] Owen, *Vindicae Evangelicae*, Prefatory Note, XX-XXX (*Works*, 12:3-4, 397-551).

[27] Owen, *Of the Death of Christ* (*Works*, 10:429-79); idem, *Of the Death of Christ, and of Justification* (*Works*, 12:591-616).

[28] Owen owned a wide range of Bellarmine's works. See *BO*, Libri Theologici in Folio, 124, Libri Theologici in Octavo, Duodecimo, &c., 125, 179, 198, 295.

[29] Cf. Owen, *The Doctrine of Justification*, General Considerations, VI, XVIII, XX (*Works*, 5:55-57, 154-55, 344-47, 390-92); idem, *The Doctrine of the Saint's Perseverance*, Preface (*Works*, 11:25-26, 73); idem, *Exposition of Hebrews*, Exercitations, IV.xxvi.25 (*Works*, 18:40-41).

obedience-only position. In the opening section of his treatise on justification, Owen observed:

> There hath been a controversy more directly stated among some *learned divines* of the Reformed churches (for the Lutherans are unanimous on the one side), about the *righteousness of Christ* that is said to be imputed unto us. For some would have this to be only his *suffering of death*, and the satisfaction which he made for sin thereby, and others include therein the *obedience of his life* also.[30]

Referring to the same controversy in Chapter VII of the treatise, he acknowledged that there were differences "among persons learned, sober, and *orthodox*…in the way and manner of the explication of the doctrine of justification by the *imputation of the righteousness of Christ*", and affirmed the agreement that existed among them "in the substance of it."[31] This is a clear indication that on the question of the *matter* of satisfaction and not the essential aspects of the doctrine, Owen perceived that there was room for divergence among the Reformed divines. Thus, in his assessment of the subject, the passive-obedience-only position was not a closed option to him. He could have easily settled for this minority view among the Reformed orthodox, appealed to the authority of influential divines like Thomas Gataker,[32] and still be considered as standing within the ambit of Reformed orthodoxy, at least in the context of England.

The reasons for Owen not doing so require further investigation. In the light of the present task to give an account of Owen's atonement theology, it is necessary to explore the theological framework behind his decision for Christ's whole obedience in sin's satisfaction and its related issues. Various polemical reasons will also be explored, but it is done with the aim of demonstrating the way in which Christ's priesthood was of primary importance to the issues at hand.

The Obedience of Christ the Mediator

Owen was not averse to employing the active/passive distinction to Christ's obedience. However, he duly acknowledged the difficulties which attend the

---

[30] Owen, *The Doctrine of Justification*, General Considerations (*Works*, 5:63).

[31] Owen, *The Doctrine of Justification*, VII (*Works*, 5:164-65). In the preceding paragraph, Owen referred to the "judgment of the Reformed churches" (164) on the matter, indicating that his following reference to persons "learned, sober, and *orthodox*" was to the Reformed divines.

[32] Known for his great learning as a linguist and philologist, Gataker was reputed "the most celebrated among the Assembly of Divines" and "a writer of infinite learning and accurate judgment." James Reid, *Memoirs of the Lives and Writings of Those Eminent Divines Who Convened in the Famous Assembly at Westminster in the Seventeenth Century* (Paisley: Printed by Stephen and Andrew Young, 1811; repr. Edinburgh: Banner of Truth, 1982), 308. Gataker argued for the passive-obedience-only position. See footnote 18 above.

use of these terms. His general unease with the distinction was generated by the testimony of Scripture on the suffering of Christ. Owen insisted that "Scripture testimonies are not to be regulated by philosophical artifices and terms."[33] It was improper, for instance, to speak of Christ's suffering as entirely passive, "for he exercised the highest active obedience in his suffering, when he offered himself to God through the eternal Spirit", alluding to Hebrews 9:14.[34] This caveat is supported by Hebrews 5:7-8, where learning obedience through suffering was an essential experience of the Son in his earthly life.[35] The inseparable connection that exists between Christ's entire life of obedience and his suffering suggests that suffering ought not to be confined to the event of the cross. Owen's exercise of a Biblically informed caution is in keeping with the anti-speculative sentiments inherent in the Scripture principle of the Reformation. Thus, it is important that Owen's qualified use of the active/passive distinction be borne in mind when the distinction is employed during the course of the following exposition.

A fundamental point asserted by Owen concerning Christ's obedience is that it is the obedience of his person as Mediator. The significance of this assertion surfaces once the contexts from which it arose are taken into account. In 1594, Faustus Socinus (1539-1604) published what was to be "the most important Socinian work against the doctrine of satisfaction", *De Jesu Christo Servatore*.[36] In the treatise, he called into question the possibility of imputation and denied the satisfactory value of Christ's obedience.[37] What drove Socinus' critique was his Christology. Since Jesus was only a man in his earthly life, his obedience to the law was the fitting response of a creature to the demands of the Creator. Within the context of the Creator-creature relationship, Jesus' obedience to the law, like the obedience of any man, was due *from himself* and performed *for himself*. As such, Socinus reasoned that Christ's obedience could not have been substitutionary in nature with imputation as a concomitant. Since Socinus' logic stemmed from his heterodox view of Christ's person, Owen's response thus involved the deployment of orthodox Christology on the question of Christ's obedience. Owen comments:

> The obedience we treat of was the obedience of Christ the Mediator: but the obedience of Christ, as 'the mediator of the covenant', was the obedience of his

---

[33] Owen, *The Doctrine of Justification*, XII (*Works*, 5:254).
[34] Owen, *The Doctrine of Justification*, XII (*Works*, 5:253).
[35] Owen, *The Doctrine of Justification*, XII, XVIII (*Works*, 5:253-54, 336).
[36] Alan W. Gomes, "*De Jesu Christo Servatore*: Faustus Socinus on the Satisfaction of Christ," *WTJ* 55, no. 2 (1993), 209.
[37] Faustus Socinus, *De Jesu Christo Servatore*, 3.5, cited in Owen, *The Doctrine of Justification*, XII (*Works*, 5:254-55). Cf. Gomes, "*De Jesu Christo Servatore*", 209-31. Grotius, the famous Dutch jurist, wrote an influential work, *De Satisfactione Christi*, against Socinus. For the English translation, see Hugo Grotius, *A Defence of the Catholic Faith Concerning the Satisfaction of Christ, against Faustus Socinus*, trans. Frank Hugh Foster (Andover: Warren F. Draper, 1889).

person; for 'God redeemed his church with his own blood,' Acts xx. 28. It was performed in the human nature; but the person of Christ was he that performed it.[38]

These comments indicate that Owen located the issue of Christ's obedience under the rubric of Christ's mediatorial work.[39] Within this mediatorial framework, Owen affirmed that the person of the Mediator is the *theanthropos* by virtue of the hypostatic union, whose work of mediation is accomplished according to the operations of his distinct natures for the *apotelesma* of satisfaction.[40] The *apotelesma* relates directly to Christ's person and not to his natures in the abstract. Since the *apotelesma* is satisfaction for sin in the immediate context, by locating Christ's obedience within this mediatorial framework, Owen established that the obedience of Christ for sin's satisfaction was the obedience of his person. The significance of relating Christ's obedience to his person is as follows:

> Wherefore, the obedience whereof we treat, being not the obedience of the *human nature abstractedly*, however performed in and by the human nature; but the *obedience of the person of the Son of God*, however the human nature was subject to the law...it was not for himself, nor could be for himself; because his whole person was not obliged thereunto.[41]

The validity of Owen's argument turns upon the distinction between the person of the Son in his divine nature and in his human nature, a distinction made possible on account of the hypostatic union. Although it was in the human nature that obedience to the law was rendered by the incarnate Son, nevertheless, the person of the Son remained free from the obligations of the law since it was impossible for deity to be subject to a higher rule. Accordingly, the Son's whole person was not subjected under the law, hence his obedience cannot be said to be for himself. Consequently, Owen argued that Christ's obedience was designed and intended for the elect on the basis of the *pactum salutis*.[42] Furthermore, since Christ became *viator* in his earthly life voluntarily and not necessarily, his obedience was not for himself but for those for whom he became *viator*.[43]

While the Socinian objection centred on the person for whom obedience to the law was rendered, with the denial of imputation altogether, orthodox objection on the issue was solely over the imputation of Christ's active obedience and concerned a different set of relations: the relationship of the active to the passive obedience of Christ. If the death of Christ was a full and

---

[38] Owen, *The Doctrine of Justification*, XII (*Works*, 5:255).
[39] Cf. Goodwin who does the same, in *Works of Thomas Goodwin*, 5:337-49.
[40] See Chapter 3 above.
[41] Owen, *The Doctrine of Justification*, XII (*Works*, 5:256).
[42] Owen, *The Doctrine of Justification*, XII (*Works*, 5:257-59).
[43] Owen, *The Doctrine of Justification*, XII (*Works*, 5:259).

sufficient sacrifice for sin's satisfaction, it follows that asserting the satisfactory value of Christ's active obedience would be a theologically redundant argument. Orthodox critics pointed out that there was every danger of diminishing the sufficiency of Christ's work on the cross if the satisfactory value of Christ's whole obedience was granted.[44] Thus, some Reformed orthodox viewed the active obedience of Christ as not essential to sin's satisfaction but merely as a necessary preparation for Christ's passive obedience.[45]

Like his reply to the Socinians, Owen's response to the orthodox rejection of the imputation of Christ's active obedience was made in the light of the mediatorial framework. He understood Christ's mediatorial obedience as consisting of Christ's "*habitual righteousness*" and his "*actual* obedience."[46] By the former, he meant "the absolute, complete, exact conformity of the soul of Christ to the will, mind, or law of God."[47] Owen subdivided Christ's actual obedience into two types of laws which he kept. Firstly, Christ obeyed the "*peculiar law of the mediator*" which only the Mediator by voluntary submission was obliged to keep, as for instance, his sacrificial death.[48] Secondly, Christ obeyed "whatever was required of us by virtue of any law", such as the "law of nature, in our state of innocency", the laws of "morally positive or ceremonial institutions", and "judicial laws."[49] In short, there were laws required by God of all humanity, and the peculiar law required by God only of Christ the Mediator. The mediatorial life of Christ involved obedience within these two spheres of divine demands.

This understanding of Christ's obedience was congenial to Owen's view of imputation. If Christ obeyed the laws that humanity was obliged to keep, then denying the imputation of Christ's active obedience would imply the redundancy of Christ's obedience to those laws. Owen's more general point

---

[44] Gataker, for example, defended himself against George Walker's charge of Socinianism by citing Pareus in support of his passive-obedience-only position, who insisted: "Those that ascribe the merit of righteousnesse unto Christs active obedience or his native holinesse, do thereby derogate from the death of Christ, and do undoubtedly make it vain, or superfluous." Thomas Gataker, *An Answer to Mr George Walkers Vindication or Rather Fresh Accusation Wherein He Chargeth Mr Wotton (Besides His Former Foul Aspersions of Heresie and Blasphemy) with Arianism; Mr Gataker with Socinianism, Dr Gouge, and Mr Downame, with a False Attestation; Dr Baylie, and Mr Stock, with Self-Condemnation; All the Eight Ministers Employed in the Busines between Himself and Mr Wotton, with Partiality and Unjust Judgement* (London: Printed by E. G. for F. Clifton, 1642), 13.

[45] Owen, *Of Communion with God*, II.vi (*Works*, 2:159); cf. the arguments of Richard Vines, Francis Woodcock, and Thomas Gataker at the Westminster Assembly. Van Dixhoorn, "Reforming the Reformation", 1:297.

[46] Owen, *Of Communion with God*, II.vi (*Works*, 2:156-59).

[47] Owen, *Of Communion with God*, II.vi (*Works*, 2:156).

[48] Owen, *Of Communion with God*, II.vi (*Works*, 2:158).

[49] Owen, *Of Communion with God*, II.vi (*Works*, 2:157).

was that within the mediatorial framework, all that Christ did from his incarnation was performed as Mediator. It would not be possible then to maintain the unity of Christ's mediatorial obedience throughout the whole of his life if the vicarious nature of his active obedience was denied. Furthermore, the obedience of Christ being that of his person would mean that his active and passive obedience had infinite value, "and so cannot be considered in parts, as though one part of it were imputed unto one, and another unto another, but the whole is imputed unto every one that doth believe."[50] Thus, Christ's active obedience had satisfactory value and was not merely preparatory or the necessary condition for his death. The assumption of human nature into personal union with the Son, and the incarnate Son's habitual grace, qualified him for the work of mediation at the cross, not his obedience to the law.[51]

In the context of the seventeenth-century, Owen's arguments for the imputation of Christ's whole obedience would certainly have been convincing for the majority of the Reformed orthodox. However, this cannot be said for the Socinians. Since the collective force of Owen's arguments depends upon on the validity of the hypostatic union, it would not have been persuasive to the Socinians who dismissed the Chalcedonian doctrine as an irrational nonsense.[52] Nor were Owen's ripostes persuasive against the Socinian charge of imputation's impossibility. His arguments, as they have been adumbrated so far, merely demonstrate that within the bounds of orthodox Christology, it was legitimate to conceive of a correlation between the obedience of Christ and those for whose sake he obeyed the law. In order to assert that the nature of that correlation is imputation, more theological grounding was needed. It is to the doctrine of union with Christ that Owen looked for that grounding.

Unio Mystica and Imputation of Christ's Obedience

Owen recognized that the union between Christ and the church is described in Scripture through the use of analogies.[53] Jesus spoke of the union between the vine and its branches (John 15:1-2). The Apostle Paul described that union using analogies of the union between husband and wife (Eph. 5:25-32),

---

[50] Owen, *The Doctrine of Justification*, XII (*Works*, 5:270).

[51] Owen, *Of Communion with God*, II.vi (*Works*, 2:160-61). The terms "habitual grace", "habitual righteousness", and "habitual holiness", are synonyms in Owen's writings. They refer to the "absolute, complete, exact, conformity of the soul of Christ to the will, mind, or law of God; or his perfect habitually-inherent righteousness" which was obtained "necessarily from the grace of union" (156).

[52] Owen was aware of this weakness: "Socinus, I confess, evades the force of this argument, by denying the divine person of Christ. But in this disputation I take that for granted, as having proved it elsewhere beyond what any of his followers are able to contradict…However, I intend them only at present who concur with him in the matter under debate, but renounce his opinion concerning the person of Christ." *The Doctrine of Justification*, XII (*Works*, 5:256-57).

[53] Owen, *The Doctrine of Justification*, VIII (*Works*, 5:178-79).

between Adam and his posterity (Rom. 5.12), and among members of the human body (1 Cor. 12:12-13). Owen perceived such a multiplicity of analogies as arguing for the insufficiency of any one to convey the nature of that union.[54] His preferred terminology for summing up these mutually reinforcing analogies is that of *unio mystica*. He states:

> The principal foundation hereof is,— that Christ and the church, in this design were one mystical person; which state they do actually coalesce into, through the uniting efficacy of the Holy Spirit. He is the head, and believers are the members of that one person, as the apostle declares, 1 Cor xii. 12, 13. Hence, as what he did is imputed unto them, as if done by them; so what they deserved on the account of sin was charged upon him.[55]

In Owen's *Dissertation on Divine Justice*, the application of the mystical union takes on a judicial flavour.

> He [God] might punish the elect either in their own persons, or in their surety standing in their room and stead; and when he is punished, they also are punished: for in this point of view the federal head and those represented by him are not considered as distinct, but as one; for although they are not one in respect of personal unity, they are, however, one,—that is, one body in mystical union, yea, *one mystical Christ;*—namely, the surety is the head, those represented by him the members; and when the head is punished, the members also are punished.[56]

For Owen, Christ and the church are one mystical person in such a way that there is a mutual reckoning or imputation of action and consequence between them. As Owen went on to show, this way of expressing imputation's ground is unmistakably traditional. He produced a remarkable catena of patristic *testimonia*, both Latin and Greek, to demonstrate the catholicity of his doctrine.[57] Those cited included Leo the Great, Augustine of Hippo, Irenaeus of Lyons, Origen of Alexandria, Cyprian of Carthage, Athanasius of Alexandria, Eusebius of Caesarea, John Chrysostom and Prosper of Aquitaine. Eusebius, in particular, received special attention, for Owen found the point of his list summed up in a passage from the Bishop of Caesarea's treatise, *Demonstratio Evangelica*.[58] Summing up what was to him the thrust of that passage by Eusebius, Owen comments: "That our sins were *transferred* unto Christ and made his, that thereon he underwent the *punishment* that was due unto us for

---

[54] Owen, *The Doctrine of Justification*, VIII (*Works*, 5:179).
[55] Owen, *The Doctrine of Justification*, VIII (*Works*, 5:176).
[56] Owen, *A Dissertation on Divine Justice*, II.xv (*Works*, 10:598).
[57] Owen, *The Doctrine of Justification*, VIII (*Works*, 5:176-78); cf. Kapic, *Communion with God*, 140-41.
[58] Eusebius, *Demonstratio Evangelica*, X.1. The text in Greek is cited along with Owen's translation in *The Doctrine of Justification*, VIII (*Works*, 5:177-78). A modern translation is found in Eusebius, *The Proof of the Gospel: Being the Demonstratio Evangelica of Eusebius of Caesarea*, trans. W.J. Ferrar, 2 vols. (London: SPCK, 1920).

them, and that the ground hereof, whereunto its equity is resolved, is the *union between him and us*, is fully declared in this discourse."[59] Thus, to Owen, imputation on the grounds of the *mystica unio* was no novel doctrine.

Such grounding in the ancient doctrine allowed Owen to make certain moves. First, the sins of the church may legitimately be imputed to Christ, and second, the merit of Christ's obedience may legitimately be imputed to the church. Such a conception of imputation was not free from problems. Does the imputation of the elect's sin to Christ not make Christ a sinner? Does the imputation of Christ's righteousness to the elect not mean that they are as righteous or perfect as Christ? The urgency of addressing these difficulties was particularly acute against the backdrop of seventeenth-century antinomianism in England.[60]

Tobias Crisp (1600-1643) had argued in a sermon on Isaiah 53:6 that it was not merely sin's punishment which the Lord laid upon Christ but sin itself, that is, both the guilt and punishment of sin.[61] He boldly declared, "Christ himself becomes the transgressor in the room and stead of this person that had transgressed: so that in respect of the reality of being a transgressor, Christ is as really the transgressor as the person that did commit it was a transgressor before Christ took this transgression upon him."[62] Commenting on Christ being made sin in 2 Corinthians 5:21, Crisp was careful to qualify that the Apostle Paul was in no way referring to sin's pollution of Christ's nature nor was he suggesting that Christ performed any sinful act. Nevertheless, he insisted that Christ was a transgressor: "the Apostle's meaning was, that no transgressor in the world was such a transgressor as Christ was. But still he was a transgressor, as our transgressions were laid upon him…"[63]

On the other side of the imputation equation, Crisp reasoned: "If you will speak of one completely righteous, you must speak of this person, and know that Christ himselfe is not more righteous than this person is, that that person is not more sinfull then Christ was when hee took their sinnes on him…"; by the

---

[59] Owen, *The Doctrine of Justification*, VIII (*Works*, 5:178).
[60] Owen was aware of the criticism that the doctrine of imputation removed "the necessity of our own personal obedience, introducing antinomianism, libertinism, and all manner of evil." Owen, *The Doctrine of Justification*, XII (*Works*, 5:252); Craig, "The Bond of Grace and Duty", 44-78; for the pre-civil war context, see Theodore D. Bozeman, *The Precisianist Strain: Disciplinary Religion and Antinomian Backlash in Puritanism to 1638* (Williamsburg, Virginia: University of North Carolina Press, 2004); David R. Como, *Blown by the Spirit: Puritanism and the Emergence of an Antinomian Underground in Pre-Civil War England* (California: Stanford University Press, 2004).
[61] Tobias Crisp, *Christ Alone Exalted in Seventeene Sermons Preached in or Neare London* (n.p.: 1643), II, 69-103. Crisp was a Church of England minister whose teachings in his posthumously published sermons became associated with antinomianism. *ODNB*, Roger Pooley, "Crisp, Tobias (1600-1643)."
[62] Crisp, *Christ Alone Exalted*, II, 82.
[63] Crisp, *Christ Alone Exalted*, II, 84.

one sacrifice of Christ, "he hath perfected them that are sanctified."[64] In similar language, John Saltmarsh (*d.* 1647), in his treatise *Free-Grace* published in 1645, had stated that "a justified person is a perfect person" who by virtue of being "in Christ" is consequently "in such a perfect righteousness" before God.[65] These unqualified assertions of the justified believer's perfection were precisely the kind of evidence which lent weight to the Catholic critique that the Protestant notion of the imputation of Christ's righteousness inevitably meant that those on whom imputation terminates are as righteous as Christ and would likewise be redeemers and saviours of the world.[66]

Owen's account of imputation shared similarities with the views of his antinomian contemporaries, but it also differed from them. In Owen's exegesis of Isaiah 53:6, the laying of iniquities upon Christ was understood in the penal sense of bearing sin's punishment.[67] He further argued that guilt and punishment are so interlinked that the imputation of the *reatus poenae* to Christ entailed the imputation of the *reatus culpae*.[68] On this, Owen and Crisp are agreed. That they held such a view in common is not surprising since Protestant orthodoxy argued for a single *reatus* which includes both *culpa* and *poena*.[69] Their difference lay in the manner of stating the implication drawn from a realist account of imputation on the basis of the *unio mystica*. Where Crisp was unapologetic in stating positively that Christ was really a transgressor, Owen exercised caution by stating it in the negative, with commentary on the precise boundaries beyond which he was unwilling to trespass.

> When our sin was imputed unto him [Christ], he did not thereby become a sinner as we are, actively and inherently a sinner; but passively only, and in God's estimation. As he was made sin, yet knew no sin; so we are made righteous, yet are sinful in ourselves.[70]

---

[64] Crisp, *Christ Alone Exalted*, II, 90.

[65] John Saltmarsh, *Free-Grace or the Flowings of Christs Blood Freely to Sinners* (London: Printed for Giles Calvert, 1645), 129. Saltmarsh was a chaplain to Sir Thomas Fairfax and the parliamentary army from May 1646 to November 1647. His work, *Free-Grace*, has been identified by critics as antinomian in character. *ODNB*, Roger Pooley, "Saltmarsh, John (*d.* 1647)."

[66] Bellarmine, *De Justificatione*, II.7, cited in Owen, *The Doctrine of Justification*, XVIII (*Works*, 5:351-52); cf. Owen's answer in chapter IX (*Works*, 5:218-19).

[67] Owen, *Vindicae Evangelicae*, XXIV (*Works*, 12:443-55).

[68] Owen, *The Doctrine of Justification*, VIII (*Works*, 5:196-200).

[69] "reatus; reatus poenae" in Muller, *DLGTT*, 258. Note, however, the exception of Baxter, who understood the union between Christ and the church politically, not mystically, and accordingly denied the imputation of the *reatus culpae* to Christ, maintaining only the imputation of the *reatus poenae*. Hans Boersma, *A Hot Pepper Corn: Richard Baxter's Doctrine of Justification in Its Seventeenth-Century Context of Controversy* (Vancouver: Regent College Publishing, 2004), 236-39.

[70] Owen, *The Doctrine of Justification*, XVIII (*Works*, 5:352).

These comments form part of Owen's exegesis on the first half of 2 Corinthians 5:21, "For he hath made him to be sin for us, who knew no sin." They suggest that Owen did concede to speaking of Christ as a sinner but on different terms from saying that the elect were so. On the second half of the verse, "that we might be made the righteousness of God in him", Owen reiterated the crucial importance of the *unio mystica*: "To be righteous in him is to be righteous with his righteousness, as we are one mystical person with him."[71] Exercising similar caution, Owen was careful to qualify the comparison between Christ and the elect on the imputation of Christ's righteousness:

> To say that we are as righteous as Christ, is to make a comparison between the personal righteousness of Christ and our personal righteousness, — if the comparison be of things of the same kind. But this is foolish and impious: for, notwithstanding all our personal righteousness, we are sinful; he knew no sin. And if the comparison be between Christ's personal, inherent righteousness, and righteousness imputed unto us, inhesion and imputation being things of diverse kinds, it is fond and of no consequence. Christ was actively righteous; we are passively so.[72]

Evidently, Owen was uncomfortable with statements that spoke of Christ as a sinner or the elect being as righteous as Christ, statements exemplified in Crisp's writings. His apprehensions were also apparent in his preaching. Owen's posthumously published sermon on the same subject saw an absence of the kind of language employed by Crisp, and a consistent adherence to the caveats he had introduced.[73]

What drove Owen's cautions was his refusal to conflate imputation of sin and righteousness with their transfusion or infusion.[74] Keeping imputation distinct from infusion was part of the anti-Catholic feature of Owen's doctrine of justification.[75] However, it did bear on the antinomian problem as the comparison between Owen and Crisp demonstrates. The logic of Owen's

---

[71] Owen, *The Doctrine of Justification*, XVIII (*Works*, 5:351).

[72] Owen, *The Doctrine of Justification*, XVIII (*Works*, 5:352); cf. ibid, IX (*Works*, 5:220-21): "It was *formally* inherent in him,— is only *materially* imputed unto us; was *actively* his,— is *passively* ours; was *wrought* in the person of God-man for the whole church,— is *imputed* unto each single believer, as unto his own concernment only."

[73] Owen, *Posthumous Sermons*, IV.xvii (*Works*, 9:597-99). The sermon is a typological treatment of Leviticus 16:21 in which Aaron lays his hands on the scape-goat's head. Owen argued that the verse is "a representation of the death of Christ" which involved "a blessed change and commutation that is made between Christ and believers, *in the imputation of their sins unto him, and in the imputation of his righteousness unto them…*" (597); cf. his comments on Leviticus 16:21-22 in *The Doctrine of Justification*, General Considerations (*Works*, 5:34-35).

[74] Owen, *The Doctrine of Justification*, VII (*Works*, 5:173).

[75] For Owen's views on justification in the light of the controversy with Rome, see Kapic, *Communion with God*, 107-146, esp. 126-37.

concerns is that failure to keep imputation and infusion distinct either commits one to the personal, inherent sinfulness of Christ, or the inherent perfect righteousness of the elect. He insisted that "as Christ had no concern in sin but as God made him sin,— it was never in him inherently; so have we no interest in this righteousness,— it is not in us inherently, but only is imputed to us."[76] This is not to deny the importance of inherent, personal righteousness in justification, but that it is the material or formal cause of justification.[77] Owen was anxious to preserve the judicial, objective nature of justification against its confusion with the concomitant sanctification of the elect, a confusion engendered by Rome's teaching on justification in his perception.[78] The imputation of Christ's whole obedience that is grounded in the *unio mystica* was a carefully qualified one for Owen in the light of polemical concerns.

Christ's Suretyship and Imputation of Christ's Obedience

In addition to the *unio mystica*, Owen conceived of another ground for imputation: Christ's suretyship.[79] He argued that imputation may justly result "*ex voluntaria sponsio*", that is, "when one freely and willingly undertakes to answer for another."[80] The importance of Christ's suretyship should not be underestimated for Owen's decision in favor of the satisfactory value of Christ's active and passive obedience. Union with Christ removes the

---

[76] Owen, *The Doctrine of Justification*, XVIII (*Works*, 5:354).

[77] Owen, *The Doctrine of Justification*, VI, IX-X (*Works*, 5:152-62, 205-40); cf. Owen's notion of "infused grace" in relation to sanctification, which he defined as "grace really bestowed upon us, and abiding in us, from the Spirit of God." *Vindiciae Evangelicae*, Mr Biddle's Preface Briefly Examined (*Works*, 12:79).

[78] Owen, *The Doctrine of Justification*, IV-V (*Works*, 5:123-52). According to Trent, justification is "not remission of sins merely, but also the sanctification and renewal of the inward man, through the voluntary reception of the grace, and of the gifts, whereby man of unjust becomes just, and of an enemy a friend, that so he may be an heir according to hope of life everlasting." *Council of Trent*, Session VI.7. Jaroslav Pelikan, and Valerie Hotchkiss, ed., *Creeds and Confessions of Faith in the Christian Tradition*, 3 vols. (New Haven/London: Yale University Press, 2003), 2:829.

[79] In Latin, the terms *sponsio*, *expromissio*, and *fideiussio*, were used by the Reformed orthodox to expound the Greek ἔγγυος (surety) in Hebrews 7:22. These Latin terms were derived from Roman law and applied to Christ by Protestant orthodox theologians. Muller, *DLGTT*, 114-15, 287. In the late seventeenth-century, a controversy arose between followers of the Dutch federal theologians, Gisbertus Voetius (1587-1676) and Johannes Cocceius (1603-1669), on whether *expromissio* or *fideiussio* was the proper sense of ἔγγυος. See Willem J. van Asselt, "*Expromissio* or *Fideiussio*? A Seventeenth Century Theological Debate between Voetians and Cocceians About the Nature of Christ's Suretyship in Salvation History", *MAJT* 14 (2003), 37-57. Although Owen employed these legal terms in the course of his attempt to explicate Christ's suretyship, he showed no interest in the semantic differences between the terms as they were used in legal practice, but was concerned simply with the sense of ἔγγυος in Scriptural usage. Cf. his exegetical discussion in Owen, *The Doctrine of Justification*, VIII (*Works*, 5:181-82).

[80] Owen, *The Doctrine of Justification*, VII (*Works*, 5:170).

arbitrariness of asserting imputation between Christ and the elect by indicating the close relationship that exists between them. What the doctrine of union with Christ achieves is the provision of a theological rationale for imputation in general. However, it does not secure the specific claim that it is Christ's whole obedience that is imputed. Christ's suretyship supplies a firmer theological grounding for that claim. As will become clear, Owen's exposition of the subject reveals his sacerdotal framework in adjudicating for the imputation of Christ's whole obedience.

In Owen's *Doctrine of Justification*, his treatment of the grounds of imputation moved from union with Christ to an extended exposition of Christ's suretyship based on Hebrews 7:22.[81] It is important to note that the period during which Owen worked on his treatise on justification overlapped with that of his labours on the book of Hebrews. At certain points in his exposition of Christ's suretyship in his *Doctrine of Justification*, Owen referred readers to his commentary for further details and also imported large segments of his then unpublished commentary into the treatise in a generally unedited form.[82] Any attempt to explicate Owen's view of suretyship would therefore need to take his commentary into consideration in order that his views may be interpreted in light of the wider exegetical context of his thought.

Owen's use of Scriptural texts reveals the sacerdotal orientation of his thought on the question of imputation. That Hebrews 7:22 was given substantial treatment instead of other equally possible texts on Christ's suretyship indicates that Christ's priesthood was the governing framework. This was not consistently Owen's practice. In *The Death of Death* Romans 5:6-8, Galatians 3:13, and 2 Corinthians 5:21 were cited as the main supporting texts for Christ's suretyship while Hebrews 7:22 was relegated to secondary status.[83] The reason for privileging the first three texts becomes clear when they are set in the light of the argument that Owen tried to secure against universal redemption. He sought to show that by dying as the elect's surety, Christ did procure release from all that they had to undergo due to their sins, and that Christ did make satisfaction to God's justice for the sins of the elect. Once the actuality of Christ's atonement is secured, the case for universal redemption would be hard to maintain. If proponents of universal redemption were to affirm that satisfaction and release from sin's consequences were actually procured by Christ's death, they would also have to affirm either that all and every one will ultimately be saved — a position which his universalist opponents rejected — or that Christ's atoning death is limited in its intrinsic efficacy. For Owen, the inevitable implication of both positions is the failure of

---

[81] Owen, *The Doctrine of Justification*, VIII (*Works*, 5:175-205).
[82] Cf. for instance, the word for word replica of *Exposition of Hebrews*, Heb. 7:22, in loc. (*Works*, 21:499-504, 507-508) in *The Doctrine of Justification*, VIII (*Works*, 5:182-87, 187-88).
[83] Owen, *Salus Electorum*, III.iii (*Works*, 10:246-49).

Christ's intention to save through his work on the cross. In the context of *The Death of Death*, Owen perceived that the substitutionary nature of Christ's death was a crucial point to secure if the actuality of the atonement was to be maintained. He explained that the first three texts "do plainly signify and hold out a change or commutation of persons, one being accepted in the room of the other."[84] All three describe Christ's death as a death *uper ēmōn*, "for us",[85] the preposition *uper* being interpreted by Owen in the sense of substitution.[86] Hebrews 7:22, however, provided no *direct* exegetical support for substitution. Rather, Christ undergoing or rendering what the elect failed to render is the plain meaning of the term "surety", not his status as the elect's substitute, albeit this is clearly assumed by Owen. His passing mention of Hebrews 7:22 reflected this exegetical consideration:

> for no other reason in the world can be assigned why Christ should undergo any thing in another's stead, but that that other might be freed from undergoing that which he underwent for him. And all justice requires that so it should be; which also is expressly intimated, when our Savior is said to be ἔγγυος, "a surety of a better testament," Heb. vii. 22; that is, by being our priest, undergoing the "chastisement of our peace," and the burden of our "iniquities", Isa. liii. 5, 6. He was "made sin for us, that we might be made the righteousness of God in him," 2 Cor. v. 21.[87]

Undergoing sin's punishment "in another's stead" was the main concern, confirmed by his references to Isaiah and 2 Corinthians. Thus, it seems reasonable to understand the rationale for prioritizing the first three texts over Hebrews 7:22 to be the direct exegetical edge they had in view of Owen's argument against universal redemption.

However, in his *Doctrine of Justification*, where the issue at hand concerned imputation, Hebrews 7:22 was the key text in support of Christ's suretyship. Likewise, there was a contextual reason for this. Socinian exegesis of Christ's suretyship had identified God as its subject. To Socinians, Christ was God's surety, undertaking to perform the necessary obligations on behalf of God. The commentary of Crellius and Schlichtingius is a typical example: "Jesus is called the surety of the Covenant or Testament, because he contracted it with us in the Name of God, and ratified it on God's part, making faith of it unto us, that God would keep the promises of his Covenant. Not therefore, as if he became our

---

[84] Owen, *Salus Electorum*, III.iii (*Works*, 10:246).
[85] "…in due time Christ died for the ungodly…while we were yet sinners, Christ died for us" (Romans 5:6, 8); "Christ has redeemed us from the curse of the law, being made a curse for us" (Galatians 3:13); "For he hath made him to be sin for us, who knew no sin…" (2 Corinthians 5:21).
[86] Owen, *Salus Electorum*, III.x (*Works*, 10:289).
[87] Owen, *Salus Electorum*, III.iii (*Works*, 10:246). Cf. idem, *Salus Electorum*, III.x (*Works*, 10:288): "He that is surety for another (as Christ was for us, Heb vii. 22) is to undergo the danger, that the other may be delivered."

surety to God, and tooke upon him the payment of our debts."[88] On this reading of the text, Christ's work as surety was directed towards humanity. While such an interpretation comports well with the prophetic and kingly offices of Christ, both of which consist of the acts of Christ *"from God*; that is, in the name and authority of God *towards us"*,[89] it however fails to account for the priestly context of Hebrews 7 which demanded the God-ward direction of Christ's sacrificial offering. Perceiving the obvious threat to Christ's priesthood, Owen insisted that the work of Christ as surety in Hebrews 7:22 was the work of Christ as Priest: "It is the *priesthood of Christ* that the apostle treats of in this place, and that alone: wherefore he is a *surety as he is a priest*, and in the discharge of that office; and therefore is so with God on our behalf";[90] "...seeing the Lord Christ is a surety of the covenant as a priest, and all the sacerdotal actings of Christ have God for their immediate object, and are performed with him on our behalf, he was a surety for us also."[91] For Owen, then, Christ's suretyship was a function of Christ's priesthood.

Owen's reading of Hebrews 7:22 was not novel in the light of the orthodox exegetical tradition. William Gouge, David Dickson, Edward Leigh, and Thomas Wilson had similarly argued for the God-ward direction of Christ's suretyship.[92] However, it was also not a unanimous reading among orthodox exegetes. Owen was aware that some eminent scholars, such as Grotius and Henry Hammond, sided with the Socinian reading.[93] Diodati, the learned Genevan minister whose Italian annotations were translated into English and commissioned in 1642 by Parliament to be printed, seemed to have understood

---

[88] Johannes Crellius, *The Expiation of a Sinner in a Commentary Upon the Epistle to the Hebrewes* (London: Printed by Tho. Harper 1646), 136. McLachlan attributes the authorship of the commentary to both Crellius and Jonas Schlichtingius, and the English translation to Thomas Lushington. See *ODNB*, H.J. McLachlan, "Lushington, Thomas (1590-1661)"; cf. Owen's citation of Schlichtingius in *The Doctrine of Justification*, VIII (*Works*, 5:182-83, 186); idem, *Exposition of Hebrews*, Heb. 7:22, in loc. (*Works*, 21:499-500).

[89] Owen, *The Doctrine of Justification*, III (*Works*, 5:121).

[90] Owen, *The Doctrine of Justification*, VIII (*Works*, 5:186); idem, *Exposition of Hebrews*, Heb. 7:22, in loc. (*Works*, 21:503).

[91] Owen, *The Doctrine of Justification*, VIII (*Works*, 5:187); idem, *Exposition of Hebrews*, Heb. 7:22, in loc. (*Works*, 21:504).

[92] Trueman, *John Owen*, 111, esp. 111n42.

[93] Owen, *The Doctrine of Justification*, VIII (*Works*, 5:183). On Grotius, it was to his later annotations on the Old and New Testaments that Owen referred. The early Grotius of *Defensio fidei catholicae de satisfactione* (1617) argued for both the God-ward and man-ward directions of Christ's sacrificial death. See Grotius, *A Defense of the Catholic Faith*, X; cf. Gary J. Williams, "A Critical Exposition of Hugo Grotius' Doctrine of the Atonement in *De Satisfactione Christi*" (Ph.D. dissertation, University of Oxford, 1999), 47-49. On Hammond, see Henry Hammond, *A Paraphrase, and Annotations Upon All the Books of the New Testament, Briefly Explaining All the Difficult Places Thereof* (London: Printed for F. Flesher for Richard Davis, 1659), Heb. 7:22, in loc.

suretyship in the light of mediatorship and consequently interpreted Christ's suretyship to be on behalf of both God and humanity.[94] Diodati thus charted a middle course between the other exegetical routes. Clearly, there was a range of readings within the orthodox exegetical tradition on Hebrews 7:22. Owen's preferred interpretation demonstrates both his refusal to endorse the exegetical conclusions which gave mileage to the Socinian view on the priesthood of Christ, and his aversion to exegetical novelty.[95]

The significance of Owen's exegesis for the imputation of Christ's whole obedience lies in his understanding of what Christ undertook on behalf of the elect as priest. As surety for the elect, "the Lord Christ was, by his *voluntary undertaking*, out of his rich grace and love, to do, answer, and perform all that is required on our part…"; "he is to *pay* that which they *owe*, and to do what is to be done by them, which they cannot perform."[96] What Christ undertook to perform was tied very closely with Owen's federal theology, necessitated in part by the language of covenant in Hebrews 7:22. That Christ was surety of a "better covenant" implied the existence of a preceding covenant with which comparison was being made. Owen identified the preceding covenant as the Mosaic covenant, which had no proper surety but only its representation in the person of the high priest.[97] For Owen, the Mosaic covenant was a renovation of the "first covenant" or the *foedus operum*, in that the moral law or the law of nature, which was the material content of the *foedus operum*,[98] was republished at Sinai in the form of the Decalogue.[99] Unlike the Mosaic covenant, the *foedus operum* had neither any surety nor its representation.[100] Without a proper surety to guarantee the fulfilment of their terms, these covenants were by nature unstable. In contrast, the "better covenant", which Owen identified as the

---

[94] Giovanni Diodati, *Pious and Learned Annotations Upon the Holy Bible: Expounding the Difficult Places Thereof Learnedly, and Plainly: With Other Things of Great Importance* (London: Printed by T. B. for Nicholas Fussell, 1643), Heb. 7:22, in loc. Subsequently, an expanded version of his annotations was completed in French with an English translation in 1648. Giovanni Diodati, *Pious and Learned Annotations Upon the Holy Bible: Plainly Expounding the Most Difficult Places Thereof* (London: Printed by Miles Flesher for Nicholas Fussell, 1648).

[95] Owen was well aware that his reading had the endorsement of the majority of orthodox exegetes. *The Doctrine of Justification*, VIII (*Works*, 5:183): "the generality of expositors, ancient and modern, Roman and Protestant churches, on the place, affirm that the Lord Christ, as the *surety of the covenant, was properly a surety or undertaker unto God for us, and not a surety and undertaker unto us for God*"; idem, *Exposition of Hebrews*, Heb. 7:22, in loc. (*Works*, 21:500).

[96] Owen, *The Doctrine of Justification*, VIII (*Works*, 5:187); idem, *Exposition of Hebrews*, Heb. 7:22, in loc. (*Works*, 21:507, 504).

[97] Owen, *Exposition of Hebrews*, Heb. 7:22, in loc. (*Works*, 21:494, 499).

[98] Owen, *Exposition of Hebrews*, Heb. 7:22, in loc. (*Works*, 21:506).

[99] Owen, *Exposition of Hebrews*, Exercitations, V.iv (*Works*, 18:387-88).

[100] Owen, *The Doctrine of Justification*, VIII (*Works*, 5:186); idem, *Exposition of Hebrews*, Heb. 7:22, in loc. (*Works*, 21:502-503).

foedus gratiae, was superior because of its stability and stable because Christ is its surety.[101] The eternal ground of its stability lies in the federal transactions between the Father and the Son within the eternal *pactum salutis*.

In sum, Christ performed what the elect failed to perform under the *foedus operum* and the Mosaic covenant, and underwent what the elect ought to have undergone due to their failure to keep the terms of these covenants. Obedience to the moral law which the elect failed to keep and the bearing of punishment incurred by the elect's transgression of the law constitute the substance of what Christ undertook as surety. These aspects correspond to the active and passive obedience of Christ. Thus, while the doctrine of *unio mystica* grounds imputation in a general way, Christ's suretyship gave specification to the content of what was imputed, thereby providing firmer ground for the imputation of Christ's whole obedience. To secure this point, the priesthood of Christ was vital because the argument that Christ's suretyship involved his active and passive obedience relied upon an understanding of suretyship which only Christ's priesthood could supply: that the mediatorial acts of Christ as surety was performed on behalf of the elect and directed towards God.

The Twofold State of Christ

Related to the God-ward direction of Christ's priestly acts for the matter of satisfaction is the entire life of Christ expressed in terms of his *status humiliationis* and *status exaltationis*. Christ's twofold state informed and underpinned Owen's exposition of sin's satisfaction at certain critical points. This should come as no surprise since Christ's priesthood and twofold state are intimately connected in Owen's atonement theology.[102]

The importance of Christ's twofold state for sin's satisfaction is seen in the theological relation it has to the imputation of Christ's obedience. Arminius, for instance, following the historical sequence in the Apostle's Creed, conceived of Christ's state of humiliation as beginning from the time when Christ was taken into custody under Pontius Pilate, to his descent into hell.[103] Consequently, the events in Christ's life prior to his state of humiliation are but "forerunners of his sufferings" rather than being an integral part of his sufferings.[104] Following Arminius, the Remonstrants' formulation of the issue was no different.[105] Trueman notes the theological implication of the Arminian formulation: "The overall dogmatic impact of this was twofold: the work of Christ which was then imputed to the believer in justification did not involve his positive fulfilment of

---

[101] Owen, *Exposition of Hebrews*, Heb. 7:22, in loc. (*Works*, 21:508-509).
[102] See Chapter 2 and Chapter 4 above.
[103] Arminius, *Private Disputation* XXXVIII.2, in *Works of Arminius*, 2:103.
[104] Arminius, *Private Disputation* XXXVIII.3, in *Works of Arminius*, 2:103.
[105] *Confession of Faith of Those Called Arminians or a Declaration of the Opinions and Doctrines of the Ministers and Pastors, Which in the United Provinces Are Known by the Name of Remonstrants Concerning the Chief Points of Christian Religion, Translated out of the Original* (London: Printed for Samuel Walsall, 1684), 130-31.

the law prior to Gethsamene but was focused much more sharply upon his death and resurrection."[106] As will become clear, Owen was aware of the theological relation between Christ's twofold state and imputation although at no point in his exposition was the connection given extensive treatment.

In relation to the active and passive obedience of Christ, Owen argued that suffering obtained at every point in Christ's obedience throughout the entire course of his earthly life:

> That which we plead is, *that the Lord Christ fulfilled the whole law for us*; he did not only undergo the penalty of it due unto our sins, but also yielded that perfect obedience which it did require. ... And all his obedience, considering his person, was mixed with suffering, as a part of his exinanition and humiliation; whence it is said that 'though he were a Son, yet learned he obedience by the things which he suffered'.[107]

The "obedience" of Hebrews 5:8, which Christ "learned" by experience, was understood by Owen to have a general and particular reference. The former refers to the entire span of Christ's earthly life, and the latter to Christ's sufferings in his death.[108] These references are not alternative but complementary readings in Owen's exegesis.[109] Together, they point to the significance of the whole of Christ's earthly life in his mediatorial sufferings. As such, Owen's interpretation concurred with the Protestant orthodox concept

---

[106] Trueman, *John Owen*, 104. It needs to be pointed out that Arminius was aware of the debate over the imputation of Christ's passive or whole obedience within the Reformed churches in France but refrained from making any decisions on the matter. Arminius, *A Declaration of the Sentiments of Arminius*, IX, in *Works of Arminius*, 1:236-38.

[107] Owen, *The Doctrine of Justification*, XII (*Works*, 5:253-54); idem, *Exposition of Hebrews*, Heb. 5:8, in loc. (*Works*, 20:523): "His state in this world was a state of humiliation and exinanition; which things have suffering in their nature. His outward condition in the world was mean, low, and contemptible; from which sufferings are inseparable."

[108] Owen, *Exposition of Hebrews*, Heb. 5:8, in loc. (*Works*, 20:522-23).

[109] Owen's interpretation was a traditional one that stood in line with the *Dutch Annotations*. See *The Dutch Annotations Upon the Whole Bible: Or, All the Holy Canonical Scriptures of the Old and New Testament, Together with, and According to Their Own Translation of All the Text: As Both the One and the Other Were Ordered and Appointed by the Synod of Dort , 1618, and Published by Authority, 1637*, trans. Theodore Haak (London: Printed by Henry Hills, for John Rothwell, Joshua Kirton, and Richard Tomlins, 1657), Heb. 5:7-8, in loc.; contra the *English Annotations* in which the "obedience" of verse 8 is confined to Christ's passive obedience. *Annotations Upon All the Books of the Old and New Testament: This Third, above the First and Second, Edition So Enlarged, as They Make an Entire Commentary on the Sacred Scripture: The Like Never before Published in English. Wherein the Text Is Explained, Doubts Resolved, Scriptures Parallel'd, and Various Readings Observed; by the Labour of Certain Learned Divines Thereunto Appointed, and Therein Employed, as Is Expressed in the Preface* (London: Printed by Evan Tyler, 1657), Heb. 5:8, in loc.

of Christ's *status humiliationis*,[110] and he readily brought the concept to bear upon the satisfactory value of Christ's active and passive obedience. For the reason that Christ's *status humiliationis* was a state of suffering, Owen resisted dichotomizing the life of Christ in such a way as to confine the experience of suffering to Christ's passive obedience and to its consequent imputation alone. Although Philippians 2:8-10, being the *locus classicus* in the development of the doctrine of Christ's twofold state,[111] could have easily been employed as Owen's supporting text, nevertheless, it was to the book of Hebrews that he looked for exegetical corroboration. His choice of biblical material in support of the imputation of Christ's whole obedience served to underscore the importance of Christ's priesthood.

So fundamentally related was Christ's priesthood and twofold state, and their fundamental relation of such vital importance for a sinner's justification, that their united reality was essential to Owen's view of the object of justifying faith.

> Whatever he did on earth with God for the church, in obedience, suffering, and offering up of himself; whatever he doth in heaven, in intercession and appearance in the presence of God, for us; it all entirely belongs unto his *priestly office*. And in these things alone doth the soul of a convinced sinner find *relief*, when he seeks after deliverance from the state of sin, and acceptance with God. In these, therefore, alone the peculiar object of his faith, that which will give him rest and peace, must be comprised.[112]

In this significant statement, the mediatorial life of Christ in his state of humiliation on earth, and in his state of exaltation in heaven, is explained in terms of Christ's priestly acts of oblation and intercession. Again, the crucial importance of Christ's priesthood is apparent and communicated in the typical form which Owen's peculiar conception of that priesthood took.

---

[110] Muller, *DGLTT*, 288-89.
[111] Owen, *Two Short Catechisms*, GC, XIV (*Works*, 1:483): "Q. 1. *In what estate or condition doth Christ exercise these offices?* A. In a two-fold estate; first, of humiliation or abasement; secondly, of exaltation or glory. — Phil. ii. 8-10"; idem, *Posthumous Sermons*, XI (*Works*, 16:493-501); Muller, *DLGTT*, 288; for the development within Lutheran orthodoxy, see Schmid, *The Doctrinal Theology of the Evangelical Lutheran Church*, 382-413; Werner Elert, *The Structure of Lutheranism:The Theology and Philosophy of Life of Lutheranism Especially in the Sixteenth and Seventeenth Centuries*, trans. Walter A. Hansen (St Louis: Concordia Publishing House, 1962), 236-53.
[112] Owen, *The Doctrine of Justification*, III (*Works*, 5:121-22); cf. Kapic, *Communion with God*, 124-26.

Satisfaction and the Death of Christ

Having dealt with the whole obedience of Christ with respect to its satisfactory value, it is now appropriate to consider the peculiarities of Owen's view on the passive obedience of Christ. As with so much of Owen's writing, the polemical context played an important part in bringing critical issues to relief. For understanding Owen's view on Christ's death, it is necessary to examine his debate with Baxter. The following analysis seeks to explicate the key issues that arose in the course of the debate.

Owen's Debate with Baxter: the Nature and Effects of Christ's Death
For most of his years as Dean of Christ Church and Vice-Chancellor of Oxford University, Owen was engaged in public controversy with Baxter over the nature and effects of Christ's atoning death.[113] Precipitated by the publication of Owen's *Death of Death* in 1647, the controversy lasted close to a decade from 1649 to 1657. Boersma observes that "it was one of the few controversies in which not Baxter himself, but his opponent had the last public word."[114] While explicating the nature of Christ's satisfaction in *The Death of Death*, Owen had argued that the nature of Christ's payment for sin's satisfaction was the same as that which was in the obligation, or what in jurisprudential parlance was termed, *solutio eiusdem*.[115] This argument was advanced in opposition to the view of Grotius who had contended that the nature of Christ's payment was not the same as that which was in the obligation but an equivalent of it. Grotius argued for what was termed, *solutio tantidem*, an equivalent payment.[116] Siding with Grotius, Baxter opened the debate in the "Appendix" to his *Aphorismes of Justification* (1649).[117] There, he leveled three charges against Owen: (1) that Owen overlooked Grotius' chief argument; (2) that only two of Grotius'

---

[113] For helpful treatment of the debate, see Boersma, *A Hot Pepper Corn*, 41-44; Trueman, *Claims of Truth*, 210-25; Gary J. Williams, "The Puritan Doctrine of Atonement," in *'Where Reason Fails...', the Westminster Conference 2006* (Stoke-on-Trent, U.K.: Tentmaker Publications, 2006), 76-81.

[114] Boersma, *A Hot Pepper Corn*, 43.

[115] Owen, *Salus Electorum*, III.vii (*Works* 10:267-73). The concept is derived from Roman law and remains in use along with the idea of *solutio tantidem* even in modern law, see William L. Burdick, *The Principles of Roman Law and Their Relation to Modern Law* (Clark, New Jersey: The Lawbook Exchange, Ltd, 2004; reprint, Second), 516-20.

[116] Grotius, *A Defence of the Catholic Faith*, 122-28. Cunningham points out that there are orthodox theologians like Turretin and Mastricht, who while rejecting *solutio eiusdem*, nevertheless hold to the full equivalence of payment, and that there are the Arminians whose view of equivalence is that of a substitute payment rather than equivalence. Cunningham, *Historical Theology*, 2:301-23.

[117] Richard Baxter, *Aphorismes of Justification with Their Explication Annexed* (London: Printed for Francis Tyton, 1649), Appendix, 137-46. Due to the poor textual quality of this edition, subsequent citations will be taken from the 1655 edition.

arguments were answered; (3) that in the final analysis, Owen's position was no different from that of Grotius.[118]

Owen duly responded in *Of the Death of Christ, the Price He Paid and the Purchase He Made* (1650).[119] It was written while he was at Trinity College, Dublin, surveying the state and future prospects of the College at Cromwell's behest.[120] He described his situation at Trinity as "attended with more than ordinary weaknesses and infirmities, separated from my library, burdened with manifold employments, with constant preaching to a numerous multitude..."[121] That he saw it necessary to respond to Baxter amid such laborious duties and unfavourable conditions for polemical engagements points to the vital importance of the issues at stake. Owen appraised Baxter's criticisms as having more to do with "words than things, expressions than opinions, ways of delivering things than the doctrines themselves", but nevertheless acknowledged that "the things pointed at are in themselves weighty, and needing some exactness in the delivery to give a right apprehension of them."[122] It is certainly the case that part of what lent support to the weightiness of the debate was the Arminian threat, as is made clear in Owen's preface.[123] Answering Baxter would therefore give further occasion for Owen to clarify and strengthen his position against Arminianism.[124]

From the content of Baxter's three charges, Owen identified two issues which he deemed as pertinent to the dispute.[125] The first concerns the nature of Christ's payment, while the second relates to the immediate fruit or effect of Christ's death for the elect. *Of the Death of Christ* was structured accordingly after these soteriological issues. An opening chapter introduced the controversy, followed by three chapters which dealt with the criticisms raised in relation to Owen's argument for *solutio eiusdem*,[126] and eight chapters of responses to the issue of the elect's justification prior to its actual possession through faith's exercise.[127]

---

[118] Richard Baxter, *Aphorismes of Justification with Their Explication Annexed* (Hague: Abraham Brown, 1655), Appendix, 302-307.
[119] Owen, *Works*, 10:429-79.
[120] Toon, *God's Statesman*, 36, 39-40.
[121] Owen, *Of the Death of Christ*, XVIII (*Works* 10:479). For the broader political and military context, see Crawford Gribben, *The Irish Puritans: James Ussher and the Reformation of the Church* (Darlington, England: Evangelical Press, 2003), 95-100.
[122] Owen, *Of the Death of Christ*, I (*Works* 10:435).
[123] Owen, *Of the Death of Christ*, To the Reader (*Works* 10:431-35).
[124] Toon, *God's Statesman*, 40: "Any compromise with Arminianism, and this was what he [Owen] felt Baxter's views were, would lead people down the slippery slope to Arminianism itself, which, in turn, would lead either to popery or Socinianism."
[125] Owen, *Of the Death of Christ*, I (*Works* 10:436).
[126] Owen, *Of the Death of Christ*, II-IV (*Works* 10:437-49).
[127] Owen, *Of the Death of Christ*, V-XII (*Works* 10:449-71). The work concludes with Chapter XIII (*Works* 10:471-79) in which Owen dealt with further objections.

On the nature of Christ's payment, Owen's response to Baxter saw a more precise explanation of what he had intended in the application of *solutio eiusdem* to Christ's death than was given in *The Death of Death*. A fundamental premise that underlies his rebuttals is that the incurred penalty and the person punished need not go together in the work of atonement.[128] This is worked out in two important areas. The first is Owen's conception of *solutio eiusdem*. Payment of the *idem*, to which Owen referred, was used in relation to the penalty incurred and not to the person punished. Thus, he was able to contend that the punishment meted out to sinners was the same as the punishment Christ underwent, but the person to be punished was changed through a relaxation of the law.[129] The law demanded punishment of the offender, but in the case of the atonement, Christ took the place of the offender on the basis of a divine act constituting satisfaction to be by way of substitution and payment of the *idem*. In Baxter's view, Owen concedes the case to Grotius precisely because the law did not specify that Christ was to be the one threatened.[130] It thus follows that the payment rendered by Christ is not the *idem* but *tantundem*. For Baxter, the person punished and the penalty incurred was of one piece as far as the execution of the law was concerned.

The second area concerning the nature of Christ's payment is the duration of Christ's suffering. Owen had qualified that when he affirmed Christ to have endured the same punishment, he meant "essentially *the same* in weight and pressure, though not in all accidents of duration and the like; for it was impossible that he should be detained by death."[131] Baxter, perceiving the obvious weakness of Owen's qualification, pointed out that the payment was "therefore not the same in the obligation because not fully the same."[132] Owen responded by applying the Aristotelian distinction of essence and accident to the distinction of person and penalty: "The accidents I mentioned follow and

---

[128] Owen, *Of the Death of Christ*, IV (*Works*, 10:449): "That there is a distinction to be allowed between the penalty and the person suffering is a common apprehension, especially when the nature of the penalty is only inquired after." Owen alludes to this point as early as his catechetical work of 1645. *Two Short Catechisms*, GC, XII, Q.7 (*Works*, 1:481n3).

[129] Owen, *Salus Electorum*, III.vii (Works, 10:270-73); idem, *Of the Death of Christ*, II (*Works*, 10:440-42). Owen argues the same point in *Exercitation XXIX*, but in addition to the language of the law's relaxation, speaks also in terms of "dispensation of or with the law". *Exposition of Hebrews*, Exercitations IV.xxix, "A Digression" (*Works*, 18:128-29).

[130] Baxter, *Aphorismes of Justification*, Appendix, 302-303.

[131] Owen, *Salus Electorum*, III.vii (*Works*, 10:269-270); cf. ibid., I.iii (*Works*, 10:173): "The punishment due to our sin and the chastisement of our peace was upon him; which that it was the pains of hell, in their nature and being, in their weight and pressure, though not in tendence and continuance (it being impossible that he should be detained by death), who can deny and not be injurious to the justice of God, which will inevitably inflict those pains to eternity upon sinners?"

[132] Baxter, *Aphorismes of Justification*, Appendix, 305.

attend the person suffering, and not the penalty itself."[133] In other words, while the duration of suffering may differ with respect to person, the essence of the incurred punishment remains the same. The distinction thus safeguards Owen's case for *solutio eiusdem*.

Contrary to Boersma's suggestion that Owen's use of the Aristotelian distinction seems to be an arbitrary move made solely to safeguard *idem* with respect to penalty,[134] Owen's move appears to be motivated by his Christology. His explanation for relating the accidents of Christ's death to his person was that "it was impossible that he should be detained by death."[135] This is a necessary implication of orthodox Christology. Elsewhere, he explained that the duration of Christ's suffering was temporal because eternal suffering attends "not *sin imputed* but *sin inherent*, especially not sin imputed to him who underwent it willingly..."[136] Being inherently sinful is only true of finite creatures, not of the incarnate Mediator who is the *theanthropos*. Thus, the punishment that fell upon Christ could not have been eternal. "Eternity," Owen explained, "is not absolutely in the curse of the law, but as a finite creature is cursed thereby."[137] Furthermore, the infinite dignity of Christ's person "was such as that he could fully satisfy divine justice in a limited season; after which God in justice loosed the pains of death, for it was impossible he should be detained thereby, Acts ii.24, and that because he was able to 'swallow up death in victory'."[138] For Owen, the conditions that attend the punishment depend upon the person on whom punishment falls, be it Christ or sinners. Owen's argument at this point borrows from the Anselmian tradition on the infinite dignity of Christ's person and is consistent with his Reformed understanding of the *communicatio idiomatum*.[139] The stress on Christ's person shows that Owen's Christology played a vital role in explaining the temporality of Christ's suffering. The Aristotelian distinction of essence and accident employed in response to Baxter was a useful heuristic device to clarify the Christological point.[140]

The second issue that Owen understood as pertinent to the debate centred on the immediate fruits of Christ's death. In *The Death of Death*, Owen had argued that the fruits of Christ's death are procured *ipso facto*, but that there is a time

---

[133] Owen, *Of the Death of Christ*, IV (*Works*, 10:447); cf. David Dickson, who employed the same distinction in answer to the question of the duration of Christ's suffering in *Therapeutica Sacra*, 51-52.
[134] Boersma, *A Hot Pepper Corn*, 252n358.
[135] Owen, *Salus Electorum*, III.vii (*Works*, 10:270).
[136] Owen, *Vindicae Evangelicae*, XXVI (*Works*, 12:492-93).
[137] Owen, *Vindicae Evangelicae*, XXVI (*Works*, 12:493).
[138] Owen, *Vindicae Evangelicae*, XXVI (*Works*, 12:493); idem, *Christologia*, XVII (*Works*, 1:209): "the temporary sufferings of him who was eternal were a full compensation for the eternal sufferings of them who were temporary."
[139] Anselm, *Cur Deus Homo*, II.xiv (*LCC*, X, 163-64); cf. Chapter 3 above.
[140] Cf. Trueman, *Claims of Truth*, 216-17.

difference between their purchase and actual possession.[141] This means that there is a sense in which the fruits of Christ's death actually belong to the elect before their response of faith. Owen explained that although the moment of purchase and possession are different, "but yet that hinders not but that they have all the fruits of his death in actual right, though not in actual possession, which last they cannot have until at least it be made known to them."[142] To Baxter, Owen's view was simply a "mistake."[143] Elaborating his critique in terms of justification, Baxter countered: "*To have right to it*, and *to have possession of it in point of Law or Right*, is to me all one: For what doth Faith give us possession of in its justifying Act, but this legall right?"[144] In Baxter's estimate, the distance between the right to possess (*ius ad rem*) and its actual possession (*ius in re*) "do seeme…to be of nearer kin" than Owen allowed.[145] Beneath the surface of Baxter's critique was his antinomian concern. To distinguish rights from possession or to argue for an *ipso facto* deliverance would concede too much ground to antinomianism. Owen's argument for the purchase of redemption in terms of its rights prior to faith resembled the antinomian doctrine of eternal justification too closely for Baxter's liking.[146] Indeed, the view that Christ's death secured immediate deliverance from sin's curse was, to Baxter, "the very pillar and foundation of the whole frame and fabrick of *Antinomianisme*."[147]

Owen's defence can be summarized in two general points. First, the charge of antinomianism was readily dismissed. Owen insisted that, with respect to eternal justification, he "never once received nor intimated the least thought of in that whole treatise [*The Death of Death*]" nor in any of his writings.[148] Instead, he explicitly distanced himself from that view.[149] Thus, to have been charged with antinomianism was "a little too harsh dealing" on Baxter's part.[150]

---

[141] Owen, *Salus Electorum*, VII (*Works*, 10:268).
[142] Owen, *Salus Electorum*, VII (*Works*, 10:268); idem, *Of the Death of Christ*, XI (*Works*, 10:465-68).
[143] Baxter, *Aphorismes of Justification*, Appendix, 316.
[144] Baxter, *Aphorismes of Justification*, Appendix, 315.
[145] Baxter, *Aphorismes of Justification*, Appendix, 314-15.
[146] Eternal justification is the view that the elect are justified in eternity before the death of Christ and their response of faith. Accordingly, faith was no longer the instrumental cause of justification but a subjective attestation of one's prior justification *in foro conscientiae*. Such teachings were evident within the "imputative" strain of English antinomianism. See Como, *Blown by the Spirit*, 200-211; Boersma, *A Hot Pepper Corn*, Part III. Baxter saw a close relationship between eternal justification and justification before faith although he distinguished between them. In his view, arguments against the latter also served to repudiate the former. Richard Baxter, *Richard Baxter's Confession of His Faith* (London: Printed by R. W. for Tho. Underhil and Fra. Tyton, 1655), 220ff.
[147] Baxter, *Aphorismes and Justification*, Appendix, 319.
[148] Owen, *Of the Death of Christ*, V (*Works*, 10:449).
[149] Owen, *Salus Electorum*, III.viii (*Works*, 10:279).
[150] Owen, *Of the Death of Christ*, V (*Works* 10:449).

Second, he affirmed the validity of speaking about procurement of rights in distinction from possession by appealing to the sovereignty of God in the matter of salvation. God freely determines both the means of redemption's purchase and the particularities of redemption's actual possession in the lives of its recipients. As supreme Governor and Judge, God alone has the power to relax his law as to the person punished, and to exact the same penalty from the appointed substitute.[151] The satisfactory value of Christ's death by *solutio eiusdem* is not ultimately determined by the logic intrinsic to jurisprudential concepts, but by divine constitution.[152] Likewise, it is the divine appointment established in the *pactum salutis* that determines the precise point in time at which the fruits of Christ's death are actualized in any person: "in that very covenant and compact from whence it is that the death of Christ is a payment, God reserveth to himself this right and liberty to discharge the debtor when and how he pleaseth, — I mean as to times and seasons."[153] Confessing his ignorance of what the difficulty was for Baxter, Owen surmised that the problem may well be a self-generated one: "Men may, as oft as they please, create contradictions in their own minds, and entangle themselves with doubts in the knots which themselves have tied."[154]

Dissatisfied with Owen's clarification, Baxter published his rejoinder in *Richard Baxter's Confession of Faith* (1655), in which Owen was further impugned with antinomianism.[155] This called forth a rejoinder by Owen, appended to his *Vindicae Evangelicae* (1655).[156] By this time, the debate's emphasis had shifted from the nature of Christ's payment to the doctrine of justification as it relates to antinomian teachings. Baxter's unrelenting indictment without due acknowledgement of Owen's repeated repudiation of the antinomian views charged upon him widened the existing rift. Offended by Baxter's treatment, Owen made full mileage of a passing critique by Baxter on his commendation of William Eyre's treatise on justification where reference was made to Socinianism.[157] In response to Baxter's passing critique, Owen

---

[151] Owen, *Vindicae Evangelicae*, XXIV (Works, 12:448-49); idem, *Salus Electorum*, III.vii (*Works*, 10:270).
[152] Owen, *Of the Death of Christ*, VIII (*Works*, 10:458).
[153] Owen, *Of the Death of Christ*, VIII (*Works*, 10:458).
[154] Owen, *Of the Death of Christ*, XIII (*Works*, 10:475).
[155] Baxter, *Richard Baxter's Confession*, 215-89, esp. 219, 222, 228-229, 254-71. Having dealt with Owen, Baxter begins a new section with the following words: "And thus I have shewed you somewhat of the face of these Doctrines of the Antinomians" (289).
[156] Owen, *Of the Death of Christ, and Of Justification* (*Works*, 12:591-616).
[157] For Owen's commendation, see "Preface" in William Eyre, *Vindiciae Justificationis Gratuitae. Justification without Conditions; or the Free Justification of a Sinner, Explained, Confirmed and Vindicated, from the Exceptions, Objections, and Seeming Absurdities, Which Are Cast Upon It, by the Assertors of Conditional Justification: More Especially from the Attempts of Mr. B. Woodbridge in His Sermon Entituled*

summarized the Socinian view of justification in eleven propositions along with a string of supporting references from Socinian sources.[158] Since the propositions resembled Baxter's view and were adumbrated in the context of Owen's response to Baxter, the association between Baxter and Socinianism was inevitable. Complaining about Owen's implicit allegation of Socinianism, Baxter, in *Certain Disputations* (1657), resolved not to engage any further with him.[159] Thus, the protracted debate was brought to a close.[160]

Owen's Debate with Baxter: the Importance of Christ's Priesthood
In the light of the attempt in this study to understand the way in which Owen's conception of Christ's priesthood contributed to his atonement theology, it is necessary to demonstrate the influence that it had on the debate with Baxter. How then does Owen's formulation of Christ's priesthood bear upon this complex debate? Three points may be advanced in answer to this question. The first has to do with the precipitating problem underlying the debate. The two issues addressed by Owen — the nature and fruits of Christ's death — may be summed up as the attempt to address one major problem posed by Socinus and his followers: the incompatibility of satisfaction with forgiveness of sins. Grotius rejected *solutio eiusdem* because payment of the *idem*, according to his understanding of the commercial logic, frees *ipso facto* from the obligation. This would imply that a further act of pardon is not required on the part of God, an implication which Grotius knew to be false and which, if granted, would serve to prove Socinus' criticism true. His solution, therefore, was *solutio tantidem*, since an equivalent payment does not free *ipso facto* but requires an act of acceptance on the part of God after payment. Likewise, Owen desired to maintain the compatibility of satisfaction and sin's forgiveness, but pointed out that if Christ's death did not free *ipso facto*, this would mean that freedom from the obligation is necessarily suspended upon the performance of some condition on the part of the human subject, notwithstanding the divine prerogative to impose that condition. Thus Owen:

[Justification by Faith] *of Mr. Cranford in His Epistle to the Reader, and of Mr. Baxter in Some Passages, Which Relate to the Same Matter. Wherein Also, the Absoluteness of the New Covenant Is Proved, and the Arguments against It, Are Disproved* (London: Printed for R.I., 1654).
[158] Owen, *Of the Death of Christ, and Of Justification* (*Works*, 12:596-601).
[159] Richard Baxter, *Certain Disputations of Right to Sacraments, and the True Nature of Visible Christianity; Defending Them against Several Sorts of Opponents, Especially against the Second Assault of That Pious, Reverend and Dear Brother Mr Thomas Blake* (London: Printed by William Du Gard for Thomas Johnson, 1657), 483-88, 502, 515.
[160] It was not until after the death of Owen and Baxter that Baxter's view on the subject was again made known in public. See Richard Baxter, *Universal Redemption of Mankind, by the Lord Jesus Christ: Stated and Cleared by the Late Learned Mr. Richard Baxter. Whereunto Is Added a Short Account of Special Redemption, by the Same Author* (London: Printed for John Salusbury, 1694).

Christ delivering us by his satisfaction, not actually nor *ipso facto, is* so to make satisfaction for us as that we shall have no benefit by his death but upon the performance of a condition, which himself by that death of his did not absolutely procure. This was that which I opposed; and therefore affirmed that Christ by his death did actually, or *ipso facto,* deliver us.[161]

In Owen's view, adhering to *solutio tantidem*, denying that Christ's death delivers *ipso facto*, and advocating a conditional satisfaction, are all interrelated aspects of an atonement theology that is "destructive of the true value and virtue of the death of Christ."[162] All three were raised in connection with Owen's critique of universal redemption whose chief error, as he pointed out in *The Death of Death*, lay in the conception of Christ's priestly office.[163] Thus, what might seem to modern readers of the debate an unhelpful preoccupation with esoteric concepts was to Owen a critical point in the defence of orthodoxy against Socinianism and universal redemption.

The second point answers the question more directly. For Owen, satisfaction and forgiveness of sins are not mutually opposed because God has appointed that both, being part of the entire dispensation of grace, were to be obtained through the oblation and intercession of Christ. Earlier, it was explained that Grotius' objection to *solutio eiusdem* in the context of the Socinian argument that satisfaction is incompatible with sin's forgiveness was due to the logic that payment of the same thing frees *ipso facto*. Another way of stating this objection is to say that payment of the same thing rules out the necessity of sin's pardon or forgiveness. For if *solutio eiusdem* frees *ipso facto*, why then should God subsequently pardon sins as if pardon had not already been obtained with the payment? Owen, responding to Grotius' objection in this form, gives the following answer:

The freedom, then, of pardon hath not its foundation in any defect of the merit or satisfaction of Christ, but in three other things:—*First*, The will of God freely appointing this satisfaction of Christ, John iii.16; Rom. V. 8; 1 John iv.9. *Secondly*, In a gracious acceptation of that decreed satisfaction in our steads; for so many, no more. *Thirdly*, In a free application of the death of Christ.[164]

Owen's response reflects his trinitarian and covenantal framework in which the appointment of the Father, the satisfaction undertaken by the Son, and the application of Christ's death by the Spirit are all crucial aspects of his discussion of sin's pardon.[165] His response is also directly related to the priestly work of Christ. God's "gracious acceptation" is an act of God's will exercised

---

[161] Owen, *Of the Death of Christ*, V (*Works*, 10:450).
[162] Owen, *Of the Death of Christ*, V (*Works*, 10:450).
[163] See Chapter 4 above.
[164] Owen, *Salus Electorum*, III.vii (*Works*, 10:269).
[165] Cf. Trueman, *Claims of Truth*, 213.

with respect to Christ's oblation or "that decreed satisfaction in our steads", while the "free application" depends upon Christ's intercession. For Owen, then, the free pardon of sins is not opposed to satisfaction by *solutio eiusdem* because the basis of sin's forgiveness does not lie in the logic intrinsic to legal concepts, but in God's appointment of the kind of satisfaction he so wills, performed in the oblative and intercessory work of Christ as priest.

The third point concerns Owen's response to Baxter about the relationship between redemption's purchase and possession. The purchase/possession distinction parallels the distinction in Owen's formulation of Christ's priesthood. It is Christ's oblation that purchased redemption. The fruits of Christ's death are subsequently dispensed to believers by virtue of Christ's heavenly intercession. In the course of explaining to Baxter the way in which those who have a right to salvific blessings come to possess the blessings themselves, Owen averred:

> What spiritual blessings soever are bestowed on any soul, I mean peculiarly distinguishing mercies and graces, they are all bestowed and collated for Christ's sake; that is, they are purchased by his merit, and procured by his intercession thereupon.[166]

Here, Christ's priestly work of oblation and intercession is again apparent. When applied to the blessing of justification, Owen's insistence that the believer's possession of justification inferred the antecedent purchase of a right to justification may therefore be understood as a statement that rests upon the distinction and inseparability of Christ's sacerdotal acts. Christ's oblation purchased the right to justification, while justification itself is subsequently possessed by believers at the divinely appointed time on account of Christ's heavenly intercession.[167]

Following this priestly framework, it is important that Owen maintains a temporal sequence between *ius ad rem* and *ius in re*. As we have already seen, this was exactly what he did, contra Baxter. Its necessity is demanded by Owen's formulation of Christ's priesthood. According to Owen, Christ's oblation was performed in his state of humiliation, while Christ's intercession was performed in his state of exaltation, and "in the ordination of God, exinanition was to precede his glorious majestical exaltation, as the Scripture witnesses."[168] It follows from the historical sequence of Christ's twofold state that oblation necessarily precedes intercession. The same sequence is therefore required for redemption's purchase and possession. Viewed through the lens of Christ's priesthood, it thus makes sound soteriological sense to speak of having

---

[166] Owen, *Of the Death of Christ*, XII (*Works*, 10:469).

[167] To speak of the right to salvific benefits as something purchased by Christ's death is an acceptable manner of theological speech for Owen. See *Of the Death of Christ*, X (*Works*, 10:462).

[168] Owen, *The Doctrine of Justification*, XII (*Works*, 5:256).

ius ad rem before *ius in re* as part of the historical sequence within the economy of salvation.

Maintaining this historical sequence also made good polemical sense with respect to Socinian soteriology. For the Socinians, Christ's oblation and intercession are entirely collapsed and taken as occurring concurrently in Christ's heavenly ministry before the Father.[169] Such a conception resulted from radical modifications to the orthodox understanding of Christ's priesthood in which its content was evacuated of anything satisfactory while the form of traditional terminologies was preserved. These modifications would logically commit the Socinians to deny the existence of a time difference between redemption's purchase and possession. Thus, affirming or rejecting the historical sequence between *ius ad rem* and *ius in re*, while raised within the specific context of Owen's debate with Baxter, nevertheless has wider polemical implications that arise from Owen's peculiar formulation of Christ's priesthood. It is a point at which the clash of sacerdotal conceptualities between Owen and his opponents is acutely felt.

Owen's Contradiction?

McGrath observes that there is "a modicum of contradiction" in Owen's view of justification.[170] The contradiction arises, supposedly, from asserting on the one hand that "the death of Christ merited *ipso facto* the justification of the elect, his death was a cause independent from the faith of the believer", and of stressing on the other hand, "the necessity of faith and repentance, for in the truest sense a person was not justified before personal faith."[171] Although not explicitly affirming that a contradiction exists, Boersma acknowledges the tension identified by McGrath and adds that it is exacerbated by Owen's notion of Christ's death meriting the right to justification.[172]

The alleged contradiction could be understood in two ways. The first concerns the assumption upon which the contradiction is founded — that the death of Christ was, as McGrath puts it, "a cause independent from the faith of the believer." Presumably, this means that if Christ's death is said to be the cause of justification, it cannot then be said that faith is necessary for

---

[169] Crellius, *The Expiation of a Sinner*, 193: "But in Christ our high priest, the offering and appearance as also the intercession were really the same; if his appearance and intercession be taken not for his bare comming to his Father, but for his comming joyned with his procuration of our salvation, as here they must be taken; because in Christ the Priest and the offering were the same. For Christ by his appearance, offers himselfe: and by offering himselfe he appeares; and by offering and appearing, he intercedes."
[170] Gavin John McGrath, "Puritans and the Human Will: Voluntarism within Mid-Seventeenth English Puritanism as Seen in the Works of Richard Baxter and John Owen" (Ph.D. dissertation, University of Durham, 1989), 264.
[171] McGrath, "Puritans and the Human Will", 264.
[172] Boersma, *A Hot Pepper Corn*, 105.

justification since that would make faith into a cause as well. In this case, however, there is no real contradiction. This is because Owen thought of Christ's death and the faith of believers as different types of causes with respect to the same effect. Christ's death is the *meritorious* or *procuring cause* of justification while faith is the *instrumental cause*.[173] Both count towards justification but as causes functioning in different ways. Furthermore, saving faith, being a divine gift, is itself purchased by Christ's death and actualized at the divinely appointed time. As such, the independence posited by McGrath between the death of Christ as a cause of justification and the faith of the elect is unwarranted. Insofar as Christ's death purchased saving faith, a view which Owen avowed,[174] Christ's death is not a cause independent of faith.

The second way in which the alleged contradiction could be understood is in relation to the *ipso facto* procurement by Christ's death. From this vantage point, the contradiction in view is between the claim that justification is an immediate effect of Christ's death because procured *ipso facto*, and the claim that it is not an immediate effect since the response of faith is required at a predetermined time in the future. It does seem, on *prima facie* consideration, that the contradiction here is real. However, careful reading of Owen suggests that it is again only apparent.

In Owen's debate with Baxter, Owen argued that Christ's death is not a *physical* but *moral* cause.[175] This distinction is not made arbitrarily, nor is it Owen's own invention, but may be found in the writings of medieval and Reformed scholastics such as Suarez, Maccovius, and Voetius.[176] The effects of physical causes are produced immediately and so would require the existence of their subjects upon their exercise, as for instance, "James pushed Justin to the ground." In this example, falling to the ground is the immediate effect of the physical cause of pushing. However, moral causes do not produce their effects immediately since a "third thing" intervenes, "namely, proportion, constitution, law, covenant,—which takes in the cause and lets out the effect."[177] In relation to Christ's death as a moral cause, what intervenes is the "compact" or *pactum salutis*. The covenanted redemption is actualized in accordance with "that relation, coherence, and causality which the Lord hath appointed between the several effects, or rather parts of the same effect, of the death of Christ."[178] Thus, the effects of Christ's death are obtained immediately, but it is "with such

---

[173] Owen, *A Display of Arminianism*, IX (*Works*, 10:94); idem, *Salus Electorum*, II.iv (*Works*, 10:231); idem, *Of the Death of Christ*, XII (*Works*, 10:470).
[174] Owen, *Salus Electorum*, II.v, III.iv (*Works*, 10:234-35, 255-57).
[175] Owen, *Of the Death of Christ*, IX (*Works*, 10:459-62).
[176] Gert Van den Brink, "Impetration and Application in John Owen's Theology," in *John Owen Today Conference* (Westminster College, Cambridge: 2008), 5-8, citing Suarez's *Disputationes Metaphysicae*, Maccovius' *Distinctiones et Regulae*, and Voetius' *Selectarum Disputationum*.
[177] Owen, *Of the Death of Christ*, IX (*Works*, 10:459).
[178] Owen, *Of the Death of Christ*, IX (*Works*, 10:461).

an immediation as attends moral causes."[179] By the death of Christ, "we are immediately delivered from death with that immediation which is proper to the efficiency of causes which produce their effects by the way of moral procurement; that is, certainly, without the intervention of any other cause of the like kind."[180] Since Owen could speak of an "immediate deliverance" whose effects are later actualized, his view of moral causation allows for temporal sequencing within the divine economy in a way that is consistent with his view of Christ's priesthood.

One could legitimately argue that Owen risked being accused of having contradicted himself by his juxtaposition of the language of immediacy with Christ's death and its effects. However, it would be difficult to maintain that Owen really contradicted himself since he could assert the immediate acquisition of salvific benefits in a way that did not entail their immediate possession. Owen does this in two ways as demonstrated above: via the *ius ad rem/in re* distinction, and via his conception of moral causation.

Owen's Commercialism?

A more serious criticism of Owen's atonement theology concerns his alleged commercial theory of the atonement. Among modern Owen scholars, Clifford is the most vociferous of critics. He attributes Owen's limited atonement to the controlling influence of Aristotle's "one-end teleology", i.e. the single end of the elect's salvation. All other relevant evidences to the contrary are tarred with the same Aristotelian brush. Thus, on the nature of Christ's sufferings, Owen is accused of an "a priori, Aristotelian teleology" that "prejudices his whole approach to the question."[181] Indeed, Clifford claims that in making the sufferings of Christ "commensurate with the sins of the elect in a quantitative, commercialistic sense [Owen] explains and reinforces his teleology of the atonement."[182] Owen's defence of *solutio eiusdem* was perceived as vital to him because "the case for the doctrine of limited atonement hangs on this issue."[183]

A key feature of Clifford's criticism is his understanding of *solutio eiusdem* as a payment whose value is measured in quantitative terms. In a telling statement, Clifford asseverates: "Consistent with his commercialism, Owen insisted that God's justice was only satisfied by Christ's payment of the same *quantitative* penalty or debt owed by the elect to God on account of their sins – the *solutio ejusdem*."[184] Further considerations on Owen's teleology and Clifford's criticisms of it will be pursued in Chapter 6. Here, it will suffice to address the specific criticisms on the alleged commercialism of Owen.

---

[179] Owen, *Of the Death of Christ*, IX (*Works*, 10:461).
[180] Owen, *Of the Death of Christ*, XIII (*Works*, 10:472).
[181] Clifford, *Atonement and Justification*, 125.
[182] Clifford, *Atonement and Justification*, 112.
[183] Clifford, *Atonement and Justification*, 11.
[184] Clifford, *Atonement and Justification*, 128-29.

Clifford's interpretation is extremely problematic for three reasons. First, his crude interpretation of Owen's commercial analogy in terms of the quantitative/qualitative category is entirely foreign to Owen's thought where sin's payment is concerned. Nowhere in Owen's exposition of the subject does he use the category or allude to it. Rather, it is the Aristotelian category of essence and accidents that was deployed in defence of *solutio eiusdem* on the duration of Christ's sufferings. The decisive influence on the issue is Owen's Christology as demonstrated above.[185] Indeed, Owen's point to Baxter that the suffering undergone by Christ is the same as the obligation in essence but not in its accident of duration is clear evidence that Owen was far from thinking of sin's penalty in quantitative terms.

Second, Clifford's interpretation is problematic because Owen himself ensured that his use of the commercial analogy does not fall prey to crude reconstructions. This is evident in his exegesis on the nature of Christ's sufferings. In defence of the position that Christ suffered the *idem* and not the *tantundem*, Owen was content to draw his proof from Scripture alone without recourse to commercial or jurisprudential logic. The form of his exegetical argument is straightforward: Scripture asserts that the penalty of sin is death (Gen. 2:17), the curse of the law (Gal. 3:13), and divine condemnation (Rom. 8:3); Scripture also asserts that Christ "tasted death" (Heb. 2:9), was "made a curse for us" (Gal. 3:13), and was "condemned...in the flesh" (Rom. 8:3); therefore Christ suffered or paid the *idem*.[186] Here, his exegesis is driven by the Protestant doctrine of Scripture's perspicuity. Owen also appealed to Scripture's *sensus literalis* in his exegesis. He grants, for instance, that 2 Corinthians 5:18-20 and Romans 3:24-25 "do expressly mention the payment of this debt by Christ as the ground of God's forgiveness, remission, and pardon",[187] but immediately qualifies that the payment is "not as considered metaphorically as a debt, but the making an atonement and reconciliation for us who had committed it, considered as a *crime* and rebellion or transgression."[188] In other words, what was paid is not sin or its penalty taken in a strictly commercialistic sense. Owen is clear that the sin-as-debt language is

---

[185] See 136-37 above.

[186] Owen, *Of the Death of Christ*, IV (*Works*, 10:448-49). Other corroborating texts cited include Romans 8:32, 2 Samuel 18:33, Psalm 116:3, 22:1, Luke 22:44, Psalm 16:8-11, Acts 2:24-28, Hebrews 2:9, 14, 1 Peter 3:18, Hebrews 9:26, 28, Romans 5:10, Isaiah 53:6, 2 Corinthians 5:21, Isaiah 53:5, 1 Peter 2:24, Matthew 26:37, 38, Mark 14:33, and Hebrews 5:7. In *Vindicae Evangelicae*, XXVI (*Works*, 12:494), after advancing a similar form of exegetical argument on the same subject, he opined: "It is strange to me that we should deserve one punishment, and he who is punished for us should undergo another, yet both of them be constantly described by the same names and titles."

[187] Owen, *Vindicae Evangelicae*, XXX (*Works*, 12:544).

[188] Owen, *Vindicae Evangelicae*, XXX (*Works*, 12:544).

metaphorical language.[189] Owen's freedom in employing the commercial analogy is not exercised at the expense of exegetical assiduousness. On another occasion, when he desired to affirm the criminal nature of Christ's satisfaction in contradistinction to a strictly commercialistic construal of payment, he flatly disavowed speaking of God, sin, the law, and Christ, in commercialistic terms, albeit allowing for their illustrative function.[190]

Thirdly, Clifford's interpretation is problematic because of its reductionistic analysis without due regard to Owen's exegesis or his broader sacerdotal framework. Owen's view of the divine intention in salvation, which Clifford terms Owen's "one-end teleology", does not function as a logical axiom from which Owen's particularist view of the atonement and his commercial analogy are derived, thereby marginalizing or bypassing redemptive history altogether. The historical outworking of redemption is as crucial to Owen's atonement theology as its eternal ground. This is evident both in Owen's formulation of Christ's priesthood that takes the entire life of Christ seriously, and in the application of this formulation in his debate with Baxter. As demonstrated above, it is Owen's exegesis and his understanding of God's divine constitution within the *pactum salutis* which are the determinants of his notion of *solutio eiusdem*, not his commercialism as Clifford has mistakenly alleged.

Conclusion

In the attempt to give an account of Owen's atonement theology in this chapter, attention has been paid to key aspects of the doctrine of satisfaction in its seventeenth-century context: the obedience of Christ; the nature and effects of his death. In the above treatment of each aspect, it was argued that Christ's priesthood functioned in an important way for Owen. On the matter of satisfaction, Owen maintained the imputation of Christ's whole obedience on the grounds of the *unio mystica* and the suretyship of Christ. For him, Christ's suretyship is a function of Christ's priesthood. Related to Owen's view of imputation is his insistence that in Christ's state of humiliation, his entire

---

[189] Elsewhere Owen viewed the sin-as-debt language as an improper way of speaking. Owen, *A Brief Declaration and Vindication*, Of the Satisfaction of Christ (*Works*, 2:431-32); idem, *A Dissertation on Divine Justice*, II.ix (*Works*, 10:567): "our sins, in respect of God, are not debts only nor properly, but metaphorically so called"; idem, *Exposition of Hebrews*, Exercitations IV.xxix (*Works*, 18:131): "In brief, Christ's undergoing the punishment due unto our sins, the same that we should have undergone,—or, to speak with respect unto that improper notion, his paying the same debts which we owed,—doth not in the least take off from the freedom of our pardon."

[190] Owen, *A Brief Declaration and Vindication*, Appendix (*Works*, 2:444): "It appears, from what hath been spoken, that, in this matter of satisfaction, God is not considered as a *creditor*, and sin as a *debt*; and the law as an obligation to the payment of that debt, and the Lord Christ as paying it;—though these notions may have been used by some for the illustration of the whole matter, and that not without countenance from sundry expressions in the Scripture to the same purpose."

earthly life is characterized by mediatorial sufferings. Indeed, so important is Christ's priestly work performed in his twofold state that it was identified by Owen as the object of justifying faith.

On the nature and effects of Christ's death, Owen contended that satisfaction by *solutio eiusdem* is compatible with sin's forgiveness and the *ipso facto* procurement of justification. Christ's priesthood is important here because of the relation his oblation sustains to satisfaction, and the corresponding relation his intercession sustains to sin's forgiveness and justification. The exercise of these sacerdotal acts would require that the salvific benefits procured *ipso facto* by Christ's oblation be dispensed by virtue of his intercession for actual possession. The integration of these sacerdotal acts with the historical movement of Christ's states means that a temporal sequence exists between redemption's purchase and possession. Owen's insistence of a temporal sequence between *ius ad rem* and *ius in re* reflects both the consistency with and the influence of his peculiar formulation of Christ's priesthood. Against the framework of Owen's doctrine of satisfaction as adumbrated above, Owen's alleged self-contradiction and commercialism are examined and found to be unsustainable.

CHAPTER 6

The End of Redemption

The subject of redemption's end is of no small significance in Owen's atonement theology. It has already been alluded to in previous chapters but was not sufficiently examined in order not to divert from the main arguments of those chapters. Here it is taken up again to bring some sense of coherence to the earlier, rather disparate allusions to the subject.

The end of redemption is one of three essential components in Owen's teleological construal of Christ's saving work, the others being the Agent and means of redemption. The three doctrinal loci around which Owen's atonement theology is constructed are related teleologically: the triune God, Christ the Mediator, and sin's satisfaction. They correspond directly with Owen's understanding of the Agent, means, and end of redemption. Owen's teleological language has already been referred to in the case study of *The Death of Death* in Chapter 1. In this chapter, his understanding of teleology will be revisited against the backdrop of the contemporary discussion on the subject, after which it will be examined in relation to two areas of Owen's thought: his conception of God's glory in the display of the divine attributes, and his treatment of the saints' perseverance. As will become clear below, Christ's priesthood plays a crucial role in Owen's understanding of these matters.

Owen's Teleology: Current Perspectives

Of the many serious works on Owen, Clifford's is the first that gave prominence to the importance of teleology for understanding Owen's atonement theology.[1] His work was, in the main, positively received until Trueman published a substantial response some eight years later.[2] An important

---

[1] Clifford, *Atonement and Justification*.
[2] Trueman, *Claims of Truth*. See the generally positive reviews of Clifford's work: Alan. F. Sell, review of *Atonement and Justification*, by Alan Clifford, *CTJ* 27, no. 1 (1992), 116-117; A. Skevington Wood, review of *Atonement and Justification*, by Alan Clifford, *EQ* 63 (1991), 287-288; W.R. Ward, review of *Atonement and Justification*, by Alan Clifford, *JEH* 42, no. 2 (1991), 326-327; Alister E. McGrath, review of *Atonement and Justification*, by Alan Clifford, *JTS* 42, no. 1 (1991), 397-398; John A. Newton, review of *Atonement and Justification*, by Alan Clifford, *Theology* 94, no. 758 (1991), 140-41; cf. also the largely positive use of Clifford's thesis in Boersma, *A Hot Pepper Corn*. For critical reviews on Clifford's interpretation of Owen's Aristotelian method, see Gerald Bray, review of *Atonement and Justification*, by Alan Clifford, *Churchman* 105, no.1 (1991), 93-94, but especially Paul Helm, review of *Atonement and Justification*, by Alan

issue that Trueman addresses is Clifford's view of Owen's teleology. In view of the significant contributions of these scholars to the issue at hand, it is necessary to highlight the main points in the debate so as to indicate the precise contribution of this chapter to the current discussion.

Clifford's overarching thesis is that Owen's atonement theology is determined by the metaphysics of Aristotle. Specifically, as was already indicated in the previous chapter, Clifford contends that Aristotle's "one-end teleology" governs Owen's understanding of the atonement's design. By "one-end teleology", Clifford is referring to what he terms the "exclusive end" of Owen's atonement theology, where Christ's death was only intended for the elect. Referring to *The Death of Death*, the following paragraph captures the main ideas in Clifford's analysis:

> Owen's Aristotelian method is evident in the opening chapters of his treatise. His basic contention that the atonement is exclusively designed for the redemption of the elect is couched in the means-end terminology of Aristotle's metaphysics. As far as he is concerned, there was one exclusive 'end' or purpose in the death of Christ. However, the set of concepts which he employs to establish his case (end, means, moving cause, etc.) are derived not from the writers of the New Testament but from Aristotle. The philosopher's conception of teleology governs his understanding of the design of the atonement.[3]

Subjecting Clifford's analysis to careful scrutiny, Trueman levels three basic criticisms at Clifford's thesis. First, he calls into question Clifford's assumption that the use of Aristotelian terminologies is evidence of the influence of a form of rationalism upon Owen's theology. He points out that the use of Aristotelian categories, in and of itself, does not argue for the negative impact of rationalism since these categories functioned simply as heuristic devices in the hands of Owen.[4] Second, Trueman observes that not only did Clifford not provide any discussion of what he means by Owen's "Aristotelianism" he is also guilty of the "root fallacy" — the failure to take into account developments in the use of Aristotelian language and categories over time.[5] This failure results in an

---

Clifford, *BTr* no. 325 (1990), 29-31. Prior to Trueman's 1998 monograph, *The Claims of Truth*, there were some serious challenges to the historiography of scholasticism by Brian Armstrong on which Clifford relied in his *Atonement and Justification*. Cf. Muller, "Calvin and the 'Calvinists': Part One"; idem, "Calvin and the 'Calvinists': Part Two"; Carl R. Trueman, "A Small Step Towards Rationalism: The Impact of the Metaphysics of Tommaso Campanella on the Theology of Richard Baxter", in *Protestant Scholasticism: Essays in Reassessment*, ed. Carl R. Trueman and R.S. Clark (Carlisle, Cumbria: Paternoster Press, 1999), 181-95. However, these challenges impinge only indirectly upon Clifford's interpretation of Owen.

[3] Clifford, *Atonement and Justification*, 96.
[4] Trueman, *Claims of Truth*, 52ff., 234.
[5] Trueman, *Claims of Truth*, 234-35; cf. idem, "A Small Step Towards Rationalism", 181-84, esp. 182n3.

interpretation of Owen that is deeply flawed. Third, Trueman reveals the further failure of Clifford to come to grips with Owen's key teleological distinction between the ultimate end of God's glory in redemption and the intermediate end of the elect's salvation.[6] Owen's statement of the distinction is as follows:

> Now, the end of the death of Christ is either *supreme* and ultimate, or *intermediate* and subservient to that last end. 1. The first is the glory of God, or the manifestation of his glorious attributes, especially of his justice, and mercy tempered with justice, unto us... 2. There is an *end* of the death of Christ which is *intermediate* and subservient to that other, which is the last and most supreme, even the effects which it hath in respect of us...which, as we before affirmed, is the *bringing of us unto God*.[7]

When this distinction is taken into account, the end of Christ's death in Owen's atonement theology cannot be understood as single and exclusive in nature as Clifford alleges. Instead, it is twofold and inclusive: the end of God's glory embraces the elect's salvation as a sub-end. Apart from the third criticism that concerns the failure to read Owen closely, the other two relate to methodological issues that pertain to the historiography of Protestant scholasticism. Trueman's argument that Owen employed Aristotelian categories as heuristic devices comports well with Muller's observation of "a consensus in contemporary scholarship that 'scholasticism,' properly understood, indicates a method, capable of presenting and arguing a variety of theological and philosophical conclusions, and not a particular theology or philosophy."[8] Trueman's concern for a nuanced understanding of Owen's appropriation of Aristotle is in line with studies that demonstrate the need to distinguish between the thought of Aristotle and its modifications by medieval and Protestant scholastics.[9] This modified Aristotelianism or "Christian Aristotelianism" exercises a far more critical and nuanced appropriation of Aristotle than Clifford allows.

In the following two sections, Trueman's third criticism will be unpacked, a criticism which he only mentions in passing. An extended exposition of Owen's twofold end of redemption will be given in order to show that Owen's distinction between God's supreme and intermediate ends is not incidental to his atonement theology. Therefore to conceive of Owen's atonement theology in terms of a "one-end teleology" is a gross caricature of his thought.

---

[6] Trueman, *Claims of Truth*, 235ff.
[7] Owen, *Salus Electorum*, II.i (*Works*, 10:201-202).
[8] Muller, *PRRD*, 1:35.
[9] Richard A. Muller, "Reformation, Orthodoxy, 'Christian Aristotelianism', and the Eclecticism of Early Modern Philosophy", *NAKG* 81, no. 3 (2001), 306-25; cf. R.N. Frost, "Aristotle's Ethics: The Real Reason for Luther's Reformation?", *TJ* 18, no.2 (1997), 223-41, and Muller's response in Richard A. Muller, "Scholasticism, Reformation, Orthodoxy, and the Persistence of Christian Aristotelianism", *TJ* 19, no. 1 (1998), 81-96; Muller, *PRRD*, 1:360-82.

The Supreme End of Redemption: the Glory of God

Foundational Issues

Owen's understanding of redemption's ultimate end has to do with the revelation of God's character in the work of redemption. This is apparent from the way in which he tied the divine attributes to the work of God in redemption. The ultimate end of redemption, as indicated above, is "the glory of God, or the manifestation of his glorious attributes..."[10] Underlying this statement are certain basic commitments about the knowledge of God that informed Owen's conception of the relationship between God's essence and its revelation in the history of redemption.

Owen's commitment to the Reformed orthodox distinction between *theologia archetypa* and *theologia ectypa* meant that he understood human knowledge of God as necessarily limited.[11] This limitation is reflected in his candid acknowledgement of the impossibility of the knowledge of God as he is in himself for the human subject: "*Do we know God as he is?* A. No; his glorious being is not of us, in this life to be comprehended"; "No finite creature can have an absolute comprehension of that which is infinite. We shall never search out the Almighty to perfection, in any of his works of infinite wisdom."[12] However, granting the epistemic limitation of the human subject does not close the door entirely to the knowledge of God. Owen, along with the Reformed orthodox, taught that God has revealed himself to humanity and his revelation in Holy Scripture is the epistemological *principium theologiae*.[13] Apart from Scripture, there can be no true knowledge of God. In his *Greater Catechism*, Owen identified two ways by which God is "*chiefly made known unto us in the Word.*"[14] The first is the divine names of God, those "glorious titles, which he hath given himself, to hold forth his excellencies unto us, with some perfections whereby he will reveal himself."[15] The second is the attributes

---

[10] Owen, *Salus Electorum*, II.i (*Works*, 10:201-202).
[11] Owen, *Theologoumena*, I.iii.11-12 (*BT*, 15-16); Rehnman, *Divine Discourse*, 57-71; Trueman, *Claims of Truth*, 52-56; cf. Willem Van Asselt, "The Fundamental Meaning of Theology: Archetypal and Ectypal Theology in Seventeenth-Century Reformed Thought", *WTJ* 64, no. 2 (2002), 319-35; Muller, *PRRD*, 1:225-38; idem, *DLGTT*, 299-301.
[12] Owen, *Two Short Catechisms*, GC, II.Q3 (*Works*, 1:471); idem, *Christologia*, XIX (*Works*, 1:239).
[13] Muller, *DLGTT*, 245-46; idem, *PRRD*, I:430-45, II:151-61. Owen was aware of the effect of sin upon creaturely knowledge of God. See Owen, *Theologoumena*, I.v-vi.21-32 (*BT*, 30-47); Rehnman, *Divine Discourse*, 73-89. Here, the concern is simply to show that Owen entertained the possibility of an epistemological route from Scripture to the knowledge of God's being in his discussion on the divine attributes. In this regard, cf. also Carl R. Trueman, "John Owen's Dissertation on Divine Justice: An Exercise in Christocentric Scholasticism", *CTJ* 33 (1998), 98-102.
[14] Owen, *Two Short Catechisms*, GC, II.Q4 (*Works*, 1:471).
[15] Owen, *Two Short Catechisms*, GC, II.Q5 (*Works*, 1:471).

of God, defined as "His infinite perfections in being and working."[16] These two modes of Scriptural revelation of God in their stated order are typical of the concerns and treatment of Reformed orthodox theologians on the subject.[17]

Owen's definition of God's attributes posits a close connection between the divine attributes and the *opera Dei*, a connection that is evident in his teleological construal of redemption. As the *opera Dei* is distinguished into *ad intra* and *ad extra*, so the conception of the divine attributes divides accordingly into attributes of being and working. The importance of this distinction for Owen is seen towards the end of his catechetical section on the Trinity: "*Can we conceive these things as they are in themselves?* A. Neither we nor the angels of heaven are at all able to dive into these secrets, as they are internally in God; but in respect of the outward dispensation of themselves to us by creation, redemption, and sanctification, a knowledge may be attained of these things, saving and heavenly."[18] This catechetical item affirms the possibility of obtaining a saving knowledge of God through his external works while recognizing the impossibility of creaturely apprehension of God in his essence. Owen's naming of the divine attributes assumes this possibility. Thus, the chief attributes of God's being are identified by Owen as "eternity, infiniteness, simplicity or purity, all sufficiency, perfectness, immutability, life, will, and understanding", and the chief attributes of God's working as "goodness, power, justice, mercy, holiness, wisdom, and the like; which he delighteth to exercise towards his creatures, for the praise of his glory."[19]

This *ad intra/extra* or being/working distinction is fundamental to Owen's classification of the divine attributes. It reflects his sensitivity to the eternal/temporal dialectic which is characteristic of Reformed orthodox treatments of the subject. Muller identifies six basic forms of classification employed by Reformed orthodox theologians: absolute and relative attributes; attributes of the divine essence and life; *via negativa* and *via eminentiae* or a priori and a posteriori attributes; essential attributes, attributes of divine actuosity, and attributes of divine relationality; attributes arranged argumentatively: *quid, quantus, qualis*; incommunicable and communicable attributes.[20] Although overlaps and differences exist in these classifications, their formulations indicate the awareness of the eternal/temporal dialectic and the significance it has upon the divine attributes conceived within the context of

---

[16] Owen, *Two Short Catechisms*, GC, II.Q6 (*Works*, 1:471).
[17] Cf. the analysis of Zanchius' *De Natura Dei* (1577) in Harm Goris, "Thomism in Zanchi's Doctrine of God", in *Reformation and Scholasticism: An Ecumenical Enterprise*, eds. Willem J. Van Asselt and E. Dekker, Texts and Studies in Reformation and Post-Reformation Thought (Grand Rapids, Mich.: Baker Academic, 2001), 122-36, and the analysis of Cocceius' *Summa Theologiae* (1665) in Van Asselt, *The Federal Theology of Johannes Cocceius*, 156-74.
[18] Owen, *Two Short Catechisms*, GC, III.Q7 (*Works*, 1:473).
[19] Owen, *Two Short Catechisms*, GC, II.Q8 (*Works*, 1:472).
[20] Muller, *PRRD*, 3:216-26.

the divine-human dynamic. Owen's preferred classification is of the first type, paralleling his distinction of the attributes of being and working in his *Greater Catechism*:

> The properties of God are either *absolute* or *relative*. The absolute properties of God are such as may be considered without the supposition of any thing else whatever, towards which their energy and efficacy should be exerted. His relative are such as, in their egress and exercise, respect some things in the creatures, though they naturally and eternally reside in God.[21]

Having discussed some of the foundational issues in Owen's conception of the divine attributes, the following section proceeds to examine the attributes which are associated with the work of redemption.

The Divine Attributes and the Work of Redemption

Owen's understanding of the divine attributes and the way in which they are directly involved in the work of redemption may be gleaned from several treatises: *The Death of Death*, *A Dissertation on Divine Justice*, *Vindicae Evangelicae*, *Christologia*, and *Exercitations Concerning the Priesthood of Christ*. Of these writings, *The Death of Death* and *Christologia* are the two most significant works for understanding Owen's overall structure of thought on the subject of God's attributes in the work of redemption. The other treatises address the subject more narrowly, tackling specific issues in detail such as God's vindicatory justice, omnipresence, foreknowledge, and problems of predication, but without situating the discussion within the kind of overarching framework for the way the divine attributes bear upon the work of redemption that the former two treatises provide.[22] In this regard, the importance of *The Death of Death* lies in situating the subject of the divine attributes within the framework of Owen's teleology.[23] Owen's identification of the means to redemption's end as the priestly oblation and intercession of Christ indicates that for him, the relationship between Christ's priesthood and the divine attributes is a significant one. Unfortunately, this relationship is not developed

---

[21] Owen, *Vindicae Evangelicae*, II (*Works*, 12:93).

[22] Owen, *A Dissertation on Divine Justice* (*Works*, 10:481-624); idem, *Vindicae Evangelicae*, III-V (*Works*, 12:98-140).

[23] The same teleological concern is evident in Owen's view of the end of creation. Owen, *Christologia*, IV (1:61): "God made all things, in the beginning, good, exceeding good. The whole of his work was disposed into a perfect harmony, beauty, and order, suited unto that manifestation of his own glory which he designed therein. And as all things had their own individual existence, and operations suited unto their being, and capable of an end, a rest, or a blessedness, congruous unto their natures and operations—so, in the various respects which they had each to other, in their mutual supplies, assistances, and co-operation, they all tended unto that ultimate end—his eternal glory."

in any substantial way in *The Death of Death*.[24] A fuller appreciation of its precise nature will have to be obtained from the other treatises mentioned above.

In regard to *Christologia*, its importance lies in the redemptive-historical framework that Owen gave to the subject of the divine attributes. This redemptive-historical framework is compatible with and supplements Owen's teleological approach. In chapters XVI and XVII of the treatise, Owen attempted a lengthy exposition of the work of redemption.[25] His method of exposition follows the chronology of redemptive history in Scripture, highlighting in particular the events of creation, humanity's fall into sin, and its recovery from sin by the person and work of the incarnate Son. What is significant in Owen's narrative of redemptive history is the prominent role he gave to the divine attributes in his attempt to make clear the theological issues associated with each of these events. The basic redemptive-historical flow of Owen's narrative will be adopted in the following exposition, and supplemented with materials drawn from treatises other than *Christologia*. Particular attention will be paid to how the narrative throws light upon the relationship between the priesthood of Christ and the divine attributes.

The key attribute that Owen desired to adumbrate in his narrative of redemptive history is divine wisdom. Divine wisdom is, according to Owen, "the directive power or excellency of the divine nature" by which God "guides, disposes, orders, and directs all things unto his own glory, in and by their own proper ends."[26] This statement gave Owen's exposition a decidedly teleological orientation that is consistent with his statement of redemption's end in *The Death of Death*. However, the way to comprehend God's wisdom in his work *ad extra* is not to isolate the attribute of wisdom in the task of theological reflection, but to observe the connection it shares with other attributes in the context of God's external work. "We can have no view or due prospect of the wisdom of God in any of his works...unless we consider also the interest of the other holy properties of the divine nature in them."[27] This point is grounded on the understanding that the principal design of God's wisdom is the ordering of all things in such a way that God's glory will be manifested. Divine wisdom thus aims towards the display of God's attributes in his external works. This point is given further clarification in Owen's axiomatic statement of the relationship between the three relative attributes of God which were to be "principally considered in all the external works of God": goodness, wisdom, and power. Referring to wisdom's end of the glorification of divine power and goodness, Owen explained:

---

[24] See, for instance, his brief discussions on God's love and wrath. Owen, *Salus Electorum*, III.viii, ix (*Works*, 10:275-78, 283).
[25] Owen, *Christologia*, XVI-XVII (*Works*, 1:178-223).
[26] Owen, *Christologia*, XVI (*Works*, 1:180).
[27] Owen, *Christologia*, XVI (*Works*, 1:179).

And unto this end the effective property of the divine nature, which is almighty power, always accompanies, or is subservient unto, the directive or infinite wisdom, which is requisite unto perfection in operation. What infinite goodness will communicate *ad extra*—what it will open the eternal fountain of the Divine Being and all-sufficiency to give forth—that infinite wisdom designs, contrives, and directs to the glory of God; and what wisdom so designs, infinite power effects.[28]

Owen then introduced another task besides the necessity of considering the interplay of other divine attributes with divine wisdom. He insisted that it was also necessary to consider "*that state and condition of our own* wherein they are so concerned", that is, the state of humanity in sin.[29] This consideration steers Owen's exposition into his significant narrative of redemptive history where the following attributes of God were brought into prominence besides goodness, wisdom, and power: holiness, righteousness, love, grace, mercy, and justice.

According to Owen, God's creation of humanity in his own image and likeness is a work of divine goodness, wisdom, and power, a work undertaken with "consultation" among the persons of the Trinity.[30] Consistent with his trinitarian understanding of the *opera Dei*, Owen applied the principle of divine operations — that the triune God works externally according to his internal order of subsistence — to his consideration of the three relative attributes of God in the work of creation:

> In this great work, divine *goodness* exerted itself eminently and effectually in the person of the Father—the eternal fountain and spring, as of the divine nature, so of all divine operations. Divine *wisdom* acted itself peculiarly in the person of the Son; this being the principle notion thereof—the eternal Wisdom of the Father. Divine *power* wrought effectually in the person of the Holy Spirit; who is the immediate actor of all divine operations.[31]

For Owen, the Agent of creation is the triune God as is the case in the work of redemption. Owen identified three aspects to the design of the triune God in the communication of the *imago dei* to humanity. First, the image of God was given for the purpose of making "*a representation of his* [God's] *holiness and righteousness* among his creatures."[32] Second, it was communicated "that it might be a means of rendering actual glory unto him from all other parts of

---

[28] Owen, *Christologia*, XVI (*Works*, 1:179).
[29] Owen, *Christologia*, XVI (Works, 1:180).
[30] Owen, *Christologia*, XVI (*Works*, 1:181ff.). The term "consultation" is a reference to the content of Genesis 1:26, a verse that supports the doctrine of personal transactions in the Godhead in Owen's exegesis. Cf. idem, *Exposition of Hebrews*, Exercitations XXVII.1-8 (*Works*, 18:42-58).
[31] Owen, *Christologia*, XVI (*Works*, 1:182).
[32] Owen, *Christologia*, XVI (*Works*, 1:182).

creation."[33] Third, it was communicated "that it might be a means to bring man unto that *eternal enjoyment* of Himself, which he was fitted for and designed unto."[34] Humanity's enjoyment of God was to be obtained by way of a life of obedience to God, the obedience of which was the proper response of intellectual creatures to their Creator and Governor, made possible by the *imago dei*. These three aspects were, in Owen's view, "the principal ends of God in the creation of all things."[35] Clearly evident here is the teleological language of means and ends and their correspondence with the distinction of supreme and intermediate ends as proposed in *The Death of Death*. The first two aspects of God's design in creation connect directly with the supreme end of God's glory while the third relates to the intermediate end of humanity's enjoyment of God. The attribute that is directly concerned with the design of the *imago Dei* as the appropriate means for obtaining the stated ends is explicitly identified as divine wisdom.[36] Apart from the means-end terminology of Aristotle, Owen did not appeal to Aristotle's metaphysics nor did he allow his exposition to be governed by it. Rather, the material content of Aristotle's terminologies is controlled by the way Owen understood God's exercise of his attributes upon the work of creation against the backdrop of the history of redemption.

Owen gave special importance to the attributes of holiness and righteousness in his narrative of the work of creation. These attributes were closely tied to the active rendering of glory to God from his creatures. God's holiness is revealed in the law he gave to humanity.[37] The representation of God's holiness results from humanity's obedience to that law of which they were naturally obliged as intellectual creatures. God's righteousness is revealed in the promises of reward upon obedience, and the threatening of punishment upon disobedience to the law.[38] Apart from humanity's imaging of God's holiness and righteousness, creation's representation of God's glory pertained only to the display of divine goodness, wisdom, and power. Even then, creation's representation of God's glory was "but as a dead thing" that could only reveal God's glory "but passively and objectively."[39] Within the created order, only the nature of humanity was designed as the means by which glory might be actively rendered to God. If humanity was not created in God's image, there would be no

---

[33] Owen, *Christologia*, XVI (*Works*, 1:183).
[34] Owen, *Christologia*, XVI (*Works*, 1:183).
[35] Owen, *Christologia*, XVI (*Works*, 1:183).
[36] Owen, *Christologia*, XVI (*Works*, 1:182): "Three things God designed in this communication of his image unto our nature, which were his principle ends in the creation of all things here below; and therefore was divine wisdom more eminently exerted therein than in all the other works of his inferior creation."
[37] Owen, *Meditations and Discourses*, I.vi (*Works*, 1:339-40); idem, *The Doctrine of the Saints' Perseverance*, VII (*Works*, 11:295).
[38] Owen, *Exposition of Hebrews*, Exercitations IV.xxix.5 (*Works*, 18:101-102).
[39] Owen, *Christologia*, XVI (*Works*, 1:183).

knowledge of God's moral perfections among his creatures, no obedience to God's law, and therefore no representation of God's holiness and righteousness. Consequently, God's glory will not be manifested through his creatures. Thus, Owen understood the glory of God in creation to consist *principally* in the representation of divine holiness and righteousness: "Without them, he could not be known and glorified as God."[40]

Such an account of creation meant that humanity's apostasy, with the resultant rejection and defacement of God's image, had directly to do with the obscuring of God's attributes and thus of his glory. The "malignity and poison of this sin" was, for Owen, "the contempt that was cast on the *holiness of God*, whose *representations*, and all its *express characters*, were utterly despised and rejected thereunto."[41] Instead of trusting God and living a life of obedience to his moral demands, humanity voluntarily switched allegiance, thereby coming under the rule of Satan who sought to dishonour and impeach God's glory.[42] Indeed, as Owen opined: "No greater dishonour could be done unto him [God]—no endeavour could have been more pernicious in casting contempt on his counsel. For as his holiness which was represented in that image, was despoiled, so we did what lay in us to defeat the contrivance of his wisdom."[43]

Since humanity's fall into sin had especially to do with the despising of God's holiness and righteousness, recovery from sin would therefore require the reparation of God's honour and the restoration of his glory with special regard to these attributes. In relation to the attribute of holiness, that reparation consists in providing for the honour and glory of God's holiness "an exaltation answerable unto the attempt for its debasement."[44] Humanity's recovery would not be consistent with the glory of God unless the divine holiness that is represented in that recovery "be more exalted, be more conspicuously represented in the same nature, than ever it was depressed or despised thereby."[45] For such a reparation and recovery to happen, divine wisdom designed that a perfect obedience to God's law would need to be performed in the nature that sinned, and performed by one who is above the law, whose obedience is voluntary, unlike the obligatory obedience of intellectual creatures.[46] With respect to the attribute of righteousness, reparation and recovery involved the restoration of God's honour and glory in his rule and government of the world.[47] In the light of sin's entrance and the resulting disorder in the world, this recovery could not be done without the infliction of a punishment that is proportionate to the demerit of sin incurred. God's

---

[40] Owen, *Christologia*, XVI (*Works*, 1:182).
[41] Owen, *Christologia*, XVI (*Works*, 1:184).
[42] Owen, *Christologia*, XVI (*Works*, 1:187).
[43] Owen, *Christologia*, XVI (*Works*, 1:183).
[44] Owen, *Christologia*, XVI (*Works*, 1:185).
[45] Owen, *Christologia*, XVI (*Works*, 1:185).
[46] Owen, *Christologia*, XVI (*Works*, 1:197-201).
[47] Owen, *Christologia*, XVI (*Works*, 1:196).

righteousness, "as it is the rectorial virtue and power of the divine nature, required that his glory should be restored, by reducing the sinning creature again into order by punishment."[48] Thus, reparation of the glory of God's holiness and righteousness involves both sin's punishment and perfect obedience to the law that humanity transgressed.

In *A Dissertation on Divine Justice*, these two divine requirements of obedience and sin's punishment are considered in relation to the attribute of divine justice. According to Owen's taxonomy of divine justice, they fall under the respective categories of God's "justice of government" and "justice of judgment."[49] The first category refers to *"that perfection of the Divine Being whereby he directs all his actions in governing and administering created things, according to the rectitude of his rule and wisdom."*[50] The obedience that humanity owes to God arises from his moral dependence upon God as a rational creature in accordance with the divine law that governs the Creator-creature relation. Obedience to God is thus the natural obligation of humanity. Since God is the Creator and Governor of the universe, the demand for obedience from humanity is God's natural right. In this way, divine justice and humanity's obedience are tied. The second category refers to God's vindicatory or sin-punishing justice. God's justice of judgement is that divine perfection "by which God punishes the crimes of rational beings, to whom a law hath been given, according to the rule of his right."[51] For Owen, God's justice of government and judgement are not two types of divine justice, but the effects of God's perfection of justice in the created world.

Owen's conception of obedience and sin's punishment in the light of divine justice is apparent in *Christologia*. While his nuanced taxonomy of justice was not reiterated in the treatise, nevertheless, Owen made it clear that the glory of God's justice was at stake in the work of redemption. As the narrative unfolded, the two requirements of obedience and sin's punishment were presented in terms of obedience and the satisfaction of God's justice: "man must make *satisfaction* to the justice of God, and thereby a reparation of his glory, that he may be saved. This, added unto a complete return unto obedience, would effect a restitution of all things."[52] Owen's anti-Pelagian stance on sin led him to deny to fallen humanity the possibility of such a return to obedience and restitution of God's glory by satisfaction. The demerit of sin incurred is infinite because it was committed against God who is infinite in his majesty.[53] Thus, sinful humanity "could not" through impotence, and "would not" in obstinacy, return

---

[48] Owen, *Christologia*, XVI (*Works*, 1:186).
[49] Owen, *A Dissertation on Divine Justice*, I.ii (*Works*, 10:504-505); idem, *Exposition of Hebrews*, Exercitations IV.xxix.6 (*Works*, 18:102).
[50] Owen, *A Dissertation on Divine Justice*, I.ii (*Works*, 10:504).
[51] Owen, *A Dissertation on Divine Justice*, I.ii (*Works*, 10:504-505).
[52] Owen, *Christologia*, XVI (*Works*, 1:194).
[53] Owen, *Christologia*, XVI (*Works*, 1:203-204).

to a state of obedience; "as that return was impossible unto man, so was this satisfaction of the injury done by sin much more."[54] Indeed, "it was just, equal, righteous with God...that mankind should perish eternally in that condition whereinto it was cast by sin."[55] The heinousness of humanity's apostasy was such that "God thereon might righteously, and suitably unto all the holy properties of his nature, leave mankind to perish eternally in that condition whereunto they had cast themselves."[56]

Despite the sinfulness of humanity and its eternal consequences, God acted to redeem a portion of the human race from eternal destruction and to restore the glory of his attributes. Owen's theological grounds for the reparation of God's glory lay in the issue of "condecency" or fittingness to the divine perfections in the work of redemption. There was a fittingness to the goodness and wisdom of God that a portion of the human race be saved.[57] This "condecency" is seen, for instance, in the manifestation of the attributes of love, grace, and mercy in the work of redemption, attributes which were not manifested in the work of creation. "With these it was that the reparation of our nature was compliant—unto them [love, grace, and mercy] it had a condecency; and the glory of them infinite wisdom designed therein."[58] There was also a fittingness to divine goodness in the work of redemption as to the *extent* of its exercise. Being the "communicative property of the divine nature", it was fitting that the perfection of goodness be exercised to its full extent in terms of its effects.[59] However, in the work of creation, "it had not done so perfectly—it had not done so to the uttermost...there yet remained another effect of it; which was, that *God should be made man*, as the way unto, and the means of, our recovery."[60]

The turning point in Owen's narrative is the introduction of the incarnate Son into the history of redemption. While humanity is still in a state of sin,

> *infinite Wisdom* interpose itself, in that glorious, ineffable contrivance of the person of Christ—or of the divine nature in the eternal Son of God and of ours in the same individual person. Otherwise this work could not be accomplished;—at least all other ways are hidden from the eyes of all living, no created

---

[54] Owen, *Christologia*, XVI (*Works*, 1:192-93, 194).
[55] Owen, *Christologia*, XVI (*Works*, 1:185).
[56] Owen, *Christologia*, XVI (*Works*, 1:190).
[57] Owen, *Christologia*, XVI (*Works*, 1:188-92). This is not tantamount to saying that the salvation of humanity is a necessary act of God's will. Owen understood the salvation of humanity to be a free act of God's will and the effects of sovereign grace and mercy. See *Works*, 1:190.
[58] Owen, *Christologia*, XVI (*Works*, 1:191).
[59] Owen, *Christologia*, XVI (*Works*, 1:191).
[60] Owen, *Christologia*, XVI (*Works*, 1:191).

understanding being able to apprehend any other way whereby it might so have been, unto the eternal glory of God.[61]

In the wisdom of God, the Son, not the Father or the Spirit, was appointed to be the Mediator between God and humanity. Owen observed that it was fitting to divine wisdom that this be so and gave three reasons. First, in view of the loss of God's image by sin, it was fitting to divine wisdom that the work of redemption be undertaken by the Son, the "essential image of God."[62] Second, it was fitting that the loss of humanity's title of *sonship* be recovered by the eternal *Son* by adoption.[63] Third, it was fitting to divine wisdom for the Son to undertake the work of redemption on account of the principle of divine operations. Redemption is a work that originates in the authority, love, and power of the Father. "The Son," Owen reasoned, "who is the second person in the order of *subsistence*, in the order of *operation* puts the whole authority, love, and power of the Father in execution."[64]

Thus, the incarnate Son fulfilled all that was necessary for the recovery of humanity from sin and for the reparation of God's glory.[65] He obeyed the laws of God perfectly and so expressed the glory of God's holiness. Although sinless, he paid the penalty incurred by the sin of humanity and thus satisfied divine justice and expressed the glory of God's righteousness. The infinite dignity of his person as the God-man gave infinite worth to his work as Mediator, thus rendering more glory to God by his obedience than the dishonour brought about by humanity's disobedience.

The Necessity of Christ's Priesthood

How then does Christ's priesthood feature in Owen's narrative? The special prominence that Owen gave to the attributes of holiness and righteousness, along with their corresponding expressions in the demand for obedience and sin's punishment, point to the vital importance that the satisfaction of divine justice has for the reparation of God's glory. From the standpoint of Christ's mediatorial office, satisfaction of divine justice belongs to the priestly work of Christ, not his prophetic or kingly work. There is, therefore, a necessity for Christ's priesthood if the supreme end of redemption is to be obtained. This relationship between divine justice and the necessity of Christ's priestly work is enunciated more substantially in *A Dissertation on Divine Justice* and *Exercitations Concerning the Priesthood of Christ*.

In the former treatise, Owen argued against the position of certain prominent proponents on the subject of the necessity of sin's satisfaction. These

---

[61] Owen, *Christologia*, XVI (*Works*, 1:205).
[62] Owen, *Christologia*, XVII (*Works*, 1:218-19).
[63] Owen, *Christologia*, XVII (*Works*, 1:219).
[64] Owen, *Christologia*, XVII (*Works*, 1:219).
[65] Owen, *Christologia*, XVII (*Works*, 1:206-23); cf. idem, *Meditations and Discourses*, I.vi (*Works*, 1:338-42).

proponents include Socinus and his followers, as well as leading Reformed orthodox figures such as William Twisse (1577/8-1646) and Samuel Rutherford (c. 1600-1661).[66] Common to them is the view that God could, by an act of his will, pardon sins without exacting punishment. There was, in other words, no absolute necessity for sin's satisfaction. This is a view that Owen embraced early in his theological career, notably in *The Death of Death*. Against the Arminian argument that God could not show mercy without the satisfaction of Christ, Owen insisted that such a view is "an unwritten tradition, the Scripture affirming no such thing, neither can it be gathered from thence in any good consequence."[67] Owen's early position had a distinguished pedigree that boasted of eminent adherents like Aquinas and major Reformed theologians such as Calvin, Twisse, and Rutherford.[68] However, in the light of Socinianism, Owen changed his mind by the early 1650s and gave a robust defence of his new position in *A Dissertation on Divine Justice* (1653).[69] In this treatise, Owen defended two basic theses. First, he contended that vindicatory or sin-punishing justice is essential to God.[70] Second, that on the supposition of sin, it is necessary that God punishes sin.[71] Both theses are argued in detail in Part I of the treatise and brought to bear upon the views of a selected number of Owen's opponents in Part II. Only the arguments that are of immediate relevance to the issue at hand will be examined below.

In defence of the first thesis, Owen put forward four types of arguments: arguments from Scripture, the general consent of mankind, providence, and Christology. Owen's Christological argument is concerned with "the revelation

---

[66] Twisse was the prolocutor of the Westminster Assembly and Rutherford one of its leading Scottish commissioners. *ODNB*, E.C. Vernon, "Twisse, William (1577/8-1646)"; *ONDB*, John Coffey, "Rutherford, Samuel (c. 1600-1661)"; Reid, *Memoirs of the Westminster Divines*, 37-67, 345-62.

[67] Owen, *Salus Electorum*, II.ii (*Works*, 10:205).

[68] Trueman, "John Owen's *Dissertation on Divine Justice*", 88n3, 90. The historical backdrop to the issue went back to debates among medieval scholastics over the question of the priority of the divine will over the intellect or vice versa, and the scholastic notion of God's *potentia absoluta* and *potentia ordinata*. Cf. Muller, *PRRD*, 3:517-40; Trueman, *Claims of Truth*, 105-11.

[69] Owen, *A Dissertation on Divine Justice*, I.ii (*Works*, 10:508): "But this I cannot forbear to mention, that those very divines who oppose our opinion, when hard pushed by their adversaries, perpetually have recourse in their disputations to this justice as to their sacred anchor, and assert that without satisfaction God could not pardon sin consistently with his nature, justice and truth. But as these are very great absurdities, it would have seemed strange to me that any men of judgment and orthodoxy should have been so entangled in some of these sophisms as to renounce the truth on their account, *unless I had happened at one time myself to fall into the same snare; which, to the praise and glory of that truth, of which I am now a servant, I freely confess to have been my case.*" Emphasis added. Cf. Trueman, "John Owen's *Dissertation on Divine Justice*", 87-103.

[70] Owen, *A Dissertation on Divine Justice*, I.iii-v (*Work*, 10:512-49).

[71] Owen, *A Dissertation on Divine Justice*, I.vi-vii (*Works*, 10:549-60).

of that *name*, glory, and nature, which God hath exhibited to us in and through Christ."[72] According to Owen, apart from Christ, sinful humanity will have no knowledge of certain divine attributes such as God's love to his people, his sparing mercy, and his free and saving grace. Even the traces of God's power, wisdom, goodness, justice, and long-suffering, all of which were represented in the works of creation, legislation, and providence, could not be known in a perspicuous and saving manner apart from Christ. More specifically, Owen averred that in the appointment of the Son to be Mediator and in the accomplishment of his mediatorial work, the attribute that was most clearly displayed is God's vindicatory justice: "in the whole matter of salvation by the Mediator, God-man, there is no excellence of God, no essential property, no attribute of his nature, the glory of which is the chief end of all his works, that he hath more clearly and eminently displayed than this punitory justice."[73] Christ's propitiatory and substitutionary sacrifice demonstrates to sinful humanity that sin-punishing justice is essential to God. If the essential nature of vindicatory justice is not maintained, even the love of God will be greatly obscured, for "what kind of love can that be which God hath shown, in doing what there was no occasion for him to do?"[74]

Owen's second thesis addressed the issue of the necessity of sin's punishment. It was also supported by four arguments. The first concerns God's hatred of sin, and the second the Scriptural description of God as a "consuming fire."[75] In Owen's third argument, he contended that the necessity of sin's punishment is founded upon the absolute necessity to preserve the glory of God. His argument was presented in the form of a syllogism: "It is absolutely necessary that God should preserve his glory entire to all eternity; but sin being supposed, without the infliction of the punishment due to it he cannot preserve his glory free from violation: therefore, it is necessary that he should punish it."[76] This argument underpinned his fourth, in which Owen adopted a negative mode of argumentation where the aim is to show up the weakness of the opponent's position. If the non-necessity of sin's punishment was granted, Owen asserted, "it will be difficult, if not impossible, to assign any sufficient

---

[72] Owen, *A Dissertation on Divine Justice*, I.v (*Works*, 10:546-47).

[73] Owen, *A Dissertation on Divine Justice*, I.v (*Works*, 10:547).

[74] Owen, *A Dissertation on Divine Justice*, I.v (*Works*, 10:548).

[75] Owen, *A Dissertation on Divine Justice*, I.vi (*Works*, 10:549-54).

[76] Owen, *A Dissertation on Divine Justice*, I.vii (*Works*, 10:554-55); cf. idem, *Exposition of Hebrews*, Exercitations IV.xxx.5 (*Works*, 18:135): "It is necessary that God should do every thing that is requisite unto his own glory. This is the perfection of his nature and existence doth require. So he doth all things for himself. It is necessary, therefore, that nothing fall out in the universe which should absolutely impeach the glory of God, or contradict his design of its manifestation. Now, suppose that God would and should let sin go unpunished, where would be the glory of his righteousness as he is the supreme ruler over all?"

and necessary *cause* of the death of Christ."[77] This critique is an important one. It calls into question the adequacy of the opposing position in light of the actual severity of Christ's sufferings and the gravity of its meaning. For Owen, the necessity of satisfaction is not to be understood in abstraction from the actual historical sufferings of Christ. This is apparent in his pointed response to his opponents. If God could readily pardon sins by an act of his will, "what sufficient reason could be given, pray, then, why he should lay those sins, so easily remissible, to the charge of his most holy Son, and on their account subject him to such dreadful sufferings?"[78] God, he answered, "had appointed, from the beginning his only-begotten Son, for the declaration and satisfaction of his justice, and the recovery of his glory, to open the way to heaven, otherwise shut, and to remain shut forever."[79]

Resident in the above analysis is an unmistakable connection between Christ's priesthood and the essential nature of God's vindicatory justice. This connection is evident in Owen's arguments that the propitiatory sacrifice of Christ reveals the just nature of God and that the severe sufferings of Christ argue the necessity of sin's satisfaction. When these arguments are weighed together with Owen's point that God has appointed his Son for the satisfaction of his own essential justice, the question that is begging is the precise nature of that connection between Christ's priesthood and God's justice. What Owen had established in *A Dissertation on Divine Justice* is the necessity of the satisfaction of divine justice, but in the course of his defence, he had simply assumed the necessity of Christ's priesthood for obtaining that satisfaction. In *Exercitations Concerning the Priesthood of Christ*, however, he went to some lengths in explicitly arguing the necessity of Christ's priesthood.[80]

Owen made several points which are important in this regard. First, he tied the *pactum salutis* to the manifestation of God's attributes teleologically, and in so doing, worked Christ's priesthood into the equation.[81] According to Owen, the "matter of this covenant, or the things and ends about which and for which it was entered into" is in general, "the saving of sinners, in and by ways and means suited unto the manifestation of God's glory."[82] It has already been demonstrated in Chapter 2 that Owen grounds the priesthood of Christ in the *pactum salutis*. Thus, when Owen identified the end of the eternal *pactum* as the manifestation of God's glory, he also acknowledged that Christ's priesthood is the means for obtaining that end. In this context, the attribute that "gave as it

---

[77] Owen, *A Dissertation on Divine Justice*, I.vii (*Works*, 10:556).
[78] Owen, *A Dissertation on Divine Justice*, I.vii (*Works*, 10:556); idem, *Exposition of Hebrews*, Exercitations IV.xxx.7 (*Works*, 18:137-38).
[79] Owen, *A Dissertation on Divine Justice*, I.vii (*Works*, 10:558).
[80] Especially telling is the fact that *Exercitations XXIX* and *XXX* were entitled, "The necessity of the priesthood of Christ on the supposition of sin and grace." Owen, *Exposition of Hebrews*, Exercitations IV.xxix-xxx (*Works*, 18:97-138).
[81] Owen, *Exposition of Hebrews*, Exercitations IV.xxviii.15-16 (*Works*, 18:89-91).
[82] Owen, *Exposition of Hebrews*, Exercitations IV.xxviii.15 (*Works*, 18:89).

were the *especial determination*" to Christ's priesthood as the means for manifesting God's glory is divine justice:

> for upon a supposition that God would pardon and save sinners, it was his eternal justice which required that it should be brought about by the sufferings of the Son, and it was itself expressed and exercised in those sufferings... Rom iii.25, 26, viii.3; Gal iii.13; 2 Cor v.21.[83]

The prominence given to divine justice here is not to the exclusion of other attributes in Owen's considerations. Owen held to the oneness of the attributes in God's essence such that the exercise of any one attribute would entail the glorification of all the rest.[84] This, however, is Owen's view of the divine attributes considered *ad intra*. When the attributes are considered *ad extra*, he observed that certain attributes are displayed more eminently and immediately than the rest with respect to certain external works of God:

> in several particular works of God, his design is firstly, immediately, and directly to exercise in a peculiarly eminent manner, and therein to advance and glorify, one or more of his glorious properties, and the rest consequentially in and by them. So in some of his works he doth peculiarly glorify justice, in some mercy, in some his power.[85]

Divine wisdom, justice, and grace were identified by Owen as the attributes which are peculiarly displayed in the execution of the *pactum salutis*.[86] Thus, a range of divine attributes is tied to Owen's discussion of the historical outworking of the eternal *pactum*, but it is the priestly work of Christ expressed in the sufferings of the Son that displayed God's justice in a "peculiarly eminent manner", to employ Owen's parlance.

Second, Owen understood the nature of this relation between Christ's priesthood and divine justice to be one of necessity.[87] For him, the necessity of Christ's priesthood arises from the necessity of sin's punishment, which in turn is rooted in the essential nature of God's vindicatory justice. The necessity of sin's punishment is not to be considered abstractly in itself, but is a state of affairs that is predicated upon several things: God's creation of all things; the creation of rational creatures who are morally dependent on God and are capable of responding in obedience; God's giving of the law to these rational creatures; God's natural right of governance over these creatures according to his law; the sin of these creatures.[88] On the supposition of these things, Owen argued that sin's punishment according to God's justice is necessary. Likewise

---

[83] Owen, *Exposition of Hebrews*, Exercitations IV.xxviii.16 (*Works*, 18:91).
[84] Owen, *Exposition of Hebrews*, Exercitations IV.xxviii.16 (*Works*, 18:90).
[85] Owen, *Exposition of Hebrews*, Exercitations IV.xxviii.16 (*Works*, 18:90-91).
[86] Owen, *Exposition of Hebrews*, Exercitations IV.xxviii.16 (*Works*, 18:91).
[87] Owen, *Exposition of Hebrews*, Exercitations IV.xxviii.1-23 (*Works*, 18:98-124).
[88] Owen, *Exposition of Hebrews*, Exercitations IV.xxviii.7 (*Works*, 18:102-103).

for Owen, the necessity of Christ's priesthood is one that obtains upon the supposition of certain things: "The priesthood of the Son of God was necessary, not absolutely and in itself, but on the supposition of the law and entrance of sin, with the grace of God to save sinners."[89]

In emphasizing the necessity of Christ's priesthood, Owen was careful not to deny the freedom of God. As a free agent, God acts freely in all his works. Owen acknowledged that God's freedom "is a necessary mode of all divine actings *ad extra*; for God does all things according to the counsel of his own will, and his will is the original of all freedom."[90] God acting to save sinners through his Son is a free act of his will so that salvation flows out of God's sovereign grace. However, on the supposition that it is necessary that sin be punished, and that God would save sinners by his Son and glorify himself, it is necessary that the Son deals with sin as a priest, bearing the punishment that sin deserves as an atoning sacrifice offered to God:

> On the grounds insisted on, argued and proved it is, that on the supposition before also laid down and explained, — namely, that God would glorify himself and his grace in the recovery and salvation of sinners, which proceeded alone from the free counsel of his will, — it was, with respect unto the holiness and righteousness of God, absolutely necessary that the Son of God, in his interposition for them, should be a priest, and offer himself for a sacrifice; seeing therein and thereby he could and did undergo the punishment which, in the judgment of God, was due unto the sins of them that were to be saved by him.[91]

Thus, for Owen, the necessity of Christ's priesthood is a *necessitas ex suppositione*, also coined by the Reformed orthodox as *necessitas consequentiae* or *necessitas ex hypothesi*.[92] God necessarily saves humanity through Christ's priesthood not from a necessity of nature, such as the Father's begetting of the Son and the procession of the Spirit, but from a necessity arising from certain supposed conditions which does not deny to God a "concomitant liberty."[93]

---

[89] Owen, *Exposition of Hebrews*, Exercitations IV.xxix.1 (*Works*, 18:98).
[90] Owen, *Exposition of Hebrews*, Exercitations IV.xxix.9 (*Works*, 18:106).
[91] Owen, *Exposition of Hebrews*, Exercitations IV.xxx.6 (*Works*, 18:136).
[92] Muller, *DLGTT*, 200; cf. Van Asselt, *The Federal Theology of Johannes Cocceius*, 207-208.
[93] Owen, *Exposition of Hebrews*, Exercitations IV.xxix.9 (*Works*, 18:105-106); Cf. idem, *A Dissertation on Divine Justice*, II.xiii (*Works*, 10:589): "There is also a necessity arising from a supposed condition, and which deprives not the agent of a concomitant liberty. God could not but create the world; but God did not create the world from an absolute necessity, although it was necessary upon a supposition that it should be created. It is necessary that God should speak truly, but he doth not speak from an absolute necessity; but it being supposed that he wills to speak, it is impossible that he should not speak truly."

Third, in addition to and support of the previous point, Owen observed that besides the demand of divine justice, the necessity of Christ's priesthood also arises from the requirement of voluntary obedience for sin's satisfaction that only the incarnate Son is able to perform. For Owen, the obedience of Christ with respect to sin's satisfaction is the obedience of Christ's entire life in his state of humiliation. This has already been demonstrated at length in Chapter 5. Within the larger compass of God's work of redemption in *Christologia*, Owen understood the obedience of Christ in his state of humiliation as part of God's design to manifest his glory in a way that exceeds the representation of his glory by the obedience of un-fallen humanity and the angelic host:

> God would glorify a state of obedience…He would render it incomparably more amiable, desirable, and excellent, than ever it could have appeared to have been in the obedience of all the angels in heaven and men on earth, had they continued therein. This he did in this way of our recovery,—in that his own eternal Son entered into a state of obedience, and took upon him the 'form' or condition 'of a servant' unto God.[94]

Owen's allusion to Philippians 2:7 makes it clear that by "state of obedience", he was referring to the obedience of Christ in his state of humiliation.[95] In *Exercitation XXIX*, the obedience of Christ for humanity's recovery was conceived as an expression of Christ's priestly work. Sin's satisfaction, Owen argued, could not be done "by mere suffering or enduring punishment, which is a thing in its own nature indifferent", but "the will and obedience of Christ in the manner of undergoing it was also required."[96] It is this requirement of voluntary obedience for sinful humanity's recovery that "made his priesthood necessary, whereby whilst he underwent the punishment due unto our sins, *he offered himself an acceptable sacrifice* for their expiation."[97] Here, Christ's voluntary obedience is a function of his self-offering or priestly oblation. The obvious connection in Owen's mind between Christ's priestly office and his state of obedience is evidence of the integration between Christ's oblation and his state of humiliation found in his formulation of the priesthood of Christ.

---

[94] Owen, *Christologia*, XVII (*Works*, 1:212).

[95] Cf. the following catechetical entry where Christ's obedience is an essential part of his state of humiliation. Owen, *Two Short Catechisms*, GC, IV.Q.2 (*Works*, 1:484): "*Wherein consisteth the state of Christ's humiliation?* A. In three things; first, in his incarnation, or being born of woman; secondly, his obedience, or fulfilling the whole law, moral and ceremonial; thirdly, in his passion, or enduring all sorts of miseries, even death itself."

[96] Owen, *Exposition of Hebrews*, Exercitations IV.xxix.8 (*Works*, 18:104).

[97] Owen, *Exposition of Hebrews*, Exercitations IV.xxix.8 (*Works*, 18:104).

The Intermediate End of Redemption: the Saints' Perseverance and Salvation

Earlier, reference was made to Owen's conception of the intermediate end of redemption as the *"bringing of us unto God"*,[98] or according to the Latin title of *The Death of Death, salus electorum*. Chapters 2 to 5 can be seen as an extended commentary on this phrase from the standpoint of what God does for his elect people. The Father enters into covenant with his Son by the Spirit in the *pactum salutis* to save a portion of sinful humanity (Chapter 2); the Son becomes incarnate and performs the work of mediation as the *theanthropos* (Chapter 3); the incarnate Son fulfils his priestly office by offering himself as a sacrifice for sin to God in his active and passive obedience on behalf of the elect, thus obtaining satisfaction for sin (Chapters 4 and 5). This section continues the same line of thought but looks at redemption's intermediate end through the lens of what God does in relation to the believer's perseverance in the faith. Specifically, it examines Owen's understanding of the believer's perseverance as a spiritual blessing that is procured by Christ's oblation and applied to believers by virtue of Christ's intercession.

During Owen's career as Vice-Chancellor of Oxford University, he produced a substantial treatise on the believer's perseverance entitled *The Doctrine of the Saints' Perseverance* (1654).[99] It was written in response to the treatise of John Goodwin (*c.* 1594-1665), *Redemption Redeemed* (1651), which had argued that those for whom Christ died included those who will ultimately perish even though they could have been in a state of grace for a period of time.[100] Goodwin's universalist position on the atonement had obvious implications for his understanding of the believer's perseverance. According to

---

[98] Owen, *Salus Electorum*, II.i (*Works*, 10:202).
[99] *Works*, 11:1-666.
[100] John Goodwin, *Apolytrosis Apolytroseos, or, Redemption Redeemed. Wherein the Most Glorious Work of the Redemption of the World by Jesus Christ, Is by Expressness of Scripture, Clearness of Argument, Countenance of the Best Authority, as Well Ancient as Modern, Vindicated and Asserted in the Just Latitude and Extent of It, According to the Counsel and Most Gracious Intentions of God, against the Incroachments of Later Times Made Upon It, Whereby the Unsearcheable Riches and Glory of the Grace of God Therein, Have Been, and yet Are, Much Obscured, and Hid from the Eyes of Many.* (London: Printed by John Macock, for Lodowick Lloyd and Henry Cripps, 1651). Goodwin was an Independent minister who taught universal redemption. *ODNB*, Tai Liu, "Goodwin, John (*c.* 1594-1665)." For the wider context of seventeenth-century English debates on the doctrine of perseverance, see Richard Baxter, *Richard Baxter's Account of His Present Thoughts Concerning the Controversies About the Perseverance of the Saints. Occasioned by the Gross Misreports of Some Passages in His Book, Called, the Right Method for Peace of Conscience, &C; Which Are Left out in the Last Impression to Avoid Offence, and This Here Substituted, for the Fuller Explication of the Same Points* (London: Printed for Tho. Underhill, 1658). Baxter lists twelve different positions on the doctrine before giving his own assessment of them in which his own nuanced position is revealed, thus making it the thirteenth position.

Goodwin, some for whom Christ died will not persevere to the end while others would. In teleological terms, the intermediate end of Christ's death is not to actually "bring us to God" but to merely obtain the potential for that end. Owen's treatise on perseverance was written in response to Goodwin's denial of the believer's perseverance. Like Augustine, Owen held to the gratuitous nature of the saints' perseverance, allowed for the possibility that believers may partially lapse into sin, but denied the ultimate victory of sin over the believer.[101] Due to the significant bearing that Christ's atonement has upon the subject, Owen's treatment of perseverance included lengthy discussions on the influence of Christ's priesthood upon the believer's perseverance. It is with these discussions that the following exposition of Owen's thought is concerned.

Owen had a very specific understanding of perseverance. "That which we intend when we mention 'the perseverance of the saints,' is their continuance to the end in the condition of saint-ship whereunto they are called."[102] Two aspects of saint-ship were identified as the elements that constitute the condition in which believers persevere: first, "That holiness which they receive from God", or "real holiness", and second, "That favour which they have with God, being justified freely by his grace, through the blood of Christ", or "gracious acceptation."[103] The latter aspect is "purely *extrinsical*", while the former is "*within* us, and that is our sanctification, our portion from God by the Spirit of holiness, and the fruits thereof, in our faith, love and obedience unto him."[104]

Isaiah 4:1-6 provided the exegetical anchor for laying out Owen's understanding of the heart and branches of the doctrine of perseverance, albeit not the only textual support for it.[105] It is a passage that recounts the gracious promises of God to Israel in the light of her painful experience of exile. At the heart of this passage is the messianic promise concerning the "Branch of the LORD" (v.2) and the "Fruit of the earth" (v.2) that will be given to the remnant of Israel, both of which were identified by Owen as referring to the Lord Jesus Christ.[106] Owen pointed out that the promises of justification (v.2), sanctification (vv.3-4), and perseverance (vv.5-6) were given to the remnant on account of Christ. The significant phrase for Owen is found at the close of verse 5: "upon all the glory shall be a defence." For him, the content of this phrase is

---

[101] Henry M. Knapp, "Augustine and John Owen on Perseverance", *WTJ* 62 (2000), 65-87.
[102] Owen, *The Doctrine of the Saints' Perseverance*, I (*Works*, 11:99).
[103] Owen, *The Doctrine of the Saints' Perseverance*, I (*Works*, 11:99).
[104] Owen, *The Doctrine of the Saints' Perseverance*, I (*Works*, 11:117).
[105] Another significant text, for instance, is Hebrews 6:4-6. See Owen, *Exposition of Hebrews*, Heb. 6:4-7, in loc. (*Works*, 21:66-91); idem, *On the Nature and Causes of Apostasy*, I (*Works*, 7:11-51). cf. Henry M. Knapp, "John Owen's Interpretation of Hebrews 6:4-6: Eternal Perseverance of the Saints in Puritan Exegesis", *SCJ* 34, no. 1 (2003), 29-52.
[106] Owen, *The Doctrine of the Saints' Perseverance*, I (*Works*, 11:114).

"a suitable bottom" to his whole treatise on the doctrine of perseverance. It comprises "the whole of my aim, with the way or method wherein it may conveniently be delivered..."[107] Owen understood "glory" typologically as referring to Christ, and "defence" as either the protection of God's remnant people by "the refreshment that the Lord Christ, the great bride-groom, gives to his bride in his banqueting-house", alluding to Canticles 2:4, or rather, as he preferred, to the protection of the "spiritual glories" of that remnant people.[108] These "spiritual glories" entail the intrinsic and extrinsic aspects of saint-ship referred to above. By an act of divine power in "defence" of these "spiritual glories", God safeguards the internal spiritual glory of believers in Christ (sanctification) and their external spiritual glory (justification). Thus, Owen saw in Isaiah 4 a key exegetical support that summed up the doctrine of the saints' perseverance.

Owen's theological grounds for the doctrine may be divided into two sets of arguments that reflect his understanding of the relationship between eternity and time: arguments that ground the doctrine in eternity and those that ground it in history. For the former, the believer's perseverance is rooted in the immutability of the divine nature, eternal decrees, and eternal purposes.[109] For the latter, it is grounded in the covenant of grace, the Gospel promises, God's oath, the mediation of Christ, and the indwelling of the Holy Spirit in believers with their consequent union with Christ.[110] Both sets of arguments are intimately related and reflect Owen's trinitarian frame of thought. What the triune God does in history are expressions and accomplishments of his eternal determinations according to his nature. The covenant of grace, for instance, is stable because God himself who is immutable, "who is faithful, who cannot lie, who cannot deceive, who will make all his covenant engagements good to the most", is the one who fulfils that covenant in Christ.[111] The Gospel promises given in time, upon which the covenant of grace is established, are likewise immutable and certain because God is immutable and faithful.[112] For Owen, time is not swallowed up by eternity into a cipher but is the context in which God's eternal decisions are worked out in accordance with the perfections of the divine nature. Owen argued the impossibility of the believer's final fall from a state of grace upon the supposition of these two sets of theological grounds.

---

[107] Owen, *The Doctrine of the Saints' Perseverance*, I (*Works*, 11:116).
[108] Owen, *The Doctrine of the Saints' Perseverance*, I (*Works*, 11:117).
[109] Owen, *The Doctrine of the Saints' Perseverance*, II-III (*Works*, 11:120-204).
[110] Owen, *The Doctrine of the Saints' Perseverance*, IV-VI, VII-IX (*Works*, 11:204-88, 288-379). "God's oath" and "union with Christ" were absent in the chapter on perseverance in the *Westminster Confession* but were inserted into the *Savoy Declaration*. This is a clear indication of their importance for Owen and reflects his influence at Savoy. Cf. *Westminster Confession*, XVII.2; *Savoy Declaration*, XVII.2.
[111] Owen, *The Doctrine of the Saints' Perseverance*, IV (*Works*, 11:210).
[112] Owen, *The Doctrine of the Saints' Perseverance*, V (*Works*, 11:231).

From the vantage point of the historical economy, Owen saw the mediation of Christ as the decisive event that procured the believer's perseverance. The distinguishing character of the covenant of grace in contradistinction to the covenant of works is the certainty of its fulfilment in and by Christ, the Surety and Mediator of his elect people.[113] The Gospel promises are "made *through Christ*, as the only *medium* of their accomplishment, and the only *procuring cause* of the good things that...are inwrapped and tendered in them, 2 Cor. i. 20."[114] Even for the subject of God's oath, which Owen had intended to discuss but eventually did not, Christ's suretyship was at the heart of his intended exposition.[115] Thus, the mediation of Christ is of decisive significance for securing the perseverance of the saints.

What is soteriologically significant in Owen's considerations of the influence of Christ's mediation upon the believer's perseverance is the centrality of Christ's priesthood. In the introductory chapter to his treatise, Owen averred that the certainty and assurance of the saints' perseverance "is not *mentis* but *entis*, not subjective but objective, not always in the person persevering, but always relating to the thing itself."[116] Owen's objective, soteriological ground for the certainty and assurance of perseverance was argued not on the basis of the *munus triplex*, but specifically on the basis of Christ's priesthood. The title of his treatise indicates unequivocally that the priesthood of Christ in his acts of oblation and intercession is the key christo-soteriological ground from which the doctrine of the saints' perseverance is "manifested and proved."[117] This attention to Christ's priesthood reflects the general sacerdotal cast of the Reformed ecclesiological statements on the doctrine of perseverance.[118] The Synod of Dort affirmed "God's free mercy" to be the cause of perseverance and denied the possibility that "the merit, intercession and preservation of Christ be rendered ineffectual..."[119] The Westminster divines and the Independents at the Savoy Conference described the christo-soteriological ground of perseverance as "the efficacy of the merit

---

[113] Owen, *The Doctrine of the Saints' Perseverance*, IV (*Works*, 11:208, 210-11).

[114] Owen, *The Doctrine of the Saints' Perseverance*, I (*Works*, 11:230).

[115] See Owen, *The Doctrine of the Saints' Perseverance*, VII (*Works*, 11:289). It was Owen's intention to leave the treatment of God's oath till the end of the treatise as "the last word in this contest" (289). Unfortunately this never came to fruition in the treatise. Goold suggests that Owen's failure was probably due to the interruption by the Council of State during the course of his work on the treatise, requesting that he respond to the catechism of the Socinian, John Biddle (*Works*, 11:3). Owen's response eventually took the form of the anti-Socinian treatise, *Vindicae Evangelicae*.

[116] Owen, *The Doctrine of the Saints' Perseverance*, I (*Works*, 11:119).

[117] Owen, *The Doctrine of the Saints' Perseverance* (*Works*, 11:1).

[118] The *Bremen Confession* (1598), however, grounds perseverance in both the priestly and kingly offices of Christ. Heppe, *Reformed Dogmatics*, 583; Schaff, *Creeds of Christendom*, 1:564.

[119] *Canons of Dort*, V, Art. viii; Schaff, *Creeds of Christendom*, 3:594.

and intercession of Jesus Christ..."[120] Arguably, the most poignant of ecclesiological statements on perseverance is found in the answer to the opening question of the *Heidelberg Catechism* (1563):

> What is thy only comfort in life and death? Answer: That I, with body and soul, both in life and in death, am not my own, but belong to my faithful Saviour Jesus Christ, who with his precious blood has fully satisfied for all my sins, and redeemed me from all the power of the devil; and so preserves me that without the will of my Father in heaven not a hair can fall from my head...[121]

Ursinus made it clear that the above-mentioned preservation on the basis of Christ's priestly oblation refers to the believer's perseverance or, in his words, the *"perpetuall preservation and maintenance of our reconcilement, freedome, and whatsoever other blessings Christ has once purchased for us."*[122] Owen's treatment of the issue stood within this traditional, sacerdotal perspective.

Consistent with Owen's formulation of Christ's priesthood, as indicated in the central proposition of this study, he conceived of Christ's priesthood in terms of his oblation and intercession. The "main foundation" of perseverance, Owen insisted, "is the eternal purpose of God, which his own nature requireth to be absolutely immutable and irreversible," however,

> For the accomplishment of this eternal purpose, and for the procurement of all the good things that lie within the compass of its intendment, are the oblation and intercession, the whole mediatory undertaking of Christ, taking away sin, bringing in life and immortality, interposed, giving farther causal influence into the truth contended for.[123]

This prefatory statement to Owen's treatise is indicative of the broad scope of Christ's priestly acts that inhered in Owen's mind. He explained the priesthood of Christ in terms of "the whole mediatory undertaking of Christ" and its effects of sin's removal and the giving of eternal life. For Owen, these blessings are distinct and depend on distinct causes: "the disposal of men unto this state and condition of right unto life and salvation, doth not depend on nor proceed from the pardon of sin, but hath another cause; which is, the imputation of the righteousness of Christ unto us, as he fulfilled the law for us."[124] The cause of a believer's right to the blessing of life and salvation is the imputation of Christ's *obedientia activa*. The cause of sin's pardon, however, is the imputation of

---

[120] *Westminster Confession*, XVII.2; *Savoy Declaration*, XVII.2.
[121] *Heidelberg Catechism*, Q.1; Schaff, *Creeds of Christendom*, 3:307-308.
[122] Zacharias Ursinus, *The Summe of Christian Religion, Delivered by Zacharias Ursinus, First, by Way of Catechism, and Then Afterwards More Enlarged by a Sound and Judicious Exposition, and Application of the Same. Wherein Also Are Debated and Resolved the Questions of Whatsoever Points of Moment Have Been, or Are Controversed in Divinitie* (London: Printed by James Young, 1645), 32.
[123] Owen, *The Doctrine of the Saints' Perseverance*, Preface (*Works*, 11:22).
[124] Owen, *The Doctrine of Justification*, XII (*Works*, 5:269).

Christ's *obedientia passiva*.[125] As such, Owen's conception of "the whole mediatory undertaking of Christ" assumes the active and passive obedience of Christ or oblation in his state of humiliation. By Christ's intercession, Owen meant "his appearance for us in the presence of God", citing Hebrews 9:24 and 1 John 2:1, thus making plain that it was Christ's intercession in the state of exaltation to which he referred.[126] Owen's conception of Christ's oblation and intercession in the context of "the whole mediatory undertaking of Christ" is therefore to be understood as involving Christ's twofold state of humiliation and exaltation.

Owen discussed the specific manner in which the saints' perseverance is grounded in the priestly work of Christ in chapters VII and IX of his treatise. He picked up, in chapter VII, the theme of Christ's oblation, and, in chapter IX, his intercession. Owen argued a twofold influence of Christ's priestly oblation upon the believer's perseverance: the removal of all causes of separation between God and believers which consist of sin's guilt, and the power of sin and Satan;[127] the procurement of the Holy Spirit for believers.[128] On Christ's priestly act of intercession, Owen was concerned to prove the following: "That Christ intercedes for the preservation of believers in the love and favour of his Father to the end..."[129] There are several things which are noteworthy in Owen's account of these priestly acts.

First, the intimate connection between Christ's oblation and intercession was maintained in order to stress the actuality or efficacy of Christ's priestly work for the perseverance of the saints. This point is argued by appeal to the typological relationship between the work of the high priest in the Old Testament and that of Christ. The Scriptural context for Owen's typological exegesis is Hebrews 7-9. According to Owen, numerous things that pertained to the Aaronical priesthood such as the animal sacrifices were types of Christ's oblation, while the entrance of the high priest into the Holy of Holies on the Day of Atonement was the principal type of Christ's intercession in the Old Testament.[130] The focus of Owen's exegesis is on the parallel between the

---

[125] Owen, *The Doctrine of Justification*, XII (*Works*, 5:266): "And as the Lord Christ could not by his most perfect obedience satisfy the curse of the law, 'Dying thou shalt die;' so by the utmost of his suffering he could not fulfil the command of the law, 'Do this, and live'...Wherefore, as we plead that the death of Christ is imputed unto us for justification, so we deny that it is imputed unto us for righteousness. For by the imputation of the sufferings of Christ our sins are remitted or pardoned, and we are delivered from the curse of the law, which he underwent; but we are not thence esteemed just or righteous, which we cannot be without respect unto the fulfilling of the commands of the law, or the obedience by it required."

[126] Owen, *The Doctrine of the Saints' Perseverance*, IX (*Works*, 11:366).

[127] Owen, *The Doctrine of the Saints' Perseverance*, VII (*Works*, 11:290-308).

[128] Owen, *The Doctrine of the Saints' Perseverance*, VII (*Works*, 11:308-10).

[129] Owen, *The Doctrine of the Saints' Perseverance*, IX (*Works*, 11:365).

[130] Owen, *The Doctrine of the Saints' Perseverance*, IX (*Works*, 11:366-67).

intention of the high priest and the intention of Christ the great High Priest. As the high priest entered the holy place, his intention was "to carry on the work of expiation and atonement to perfection, and complete peace with God in the behalf of them for whom he offered without" as Hebrews 9:7 suggests.[131] The intention of the high priest reveals that his work in the Holy of Holies is "but a continuation of his oblation begun without unto a complete atonement", thus indicating the intimate connection between oblation and intercession.[132] On the basis of this connection, Owen argued, "there is no real difference between the efficacy of the death of Christ, and that of this intercession upon the actual accomplishment of it."[133] Here, the efficacy of Christ's priesthood is argued by appeal to the unity of Christ's priestly acts.

Second, the role of the Holy Spirit is taken seriously in Owen's exposition of the influence of Christ's priestly acts upon the believer's perseverance. The obvious evidence for this is his discussion of the procurement of the Spirit in Christ's oblation and his extended digression on the Spirit's indwelling in the lives of believers.[134] Owen's treatment of the Spirit is marked by his trinitarian frame of thought, brought into focus by the *pactum salutis*. Referring to Christ's priestly procurement of the promised "eternal inheritance" in Hebrews 9:15 and its explanation in Acts 2:33 as the Holy Spirit, Owen averred:

> The promise which Jesus Christ received of the Father, upon his exaltation, was that of the Holy Ghost, having purchased and procured the bestowing of him by his death. Upon his exaltation, the dispensation thereof is committed to him, as being part of the compact and covenant which was between his Father and himself, the grand bottom of his satisfaction and merit. This is the great, original, radical promise of that eternal inheritance. By the promised Spirit are we begotten anew unto a hope thereof, made meet for it, and sealed up unto it...[135]

In this passage, the trinitarian context of the Spirit's procurement and application is clearly set out: Christ procures the Spirit by his oblation, receives the promised Spirit from the Father in his state of exaltation, and dispenses the Spirit to believers. This set of relations finds its origin in the intratrinitarian covenant of redemption. Although the intercession of Christ is not explicitly mentioned, it is certainly assumed by Owen on account of his peculiar formulation of Christ's priesthood. This reading is confirmed by Owen's own summary statement of the discussion: "the Holy Spirit is purchased for us by

---

[131] Owen, *The Doctrine of the Saints' Perseverance*, IX (*Works*, 11:367); idem, *Exposition of Hebrews*, Heb. 9:6-7, in loc. (*Works*, 22:222-33).

[132] Owen, *The Doctrine of the Saints' Perseverance*, IX (*Works*, 11:367).

[133] Owen, *The Doctrine of the Saints' Perseverance*, IX (Works, 11:367). Here, Owen assumes the perfection of Christ's oblation of which its efficacy is a product. This perfection is defended in chapter VII on the basis of Hebrews 10 (See *Works*, 11:290-93).

[134] Owen, *The Doctrine of the Saints' Perseverance*, VII-VIII (*Works*, 11:308-65).

[135] Owen, *The Doctrine of the Saints' Perseverance*, VII (*Works*, 11:309).

the oblation of Christ, and bestowed on us through his intercession..."[136] Evidently, Owen relied upon his understanding of the integration of Christ's intercession and his state of exaltation in the purchase and bestowal of the Spirit for the saints' perseverance.

Third, Owen was fully aware of the decisive impact of Christ's priestly work upon Satan and his work. These diabolical forces were identified as the efficient cause of separation from God, and their destruction is achieved by way of the priesthood of Christ. Hebrews 2:14, Genesis 3:15, and Colossians 2:15 were cited to show that it is by the power of Christ that Satan has been overcome and destroyed. Owen explained that this was done in two ways. Christ subdued Satan by "taking away all that *right* and *title* which he had by sin to rule over them: I speak of the elect of God", and by removing "the *exercise of his power*, and that to the utmost...";[137] Christ's oblation destroyed Satan's works by abolishing that "corrupted principle of nature" or "the ruling of original sin" in the elect, the very principle and rule on which Satan capitalizes in his seduction of humanity into various sinful acts.[138]

That Owen tied the destruction of Satan and his work specifically to Christ's priestly oblation was no arbitrary move but a reflection of his understanding of God's self-glorification in the economy of salvation. Owen was mindful of the unrighteous nature of Satan's power over sinful humanity. He observed that it is a power that was obtained by fraud and deceit, unjustly possessed from God, and exercised in unrighteousness.[139] As such, it is not the intention of God to destroy Satan by the mere exercise of divine power, "for he would yet glory in his craft and the success of it,—that there was no way to disappoint him, but by crushing him with power, without respect unto righteousness or demonstration of wisdom."[140] God in his wisdom designed Satan's destruction in such a way "wherein he might see, unto his eternal shame and confusion, all his arts and subtleties defeated by infinite wisdom, and his enterprise overthrown in a way of right and equity."[141] The means by which the glory of God's justice and wisdom is manifested and Satan defeated is the priestly oblation of Christ. Christ's oblation satisfied divine justice and thus manifests the glory of its perfection. Since such a means of redemption did not cross the mind of Satan or of any creature but was conceived by divine wisdom alone, consequently the glory of divine wisdom is manifested. In Owen's understanding, then, the power of Christ by which Satan is defeated, mentioned at the beginning of this third point, is a power exercised not apart from but on account of divine justice.

---

[136] Owen, *The Doctrine of the Saints' Perseverance*, VIII (*Works*, 11:329).
[137] Owen, *The Doctrine of the Saints' Perseverance*, VII (*Works*, 11:305, 307).
[138] Owen, *The Doctrine of the Saints' Perseverance*, VII (*Works*, 11:307).
[139] Owen, *Christologia*, XVII (*Works*, 1:217).
[140] Owen, *Christologia*, XVII (*Works*, 1:216).
[141] Owen, *Christologia*, XVII (*Works*, 1:216).

The removal of diabolical forces against the saints' perseverance by Christ's priestly oblation serves the supreme end of God's glory.

Conclusion

From the above treatment of Owen's conception of God's glory in redemption and of his doctrine of the saints' perseverance, it is clear that to conceive of his atonement theology in terms of a "one-end teleology" is misguided. Owen not only distinguishes between redemption's supreme and intermediate end, but also develops their content substantially in his atonement theology. His account of the way the perfection of God's attributes is at stake in redemption is substantially articulated according to the Scriptural flow of redemptive history. Also evident is the connection between Owen's doctrine of the saints' perseverance and his account of Satan's destruction.

As demonstrated above, Christ's priesthood is of central importance in Owen's articulation of redemption's supreme and intermediate end. For the former, this is seen in the crucial importance Owen gave to the manifestations of divine holiness and righteousness in his narrative of redemption. Both attributes are entailed in his conception of divine justice, are central to humanity's glorification of God before the fall, and are therefore central to God's work of redemption by Christ. Christ's priesthood is crucial because it is the necessary means by which divine justice is satisfied and displayed. Owen argues for this necessity on the grounds that vindicatory justice is essential to God and that satisfaction requires a voluntary obedience that only the incarnate Son is able to perform. Since the obedience of Christ is the obedience of his entire life in his state of humiliation, Owen's argument for the necessity of Christ's priesthood relies on his peculiar formulation of that office.

With respect to redemption's intermediate end, Owen argues for the saints' perseverance on eternal and historical grounds. Christ's priestly work is a vital part of the latter and is rooted in the former. According to Owen, the saints' perseverance rests upon the efficacy of Christ's priesthood. Christ's oblation, performed in his state of humiliation, procures the Holy Spirit for believers; Christ's intercession, performed in his state of exaltation, dispenses the Spirit to believers. By the oblation of Christ, divine justice is satisfied and the principle of sin which Satan exploits in order to tempt and deceive believers is abolished. In this way, Satan and his works are destroyed and the glory of God manifested. For Owen, then, the priesthood of Christ performed in his twofold state is central to God's preservation of the saints for their eternal salvation.

CHAPTER 7

Conclusion

This study provides an extended exposition of Owen's atonement theology in his intellectual milieu of Reformed orthodoxy and the wider context of the Western trinitarian tradition. Every effort has been made to offer a critical and contextually informed reading of Owen's writings. However, it has not been the aim of the present study to offer criticisms of his atonement theology. It is not possible that such an exercise be responsibly or constructively executed without first listening to Owen with care in his context and articulating his thoughts accurately within that context. "Listening to the past" has been the burden of the present study, to borrow the title of Holmes' book.[1] Having arrived at the close of this study, it is appropriate to summarize the key findings and offer some concluding observations.

Following Owen's flow of thought in *The Death of Death*, an account of his atonement theology was articulated according to the order of the following doctrinal loci: the triune God, Christ the Mediator, and satisfaction for sin. For Owen, all three concerns aim towards the glory of God in the salvation of the elect. The central proposition of this study is that Owen's conception of the priesthood of Christ, in terms of Christ's united acts of oblation and intercession performed in his twofold state of humiliation and exaltation, lies at the heart of his atonement theology. This proposition is argued by demonstrating that Owen's peculiar formulation of Christ's priesthood is of central importance to his exposition of each doctrinal locus and in his conception of redemption's end.

Discussion of the first locus (Chapter 2) showed that Owen understood the mediatorial work of Christ to be conceived by the triune God and constituted in the *pactum salutis*. Evident in Owen's exposition is his reliance on the principles inherent in the trinitarian orthodoxy of the West. Owen expressed the content of the eternal *pactum* in terms of the various elements of Christ's priesthood conceived in relation to the historical movement of Christ's states of humiliation and exaltation. As such, there is an unmistakable prominence accorded to the priestly office of Christ in Owen's conception of the *pactum salutis*. This prominence is carried over into Owen's treatment of Christ's person and mediatorial work in history – the concern of the second locus (Chapters 3 and 4).

---

[1] Stephen R. Holmes, *Listening to the Past: the Place of Tradition in Theology* (Carlisle: Paternoster/Grand Rapids: Baker, 2002).

Crucial to Owen's Christology is the mediatorial framework that holds the person and work of Christ together (Chapter 3). The governing category of Owen's Christology is the mediatorial office of Christ. This is seen in the concerns and structure of *Christologia*. Owen articulated his Christology in the light of the Socinian challenge of his day, drawing from the Reformed resolution of the problems that arose in the Christological debates between the Lutherans and the Reformed over the sacraments, and the Stancaro controversy over the participation of Christ's natures in his mediatorial work. Owen's Reformed Christology is evident from his conception of the *communicatio idiomatum* and his insistence on the involvement of both the divine and human natures of Christ in his mediatorial work. Consistent with his trinitarianism, Owen's Christology has a strong pneumatological element. His Spirit Christology reflects his Reformed concern to preserve the integrity of the two natures of Christ. With the Reformed, Owen understood the acting subject of all mediatorial work to be the God-man and consistently predicated mediatorial operations of Christ's person and not of his natures in the abstract. His Christology is foundational to his understanding of the threefold office of Christ.

While it is clear that Owen employed the threefold office of prophet, priest, and king to elucidate his Christology, nevertheless, it is the priestly office that occupied his labours in the construction of his atonement theology against the threat of universal redemption (Chapter 4). He identified the chief error of the universal redemptionists to be the division between the oblation and intercession of Christ. In Owen's analysis, this division arose from an asymmetrical construal of the scope of Christ's priestly acts of oblation and intercession: Christ was, for instance, an oblation for both the elect and non-elect but intercedes only for the elect. In turn, this division in scope suggests an asymmetrical construal of the divine intention: God intends to save every person through the death of Christ and also intends to save only the elect. Analyses of the positions of the Arminians, Saumurians, and Thomas More on the atonement demonstrated that Owen's perception of the controversy in terms of the division between Christ's oblation and intercession is contextually justified. Lending weight to the central proposition of this study is Owen's preoccupation with and employment of his peculiar formulation of Christ's priesthood in various contexts throughout the course of his theological career. What is evident from a sampling of Owen's early and mature writings on the subject is the consistency of his formulation and its crucial significance in polemical engagements with the Arminians, Saumurians, and Thomas More. Owen's formulation involves the integration of Christ's priestly acts of oblation and intercession with his twofold state of humiliation and exaltation as indicated in his conception of the *pactum salutis*.

Discussion of the third locus, which concerns sin's satisfaction, centred on the mediatorial obedience of Christ and the nature and effects of his death (Chapter 5). Owen's understanding of Christ's obedience was explored against the backdrop of seventeenth-century debates over the satisfactory value of Christ's obedience. Unlike the views of a minority of the Reformed orthodox who restricted imputation to the passive obedience of Christ, Owen stood with the majority on the issue. He argued for the satisfactory value of Christ's active and passive obedience on the grounds of the unity of Christ's mediatorial obedience, of the mystical union between Christ and the elect, and that Christ is the elect's surety. While the first and second grounds buttress the imputation of Christ's whole obedience in general, Christ's suretyship specifies the content of what is imputed, thus strengthening Owen's case. As a function of Christ's priesthood, his suretyship involves perfect obedience to the law which the elect are unable to perfectly keep, and his death on the cross as the penalty of sin borne on behalf of the elect. The object of justifying faith, for Owen, is Christ in his mediatorial office as priest, which entails both his oblation on earth and intercession in heaven.

On the nature and effects of Christ's death, Owen's debate with Baxter demonstrates the central importance of Christ's priesthood for him. He argued that satisfaction by *solutio eiusdem* is compatible with sin's forgiveness and the *ipso facto* procurement of justification. The priesthood of Christ is vital for Owen here because of the relation Christ's oblation sustains to satisfaction and his intercession to sin's forgiveness and justification. The exercise of these priestly acts would require that the *ipso facto* procurement of salvific benefits by Christ's oblation be dispensed and applied by virtue of his intercession. On account of the temporal sequence between Christ's state of humiliation and exaltation in Owen's formulation, it is necessary that a corresponding sequence exists between redemption's purchase and possession. Owen's contention for temporal sequencing between the right to justification (*ius ad rem*) and the right to its possession (*ius in re*) reflects the impact of his formulation in his conception of the effects of the atonement.

On the subject of redemption's end (Chapter 6), Owen's teleological construal of redemption was examined according to his distinction of the supreme end of God's glory and the intermediate end of the elect's salvation. For the former, the necessity of Christ's priesthood for sin's satisfaction and the consequent manifestation of God's justice argue the importance of this office for Owen. One of Owen's grounds for the necessity of Christ's priestly mediation is Christ's voluntary obedience in his state of humiliation, which indicates the importance of his formulation. Owen's treatment of redemption's intermediate end was explored through the lens of his doctrine of the saints' perseverance. The soteriological foundation on which Owen's doctrine of perseverance is grounded is the priesthood of Christ. By Christ's priestly acts performed in his twofold state, the Holy Spirit is procured for and given to believers, and the principle of sin in humanity by which Satan works is abolished. Consequently, Satan and his works are destroyed and God glorified.

Having summarized the findings of this study, two observations regarding certain modern interpretations of Owen's atonement theology and one observation on a late theme in Owen's thought will be offered by way of conclusion.

First, in the light of this study, it is fallacious to argue that Owen's doctrine of limited atonement is the direct result of starting with certain logical and unbiblical or Aristotelian premises about God. Torrance asserts that it is Aristotelian logic that "led later Calvinists like John Owen to formulate the doctrine of 'limited atonement.'"[2] He insists that the doctrine of limited atonement emerges "where we draw inferences from certain 'logical premises' or isolated texts or an Aristotelian idea of God."[3] One of the ways this exercise of logical inference is executed is as follows: "The scholastic Calvinists made *election prior to grace*, beginning with the doctrine of a double decree as a major premiss, and then moving on to formulate the doctrines of grace, incarnation and atonement, as God's way of executing the eternal decrees – thereby 'logically' teaching that Christ died only for the elect, to secure infallibly the salvation of the elect."[4] This is certainly not the "logic" employed by Owen. For Owen, the eternal ground of the atonement is the *pactum salutis*. Election is not a doctrine to be abstracted from this trinitarian and covenantal foundation. Owen's doctrine of the eternal *pactum*, as argued in Chapter 2, has its basis in Scripture and tradition. It is informed by exegetical considerations on the basis of etymological analyses and the collation of representative Scriptural texts, and worked out according to orthodox trinitarian principles in the context of the developing federal theology in the Reformed tradition. What is done in redemptive history for the atonement of sins is the accomplishment and implementation of the eternal *pactum* through the united acts of Christ's priestly oblation and intercession performed in his twofold state by the power of the Spirit. Any attempt to engage critically with the particularity of the atonement as Owen understood it needs to engage his doctrines of the *pactum salutis* and Christ's priesthood so as not to be found engaging an Aristotelian strawman. Of course, this is not to make any judgement for or against the correctness of Owen's atonement theology. Nor is it to deny the need for critically engaging Owen. It is simply a plea for careful listening to and interpretation of the past in order to engage constructively with the theological formulations of such theologians as Owen.

---

[2] James B. Torrance, "The Incarnation and 'Limited Atonement'", *Evangelical Quarterly* 55, no. 2 (1983), 84.
[3] Torrance, "The Incarnation and 'Limited Atonement'", 86.
[4] Torrance, "The Incarnation and 'Limited Atonement'", 87; cf. Grensted, who sees Owen as representing "the extremest form of English Calvinism, as developed in opposition to Arminian influence" in which the doctrine of limited atonement was allegedly held as "a corollary from that of election..." L.W. Grensted, *A Short History of the Doctrine of Atonement* (Manchester: Longmans, Green & Co., 1920), 275.

Second, great care ought to be taken when speaking of Owen's atonement theology in terms of a "commercial theory" or "theory of limited satisfaction".[5] Theories are helpful insofar as they help to explain the way in which the Biblical metaphors on the atonement are expressed in ways other than the bare words of Scripture in Owen's writings. However, mere descriptions of the commercial "mechanics" of the atonement in words other than those in Scripture does not warrant the conclusion that Owen thought in terms of a certain atonement theory and consequently read the Scriptural data through the lens of that theory. It was argued in Chapter 5 that Owen's conception of satisfaction by *solutio eiusdem* is not regulated by the logic that is intrinsic to this legal and commercial concept, but by the *pactum salutis*, his formulation of Christ's priesthood, and the plain meaning of Scriptural texts. It was also shown that Owen was clearly aware that in Scripture, the notion of sin as a debt to be paid is metaphorical and therefore an improper way of speaking about sin. Thus, to develop Owen's use of the commercial metaphor into a commercial theory and read the features and logic of that theory back into Owen's writings on the atonement is not to interpret his writings but to misinterpret them.

A more satisfying approach is to observe the way in which metaphors of the atonement overlap. In the context of his debate with Baxter, for instance, Owen employed at least three atonement metaphors: as the supreme Governor, God relaxes the law in relation to the person to be punished (governmental); as Judge, God punishes sin for what it deserves in Christ (judicial); as Creditor, God demands payment of the same debt as that which is in the obligation (commercial). In Owen's exposition of the saints' perseverance, he employed, again, at least three metaphors: the priestly work of Christ (sacrifice) removes the guilt of sin (judicial) and destroys Satan with his power (victory). Even then, care needs to be taken not to restrict a reading of Owen on the atonement to his use of atonement metaphors alone. Owen's view of the atonement takes the whole course of Christ's life seriously from the incarnation to his heavenly intercession, as his formulation of Christ's priesthood makes plain. However, this wider context of Christ's life is in danger of being sidelined if only atonement metaphors are noted.

Arguably, the concept that best captures Owen's atonement theology is that of Christ the Mediator.[6] It is the central category in his Christology as argued in Chapter 3. Within this mediatorial framework, the Father, in his love and by the Spirit, appoints the Son to be the Mediator for those to whom the Father has

---

[5] Clifford, *Atonement and Justification*, 111, 128.

[6] For more recent articulations of this theme but not in relation to Owen, see Thomas F. Torrance, *The Mediation of Christ* (Exeter: Paternoster, 1983); Robert J. Sherman, *King, Priest and Prophet: A Trinitarian Theology of Atonement* (London: T&T Clark, 2004); Robert J. Sherman, "Toward a Trinitarian Theology of the Atonement", *SJT* 52, no. 3 (1999), 346-74; Alan J. Spence, *The Promise of Peace: A Unified Theory of Atonement* (Edinburgh: Continuum International Publishing/T&T Clark, 2006).

given him, and the Son voluntarily undertakes to be the Mediator for his chosen people by the Spirit (*pactum salutis*); the Son humbled himself by becoming incarnate in order to live a life of perfect obedience by the Spirit on behalf of the elect, both "actively" by obeying the law and "passively" in his death (Christ's oblation); the incarnate, crucified Son was exalted in his resurrection and ascension, brought the fruits of his perfect life and death into his Father's presence, and now lives to make intercession for the preservation and salvation of the elect on the grounds of his earthly oblation (Christ's intercession).

Finally, it is significant that there is a theme in Owen's atonement theology that was absent from his writings for the greater part of his life. It was communicated in published form only after his death in *Meditations and Discourses on the Glory of Christ* (1684).[7] This theme is the Irenean theme of recapitulation, based on Ephesians 1:10.[8] In *The Death of Death*, Owen mentioned in passing that Christ's incarnation is related to his priestly oblation and intercession as "the foundation for both the others, being as it were the means in respect of them as the end..."[9] In *Meditations and Discourses*, this relationship was acknowledged but the design of the incarnation was extended to include the recapitulation of all things in the person of the incarnate Son.[10] Like Irenaeus, Owen appealed to the Pauline text in Ephesians. He explained his understanding of recapitulation by retelling the narrative of redemptive history in a way that was very similar to the one that was traced in Chapter 6 in relation to the divine attributes, but with one crucial difference. The focus was not merely on the history of sinful humanity and how a portion of it was redeemed by Christ. Owen's most mature narrative included the history of the other portion of intellectual creatures besides humanity, the angels.[11] Sin had brought disorder to the "union between the two families of God",[12] therefore in the reparation of that disorder, both angels and humanity are significant characters in Owen's narrative:

> The first creation in its order was a curious and glorious fabric. But every thing depending immediately on God, by virtue of the principles of its own nature and

---

[7] *Works*, 1:273-415. Two additional chapters of the treatise were found after the 1684 publication and were included in the 1691 and 1696 editions. In the Goold edition of Owen's works and its Banner reprint, these chapters are collated as Part II of the treatise with the title *Meditations and Discourses Concerning The Glory of Christ; Applied Unto Unconverted Sinners and Saints Under Spirit Decays, in Two Chapters From John XVII.24*. See *Works*, 1:417-61.

[8] Irenaeus, *Adversus Haereses*, III.xvi.6, III.xviii.1, 7 (*ANF*, 1:442-43, 446, 448); cf. Franks, *The Work of Christ*, 24-27.

[9] Owen, *Salus Electorum*, I.iv (*Works*, 10:174-75).

[10] Owen, *Meditations and Discourses*, I.xi (*Works*, 1:372). The title of Chapter XI of the treatise reads: "The Glory of Christ in the Recapitulation of all things in Him."

[11] Hints of this are found in Owen's references to angels in *Christologia*, XVI, XVII (*Works*, 1:195-96, 211).

[12] Owen, *Meditations and Discourses*, I.xi (*Works*, 1:370).

the law of its obedience, all was brought unto a loss by the sin of angels and men. But now every thing that belongs unto this new creation, even every believer in the world, as well as the angels in heaven, being gathered together in this one head, the whole and all, and every part and member of it, even every particular believer, are secured from ruin, such as befell all things before. In this new Head they have an indissoluble consistency.[13]

At the centre of his mature narrative of creation's ultimate destiny stands the glorious person of Christ, the incarnate Son of God, the "*new Head* of God's recollected family" in whom God has gathered up all things and from whom "*firmness and security is communicated unto the whole new creation.*"[14] This late theme of recapitulation points to the fact that Owen's atonement theology was a work in progress. It is so because his knowledge of God was the *theologia viatorum*, and the supreme object of his contemplation, the exalted, glorified, and reigning Christ.

---

[13] Owen, *Meditations and Discourses*, I.xi (*Works*, 1:374).
[14] Owen, *Meditations and Discourses*, I.xi (*Works*, 1:374).

Bibliography

Primary Sources

A Declaration of the Faith and Order, Owned and Practised in the Congregational Churches in England: Agreed Upon and Consented Unto by Their Elders and Messengers in Their Meeting at the Savoy, October 12 1658. London: Printed by J.P., 1659.

Ames, William. *The Marrow of Theology*. Translated by John Dykstra Eusden. Grand Rapids: Baker, 1997.

Annotations Upon All the Books of the Old and New Testament: This Third, above the First and Second, Edition So Enlarged, as They Make an Entire Commentary on the Sacred Scripture: The Like Never before Published in English. Wherein the Text Is Explained, Doubts Resolved, Scriptures Parallel'd, and Various Readings Observed; by the Labour of Certain Learned Divines Thereunto Appointed, and Therein Employed, as Is Expressed in the Preface. London: Printed by Evan Tyler, 1657.

Aquinas, Thomas. *Summa Theologiae: Latin Text and English Translation, Introduction, Notes, Appendixes and Glossaries*. 61 vols. London: Blackfriars in conjunction with Eyre & Spottiswoode, 1964-1981.

Arminius, James. *The Works of James Arminius*. Translated by James Nichols and W.R. Bagnall. 3 vols. London ed. Grand Rapids: Baker, 1986.

Baxter, Richard. *Aphorismes of Justification with Their Explication Annexed*. London: Printed for Francis Tyton, 1649.

—. *Aphorismes of Justification with Their Explication Annexed*. Hague: Abraham Brown, 1655.

—. *Richard Baxter's Confession of His Faith*. London: Printed by R.W. for Tho. Underhil and Fra. Tyton, 1655.

—. *Certain Disputations of Right to Sacraments, and the True Nature of Visible Christianity; Defending Them against Several Sorts of Opponents, Especially against the Second Assault of That Pious, Reverend and Dear Brother Mr Thomas Blake*. London: Printed by William Du Gard for Thomas Johnson, 1657.

—. *Richard Baxter's Account of His Present Thoughts Concerning the Controversies About the Perseverance of the Saints. Occasioned by the Gross Misreports of Some Passages in His Book, Called, the Right Method for Peace of Conscience, &C; Which Are Left out in the Last Impression to Avoid Offence, and This Here Substituted, for the Fuller Explication of the Same Points*. London: Printed for Tho. Underhill, 1658.

—. *Catholick Communion Defended against Both Extreames: And Unnecessary Division Confuted, by Reasons against Both the Active and Passive Ways of Seperation: Occasioned by the Racks and Reproaches of One Sort, and the Impatience and Censoriousness of the Other; and the Erroneous, Tho Confident Writings of Both. And Written in Compassion, of a Distracted,*

Self-Tearing People, Tho with Little Hope of Any Great Success. In Five Parts. London: Printed for Tho. Parkhurst, 1684.

—. *Universal Redemption of Mankind, by the Lord Jesus Christ: Stated and Cleared by the Late Learned Mr. Richard Baxter. Whereunto Is Added a Short Account of Special Redemption, by the Same Author*. London: Printed for John Salusbury, 1694.

—. *Reliquiae Baxterianae, or Mr Richard Baxter's Narrative of the Most Memorable Passages of His Life and Times*. London: Printed for T. Parkhurst, F. Robinson, F. Lawrence, and F. Dunton 1696.

Beza, Theodore. *The Bible, That Is, the Holy Scripture Contained in the Old and the New Testament. Translated According to the Hebrew and Greeke, and Conferred with the Best Translations in Diuers Languages. With Most Profitable Annotations Upon All the Hard Places and Other Things of Great Importance*. London: Printed by Robert Barker, 1602.

Biddle, John. *A Twofold Catechism: The One Simply Called a Scripture-Catechism; the Other, a Brief Scripture-Catechism for Children. Wherein the Chiefest Points of the Christian Religion, Being Question-Wise Proposed, Resolves Themselves by Pertinent Answers Taken Word for Word out of the Scripture, without Either Consequences or Comments*. London: Printed by J. Cottrel, 1654.

Bucanus, William. *Body of Divinity, or Institutions of Christian Religion; Framed out of the Word of God, and the Writings of the Best Divines, Methodically Handled by Way of Question and Ansvver, Fit for All Such as Desire to Know and Practise the Will of God*. Translated by Robert Hill. London: Printed for Daniel Pakeman, Abel Roper, and Richard Tomlins, 1659.

Calvin, John. *Institutes of the Christian Religion*. Translated by Ford Lewis Battles. 2 vols., ed. John T. McNeill. Philadelphia: Westminster, 1960.

—. *Calvin's Commentaries*. 46 vols. Edinburgh: Calvin Translation Society, 1843-1855. Reprint, in 22 vols. Grand Rapids: Baker, 1996.

Cameron, John. *Certain Theses or Positions of the Learned John Cameron Concerning the Threefold Covenant of God with Man*, in Samuel Bolton, *The True Bounds of Christian Freedom, Whereunto Is Annexed a Discourse of the Learned John Camerons, Touching the Three-Fold Covenant of God with Man* (London: Printed for P.S., 1656), 351-401.

Charnock, Stephen. *Several Discourses Upon the Existence and Attributes of God*. London: Printed for D. Newman, T. Cockerill, Benj. Griffin, T. Simmons, and Benj. Alsop, 1682.

Chemnitz, Martin. *The Two Natures in Christ*. Translated by J.A.O. Preus. St Louis, Missouri: Concordia Publishing House, 1971.

Confession of Faith of Those Called Arminians or a Declaration of the Opinions and Doctrines of the Ministers and Pastors, Which in the United Provinces Are Known by the Name of Remonstrants Concerning the Chief Points of Christian Religion, Translated out of the Original. London: Printed for Samuel Walsall, 1684.

Crellius, Johannes. *The Expiation of a Sinner in a Commentary Upon the Epistle to the Hebrewes*. London: Printed by Tho. Harper, 1646.
Crisp, Tobias. *Christ Alone Exalted in Seventeene Sermons Preached in or Neare*. London, 1643.
Dickson, David. *A Short Explanation of the Epistle of Paul to the Hebrevves*. Cambridge: Printed by Roger Daniel for Francis Eglesfield, 1649.
—. *Therapeutica Sacra, Shewing Briefly the Method of Healing the Diseases of the Conscience, Concerning Regeneration*. Edinburgh: Printed by Evan Tyler, 1664.
Diodati, Giovanni. *Pious and Learned Annotations Upon the Holy Bible: Expounding the Difficult Places Thereof Learnedly, and Plainly: With Other Things of Great Importance*. London: Printed by T.B. for Nicholas Fussell, 1643.
—. *Pious and Learned Annotations Upon the Holy Bible: Plainly Expounding the Most Difficult Places Thereof*. London: Printed by Miles Flesher for Nicholas Fussell, 1648.
Edwards, Thomas. *The Second Part of Gangraena, or a Fresh and Further Dicovery of the Errors, Heresies, Blasphemies, and Dangerous Proceedings of the Sectaries of This Time*: London, 1646.
Eusebius. *The Proof of the Gospel: Being the Demonstratio Evangelica of Eusebius of Caesarea*. Translated by W.J. Ferrar. 2 vols. London: SPCK, 1920.
Fairweather, Eugene R., ed. *A Scholastic Miscellany: Anselm to Ockham*. Vol. 10, The Library of Christian Classics. London: SCM Press; Philadelphia: Westminster Press, 1956.
Gataker, Thomas. *An Answer to Mr George Walkers Vindication or Rather Fresh Accusation Wherein He Chargeth Mr Wotton (Besides His Former Foul Aspersions of Heresie and Blasphemy) with Arianism; Mr Gataker with Socinianism, Dr Gouge, and Mr Downame, with a False Attestation; Dr Baylie, and Mr Stock, with Self-Condemnation; All the Eight Ministers Employed in the Busines between Himself and Mr Wotton, with Partiality and Unjust Judgement*. London: Printed by E.G. for F. Clifton, 1642.
Gillespie, Patrick. *The Ark of the Covenant Opened; or a Treatise of the Covenant of Redemption between God and Christ, as the Foundation of the Covenant of Grace*. London: Printed for Tho. Parkhurst, 1677.
Goodwin, John. *Apolytrosis Apolytroseos, or, Redemption Redeemed. Wherein the Most Glorious Work of the Redemption of the World by Jesus Christ, Is by Expressness of Scripture, Clearness of Argument, Countenance of the Best Authority, as Well Ancient as Modern, Vindicated and Asserted in the Just Latitude and Extent of It, According to the Counsel and Most Gracious Intentions of God, against the Incroachments of Later Times Made Upon It, Whereby the Unsearchable Riches and Glory of the Grace of God Therein, Have Been, and yet Are, Much Obscured, and Hid from the Eyes of Many*. London: Printed by John Macock, for Lodowick Lloyd and Henry Cripps, 1651.

Goodwin, Thomas. *The Works of Thomas Goodwin.* 12 vols. Eureka: Tanski Publications, 1996.
Grotius, Hugo. *A Defence of the Catholic Faith Concerning the Satisfaction of Christ, against Faustus Socinus.* Translated by Frank Hugh Foster. Andover: Warren F. Draper, 1889.
Hammond, Henry. *A Paraphrase, and Annotations Upon All the Books of the New Testament, Briefly Explaning All the Difficult Places Thereof.* London: Printed for F. Flesher for Richard Davis, 1659.
Heppe, Heinrich. *Reformed Dogmatics: A Compendium of Reformed Theology.* Translated by G.T. Thomson, ed. Ernst Bizer, 1950. Reprint, London: Wakeman, n.d.
Jones, William. *A Commentary Vpon the Epistles of Saint Pavl to Philemon, and to the Hebrewes, Together with a Compendiovs Explication of the Second and Third Epistles of Saint John.* London: Printed by R.B. for Robert Allot, 1635.
Lawson, George. *An Exposition of the Epistle to the Hebrewes. Wherein the Text Is Cleared; Theopolitica Improved: The Socinian Comment Examined.* London: Printed by J.S. for George Sawbridge, 1662.
Leigh, Edward. *Annotations on Five Poetical Books of the Old Testament: Job, Psalmes, Proverbs, Ecclesiastes, and Canticles.* London: Printed by A.M. for T. Pierpoint, 1657.
Leith, John H., ed. *Creeds of the Churches: A Reader in Christian Doctrine from the Bible to the Present.* Atlanta: John Knox Press, 1982.
Matthews, A.G., ed. *The Savoy Declaration of Faith and Order 1658, with an Additional Notice by Daniel T. Jenkins.* London: Independent Press, 1959.
Millington, Edward, ed. *Bibliotheca Oweniana Sive Catalogus Librorum Plurimis Facultatibus Insignium, Instructissimae Bibliothecae Rev. Doct. Vir. Joan. Oweni, (Quondam Vice-Cancellarii & Decani Edis-Christi in Academia Oxoniensi) Nuperrime Defuncti.* London, 1684.
More, Thomas. *The Vniversallity of God's Free-Grace in Christ to Mankind. Proclaimed and Displayed from 1 Tim. 2.6. And Hebr. 2.9. According to Their Genuine Sense That All Might Be Comforted, Encouraged; Every One Confirmed and Assured of the Propitiation and Death of Christ for the Whole Race of Mankind, and So for Himself in Particular.* London: n.p., 1646.
Musculus, Wolfgang. *Common Places of Christian Religion, Gathered by Wolfgangus Musculus for the Vse of Such as Desire the Knovvledge of Godly Truth.* Translated by Iohn Man. London: Imprinted by Henry Bynneman, 1578.
Owen, John. *ΘΕΟΛΟΓΟΥΜΕΝΑ ΠΑΝΤΟΔΑΠΑ, Sive, De Natura, Ortu Progressu, Et Studio Verae Theologiae, Libri Sex Quibus Etiam Origines & Processus Veri & Falsi Cultus Religiosi, Casus & Instaurationes Ecclesiae Illustriores Ab Ipsis Rerum Primordiis, Enarrantur.* Oxoniae, 1661.
——. "Preface." In *Vindiciae Justificationis Gratuitae. Justification without Conditions; or the Free Justification of a Sinner, Explained, Confirmed and*

Vindicated, from the Exceptions, Objections, and Seeming Absurdities, Which Are Cast Upon It, by the Assertors of Conditional Justification: More Especially from the Attempts of Mr. B. Woodbridge in His Sermon Entituled [Justification by Faith] of Mr. Cranford in His Epistle to the Reader, and of Mr. Baxter in Some Passages, Which Relate to the Same Matter. Wherein Also, the Absoluteness of the New Covenant Is Proved, and the Arguments against It, Are Disproved, William Eyre. London: Printed for R.I., 1654.

—. *The Works of John Owen, with Memoirs of His Life by William Orme*. 21 vols., ed. Thomas Russell. London: Richard Baynes, 1826.

—. *The Works of John Owen*. 24 vols., ed. William H. Goold. London: Johnstone and Hunter, 1850-55.

—. *The Works of John Owen*. 23 vols., ed. William H. Goold. Reprint ed. Edinburgh: Banner of Truth, 1965-68, 1991.

—. *The Death of Death in the Death of Christ*. Reprint, Edinburgh: Banner of Truth, 1959.

—. *The Correspondence of John Owen (1616-1683): With an Account of His Life and Work*, ed. Peter Toon. Cambridge: James Clarke, 1970.

—. *The Oxford Orations of Dr. John Owen*. Edited and translated by Peter Toon. Cornwall: Gospel Communication, 1971.

—. *Biblical Theology or the Nature, Origin, Development, and Study of Theological Truth, in Six Books*. Translated by Stephen P. Westcott. Morgan, PA: Soli Deo Gloria, 1994.

Perkins, William. *A Golden Chaine, or the Description of Theologie, Containing the Order of the Causes of Saluation and Damnation, According to God's Word*. Cambridge: Iohn Legate, 1597.

—. *An Abridgement of the Whole Body of Divinity Extracted from the Learned Works of That Ever-Famous, and Reverend Divine, Mr. William Perkins* London: Printed by W. B. for Will. Hope, 1654.

Pelikan, Jaroslav, and Valerie Hotchkiss, ed. *Creeds and Confessions of Faith in the Christian Tradition*. New Have /London: Yale University Press, 2003.

Peterkin, Alexander, ed. *Records of the Kirk of Scotland, Containing the Acts and Proceedings of the General Assemblies, from the Year 1638 Downwards, as Authenticated by the Clerks of Assembly; with Notes and Historical Illustrations*. Edinburgh: John Sutherland, 1838.

Piscator, Johannes. *A Learned and Profitable Treatise of Mans Iustification, Two Bookes, Opposed to the Sophismes of Robert Bellarmine, Iesuite*. London: Thomas Creede for Robert Dexter, 1599.

Polanus, Amandus. *The Svbstance of Christian Religion Sovndly Set Forth in Two Bookes, by Definitions and Partitions, Framed According to the Rules of a Naturall Method* Translated by Thomas Wilcocks. London: Printed for Arn Hatfield for Felix Norton, 1600.

Poole, Matthew. *Annotations Upon the Holy Bible Wherein the Sacred Text Is Inserted, and Various Readings Annex'd*. Vol. 1. London: Printed by John Richardson, 1683.

Quick, John. *Synodicon in Gallia Reformata or the Acts, Decisions, Decrees, and Canons of Those Famous National Councils of the Reformed Churches in France*. London: Printed for T. Parkhurst and J. Robinson 1692.

Roberts, Alexander, and Donaldson, James, eds. *The Ante-Nicene Fathers*. 10 vols. Reprint edition. Peabody, MA: Hendrickson Publishes, 1999.

Rutherford, Samuel. *Christ Dying and Drawing Sinners to Himselfe or a Survey of Our Saviour in His Soule-Suffering, His Lovelynesse in His Death, and the Efficacie Thereof. In Which Some Cases of Soule-Trouble in Weake Beleevers, Grounds of Submission under the Absense of Christ, with the Flowings and Heightnings of Free Grace, Are Opened*. London: Printed by J. D. for Andrew Crooke, 1647.

—. *The Covenant of Life Opened or, a Treatise of the Covenant of Grace*. Edinburgh: Printed by Andro Anderson for Robert Broun, 1654.

Saltmarsh, John. *Free-Grace or the Flowings of Christs Blood Freely to Sinners*. London: Printed for Giles Calvert, 1645.

Schaff, Philip, ed. *The Creeds of Christendom: With a History and Critical Notes*. 3 vols. Grand Rapids: Baker, 1993.

—. *Nicene and Post-Nicene Fathers: First Series*. 14 vols. Reprint edition. Peabody, MA: Hendrickson Publishes, 1999.

Schaff, Philip, and Wace, Henry, eds. *Nicene and Post-Nicene Fathers: Second Series*. 14 vols. Reprint edition. Peabody, MA: Hendrickson Publishes, 1999.

Stalham, John. *Vindicae Redemptionis, in the Fanning and Sifting of Samuel Oates, His Exposition Upon Mat. 13.44, with a Faithful Search after Our Lords Meaning in His Two Parables of the Treasure and the Pearl. Endeavoured in Severall Sermons Upon Mat. 13.44, 45*. London: Printed by A.M. for Christopher Meredith, 1647.

The Bible and Holy Scriptvres Conteyned in the Olde and Newe Testament. Geneva: Printed by Roulandnald, 1560.

The Book of Concord: The Confessions of the Evangelical Lutheran Church. Translated by Charles Arand et al., ed. Robert Kolb and Timothy J. Wengert. Minneapolis: Fortress Press, 2000.

The Dutch Annotations Upon the Whole Bible: Or, All the Holy Canonical Scriptures of the Old and New Testament, Together with, and According to Their Own Translation of All the Text: As Both the One and the Other Were Ordered and Appointed by the Synod of Dort , 1618, and Published by Authority, 1637. Translated by Theodore Haak. London: Printed by Henry Hills, for John Rothwell, Joshua Kirton, and Richard Tomlins, 1657.

The Holy Bible, Conteyning the Old Testament, and the New: Newly Translated out of the Originall Tongues & with the Former Translations Diligently Compared and Revised by His Maiesties Speciall Comandement. London: Robert Barker, 1611.

The Humble Advice of the Assembly of Divines, Now by Authority of Parliament Sitting at Westminster, Concerning a Confession of Faith, with the Quotations and Texts of Scripture Annexed, Presented by Them Lately to

Both Houses of Parliament. London: Printed for the Company of Stationers; Reprinted at Edinburgh by Evan Tyler, 1647.

The Racovian Catechisme; Wherein You Have the Substance of the Confession, That No Other Save the Father of Our Lord Jesus Christ Is That One God of Israel, and That the Man Jesus of Nazareth Who Was Born of the Virgin, and No Other Besides or before Him, Is the Onely Begotton Sonne of God. Amsterledam: Printed for Brooer Janz, 1652.

Trapp, John. *A Commentary or Exposition Upon These Following Books of Holy Scripture; Proverbs of Solomon, Ecclesiastes, the Song of Songs, Isaiah, Jeremiah, Lamentations, Ezekiel & Daniel*. London: Printed by Robert White, for Nevil Simmons, 1660.

Trelcatius, Lucas. *A Brief Institvtion of the Common Places of Sacred Divinitie, Wherein the Truth of Every Place Is Proved, and the Sophismes of Bellarmine Are Reprooved*. Translated by Iohn Gawen. London: Imprinted by T.P. for Francis Bvrton, 1610.

Turretin, Francis. *Institutes of Elenctic Theology*. Translated by George Musgrave Giger. 3 vols., ed. James T. Dennison Jr. Phillipsburg; New Jersey: P & R Publishing, 1992.

Ursinus, Zacharias. *The Summe of Christian Religion, Delivered by Zacharias Ursinus, First, by Way of Catechism, and Then Afterwards More Enlarged by a Sound and Judicious Exposition, and Application of the Same. Wherein Also Are Debated and Resolved the Questions of Whatsoever Points of Moment Have Been, or Are Controversed in Divinitie*. London: Printed by James Young, 1645.

Whitfield, Thomas. *A Refutation of the Loose Opinions, and Licentious Tenets Wherwith Those Lay-Preachers Which Wander up and Downe the Kingdome, Labour to Seduce the Simple People or an Examination and Confutation of the Erronious Doctrines of Thomas More, Late a Weaver in Wells Neare Wisbitch, in His Book Entituled [the Universality of God's Free Grace in Christ to Mankinde*. London: Printed for John Bellamie, 1646.

Witsius, Herman. *The Economy of the Covenants between God and Man Comprehending a Complete Body of Divinity*. 2 vols. Kingsburg, CA: den Dulk Christian Foundation, 1990.

Wollebius, Johannes. *The Abridgment of Christian Divinitie: So Exactly and Methodically Compiled, That It Leads Us, as It Were, by the Hand to the Reading of the Holy Scriptures, Ordering of Common-Places, Understanding of Controversies, Cleering of Some Cases of Conscience*. London: Printed for T. Mab and A. Coles for John Saywell, 1650.

Secondary Sources

Armstrong, Brian G. *Calvinism and the Amyraut Heresy: Protestant Scholasticism and Humanism in Seventeenth-Century France*. Madison/Milwaukee/London: University of Wisconsin Press, 1969.

Asselt, Willem J. van. *The Federal Theology of Johannes Cocceius (1603-1669).* Studies in the History of Christian Thought. Leiden/Boston/Koln: Brill, 2001.
—. "The Fundamental Meaning of Theology: Archetypal and Ectypal Theology in Seventeenth-Century Reformed Thought." *Westminster Theological Journal* 64, no. 2 (2002): 319-335.
—. "Expromissio or Fideiussio? A Seventeenth Century Theological Debate between Voetians and Cocceians About the Nature of Christ's Suretyship in Salvation History." *Mid-America Journal of Theology* 14 (2003): 37-57.
—. "The Theologian's Toolkit: Johannes Maccovius (1588-1644) and the Development of Reformed Theological Distinctions." *Westminster Theological Journal* 68 (2006): 23-40.
Asselt, W. J. van, and E. Dekker, eds. *Reformation and Scholasticism : An Ecumenical Enterprise*, Texts and Studies in Reformation and Post-Reformation Thought. Grand Rapids, Mich.: Baker Academic, 2001.
Bangs, Carl. *Arminius: A Study in the Dutch Reformation.* Nashville: Abingdon Press, 1971.
Barth, Karl. *Church Dogmatics: The Doctrine of Reconciliation.* Vol. IV.2, eds. T.F. Torrance G.W. Bromiley. London/New York: T & T Clark International, 2004.
—. *Church Dogmatics: Index with Aids for the Preacher*, eds. T.F. Torrance G.W. Bromiley. London/New York: T&T Clark International, 2004.
Bass, William Ward. "Platonic Influences on Seventeenth Century English Puritan Theology, as Expressed in the Thinking of John Owen, Richard Baxter, and John Howe." Ph.D. dissertation, University of Southern California, 1958.
Bavinck, Herman. *Reformed Dogmatics: Sin and Salvation in Christ.* Translated by John Vriend. Vol. 3, ed. John Bolt. Grand Rapids: Baker, 2006.
Beach, J. Mark. "The Doctrine of the *Pactum Salutis* in the Covenant Thought of Herman Witsius." *Mid-America Journal of Theology* 13 (2002): 101-142.
Beeke, Joel R. *The Quest for Full Assurance: The Legacy of Calvin and His Successors.* Edinburgh: Banner of Truth, 1999.
Bierma, Lyle D. *German Calvinism in the Confessional Age: The Covenant Theology of Caspar Olevianus.* Grand Rapids: Baker, 1996.
Bobick, Michael William. "Owen's Razor: The Role of Ramist Logic in the Covenant Theology of John Owen (1616-1683)." Ph.D. dissertation, Drew University, 1996.
Boersma, Hans. *A Hot Peppercorn: Richard Baxter's Doctrine of Justification in Its Seventeenth-Century Context of Controversy.* Vancouver: Regent College Publishing, 2004.
Bozeman, Theodore D. *The Precisianist Strain: Disciplinary Religion and Antinomian Backlash in Puritanism to 1638.* Williamsburg, Virginia: University of North Carolina Press, 2004.

Bray, Gerald, ed. *Documents of the English Reformation*. Cambridge: James Clarke, 1994.

Bray, Gerald. Review of *Atonement and Justification*, by Alan Clifford. *Churchman* 105, no.1 (1991): 93-94.

Brink, Gert Van den. "Impetration and Application in John Owen's Theology." In *John Owen Today Conference*. Westminster College, Cambridge, 2008.

Burdick, William L. *The Principles of Roman Law and Their Relation to Modern Law*. Reprint, 2nd ed. Clark, New Jersey: The Lawbook Exchange Ltd, 2004.

Campbell, J. McLeod. *The Nature of the Atonement*. First published, 1856; Edinburgh: Handsel Press; Grand Rapids: Eerdmans, 1996.

Clark, R. Scott. *Caspar Olevian and the Substance of the Covenant: The Double Benefit of Christ*. Edinburgh: Rutherford House, 2005.

Clifford, Alan C. *Atonement and Justification: English Evangelical Theology 1640-1790, an Evaluation*. Oxford: Clarendon Press, 1990.

—. *Amyraut Affirmed or 'Owenism, a Caricature of Calvinism'*. Norwich: Charenton Reformed Publishing, 2004.

Como, David R. *Blown by the Spirit: Puritanism and the Emergence of an Antinomian Underground in Pre-Civil War England*. California: Stanford University Press, 2004.

Craig, Philip A. "The Bond of Grace and Duty in the Soteriology of John Owen: The Doctrine of Preparation for Grace and Glory as a Bulwark against Seventeenth-Century Anglo-American Antinomianism." Ph.D. dissertation, Trinity International University, 2005.

Cunningham, William. *Historical Theology: A Review of the Principal Doctrinal Discussions in the Christian Church since the Apostolic Age*. 2 vols. Reprint ed. St Edmonton, Canada: Still Waters Revival Books, 1991.

Daniels, Richard W. *The Christology of John Owen*. Grand Rapids: Reformation Heritage Books, 2004.

Dixhoorn, Chad B. Van. "Reforming the Reformation: Theological Debate at the Westminster Assembly, 1643-1652." Ph.D. dissertation, Cambridge, 2004.

Donnelly, John Patrick S.J., Frank A. James III, Joseph C. McLelland, eds. *The Peter Martyr Reader*. Kirksville, Missouri: Truman State University Press, 1999.

Dorner, Isaac A. *History of the Development of the Doctrine of the Person of Christ*. Translated by D.W. Simon. Vol. 2. Edinburgh: T&T Clark, 1870.

Edmonson, Stephen. *Calvin's Christology*. Cambridge: Cambridge University Press, 2004.

Elert, Werner. *The Structure of Lutheranism: The Theology and Philosophy of Life of Lutheranism Especially in the Sixteenth and Seventeenth Centuries*. Translated by Walter A. Hansen. St Louis: Concordia Publishing House, 1962.

Everson, Don Marvin. "The Puritan Theology of John Owen." Ph.D. dissertation, The Southern Baptist Theological Seminary, 1959.

Ferguson, Sinclair. *John Owen on the Christian Life*. Edinburgh: Banner of Truth, 1987.

Forbesius, Gulielmum. *Considerationes Modestae Et Pacificae Controversiarum De Justificatione, Purgatorio, Invocatione Sanctorum, Christo Mediatore, Et Eucharista Una Cum Versione Anglica*. 2 vols. Oxonii: Apud J.H. Parker, 1850-1856.

Franks, Robert S. *The Work of Christ: A Historical Study of Christian Doctrine*. London: Thomas Nelson and Sons Ltd, 1962.

Frost, R.N. "Aristotle's Ethics: The Real Reason for Luther's Reformation?" *Trinity Journal* 18 (1997): 223-241.

Gleason, Randall C. *John Calvin and John Owen on Mortification*. New York: Peter Lang, 1995.

Gomes, Alan W. "*De Jesu Christo Servatore*: Faustus Socinus on the Satisfaction of Christ." *Westminster Theological Journal* 55, no. 2 (1993): 209-231.

Goris, Harm. "Thomism in Zanchi's Doctrine of God." In *Reformation and Scholasticism: An Ecumenical Enterprise*, eds. Willem J. Van Asselt and E. Dekker, 121-139. Grand Rapids, Mich.: Baker Academic, 2001.

Grensted, L.W. *A Short History of the Doctrine of Atonement*. Manchester: Longmans, Green & Co., 1920.

Gribben, Crawford. *The Irish Puritans: James Ussher and the Reformation of the Church*. Darlington, England: Evangelical Press, 2003.

Griffith, Howard. "High Priest in Heaven: The Intercession of the Exalted Christ in Reformed Theology, Analysis and Critique." Ph.D. dissertation, Westminster Theological Seminary, 2004.

Hall, Basil. "Calvin against the Calvinists." In *John Calvin: A Collection of Distinguished Essays*, ed. Gervase Duffield, 23-27. Grand Rapids: Eerdmans, 1966.

Harrison, A.W. *The Beginnings of Arminianism to the Synod of Dort*. London: University of London Press, 1926.

Hawkes, Richard Mitchell. "The Logic of Grace in John Owen, D.D.: An Analysis, Exposition, and Defense of John Owen's Puritan Theology of Grace." Ph.D. dissertation, Westminster Theological Seminary, 1987.

Helm, Paul. Review of *Atonement and Justification*, by Alan Clifford. *Banner of Truth* no. 325 (1990): 29-31.

Holmes, Stephen R. *Listening to the Past: The Place of Tradition in Theology*. Carlisle: Paternoster/Grand Rapids: Baker, 2002.

— "Reformed Varieties of the *Communicatio Idiomatum*." In *The Person of Christ*, eds. Murray Rae and Stephen R. Holmes, 70-86. Edinburgh: T&T Clark, 2005.

Jansen, John F. *Calvin's Doctrine of the Work of Christ*. London: James Clarke, 1956.

Jong, Peter Y. De, ed. *Crisis in the Reformed Churches: Essays in Commemoration of the Great Synod of Dort, 1618-1619*. Grand Rapids: Reformed Fellowship, Inc., 1968.

Kapic, Kelly M. *Communion with God: The Divine and the Human in the Theology of John Owen*. Grand Rapids: Baker, 2007.

Kay, Brian K. *Trinitarian Spirituality: John Owen and the Doctrine of God in Western Devotion*. Studies in Christian History and Thought. Milton Keynes: Paternoster, 2007.

Kendall, R.T. *Calvin and English Calvinism to 1649*. Oxford Theological Monograph Series. Oxford: Oxford University Press, 1979.

Kennedy, Kevin Dixon. *Union with Christ and the Extent of the Atonement* Studies in Biblical Literature 48. New York/Bern/Oxford: Peter Lang, 2002.

Knapp, Henry M. "Understanding the Mind of God: John Owen and Seventeenth Century Exegetical Methodology." Ph.D. dissertation, Calvin Theological Seminary, 2002.

— "Augustine and John Owen on Perseverance." *Westminster Theological Journal* 62 (2000): 65-87.

—. "John Owen's Interpretation of Hebrews 6:4-6: Eternal Perseverance of the Saints in Puritan Exegesis." *Sixteenth Century Journal* 34, no. 1 (2003): 29-52.

Kuyper, Abraham. *The Work of the Holy Spirit*. Translated by Henri De Vries. New York; London: Funk & Wagnalls, 1900.

Letham, Robert. "John Owen's Doctrine of the Trinity and Its Significance for Today." In *"Where Reason Fails...", the Westminster Conference 2006*. Stoke-on-Trent, U.K.: Tentmaker Publications, 2006.

MacLeod, Jack N. "John Owen and the Death of Death." In *Out of Bondage*. Nottingham: The Westminster Conference, 1983. Reprint, Stoke-On-Trent: Tentmaker Publications, n.d.

Mason, Matthew. "The Significance of the Systematic and Polemic Function of Union with Christ in John Owen's Contribution to Seventeenth Century Debates Concerning Eternal Justification." M.Th. dissertation, Oak Hill College, 2005.

McCormack, Bruce L. "For Us and Our Salvation: Incarnation and Atonement in the Reformed Tradition." *Studies in Reformed Theology and History* 1, no. 2 (1993).

McLachlan, H. John. *Socinianism in Seventeenth Century England*. Oxford: Oxford University Press, 1951.

McDonald, Suzanne. "Re-Imaging Election: The Holy Spirit and the Dynamic of Election to Representation." Ph.D. dissertation, St Andrews University, Scotland, 2006.

McGrath, Alister E. *Iustitia Dei: A History of the Christian Doctrine of Justification*. 3rd ed. Cambridge/New York/Melbourne: Cambridge University Press, 2005.

McGrath, Alister E. Review of *Atonement and Justification*, by Alan Clifford. *Journal of Theological Studies* 42, no. 1 (1991): 397-398.

McGrath, Gavin John. "Puritans and the Human Will: Voluntarism within Mid-Seventeenth English Puritanism as Seen in the Works of Richard Baxter and John Owen." Ph.D. dissertation, University of Durham, 1989.

Moffatt, James, ed. *The Golden Book of John Owen*. London: Hodder and Stoughton, 1904.

Muhlen, Karl-Heinz zur. "Christology." In *The Oxford Encyclopedia of the Reformation*, ed. Hans J. Hillerbrand, 1, 314-322. New York/Oxford: Oxford University Press, 1996.

Muller, Richard A. *Dictionary of Latin and Greek Theological Terms: Drawn Principally from Protestant Scholastic Theology*. Grand Rapids: Baker, 1985.

—. *Christ and the Decree: Christology and Predestination in Reformed Theology from Calvin to Perkins*. Durham, N.C.: Labyrinth Press, 1986.

—. *God, Creation, and Providence in the Thought of Jacobus Arminius: Sources and Directions of Scholastic Protestantism in the Era of Early Orthodoxy*. Grand Rapids: Baker, 1991.

— "Calvin and the 'Calvinists': Assessing Continuities and Discontinuities between the Reformation and Orthodoxy. Part One." *Calvin Theological Journal* 30, no. 2 (1995): 345-75.

— "Calvin and the Calvinists: Assessing Continuities and Discontinuities between the Reformation and Orthodoxy. Part Two." *Calvin Theological Journal* 31, no. 1 (1996): 125-60.

—. "Scholasticism, Reformation, Orthodoxy, and the Persistence of Christian Aristotelianism." *Trinity Journal* 19, no. 1 (1998): 81-96.

—. "Reformation, Orthodoxy, 'Christian Aristotelianism', and the Eclecticism of Early Modern Philosophy." *Nederlands Archief Voor Kerkgeschiedenis* 81, no. 3 (2001): 306-325.

—. *After Calvin: Studies in the Development of a Theological Tradition* Oxford Studies in Historical Theology. New York: Oxford University Press, 2003.

—. *Post Reformation Reformed Dogmatics: The Rise and Development of Reformed Orthodoxy, ca. 1520 to ca. 1725*. 4 vols. Grand Rapids: Baker, 2003.

—. "Toward the *Pactum Salutis*: Locating the Origins of a Concept." *Mid-America Journal of Theology* 18 (2007): 11-65.

Newton, John A. Review of *Atonement and Justification*, by Alan Clifford. *Theology* 94, no. 758 (1991): 140-141.

Oliver, Robert W., ed. *John Owen: The Man and His Theology*. Darlington: Evangelical Press; Philadelphia: P&R Publishing, 2002.

Oxford Dictionary of National Biography (61 vols). Oxford: Oxford University Press, 2004. [*Oxford DNB Online* at http://www.oxforddnb.com, 2004 -.]

Packer, J.I. *A Quest for Godliness: The Puritan Vision of the Christian Life*. Wheaton, Illinois: Crossway Books, 1990.

Pannenberg, Wolfhart. *Jesus – God and Man*. Translated by Lewis L. Wilkins and Duane A. Priebe. Philadelphia: Westminster Press, 1968.

—. *Systematic Theology*. Translated by Geoffrey W. Bromiley. 3 vols. Edinburgh: T&T Clark; Grand Rapids: Eerdmans, 1991-1998.

Payne, Jon D. *John Owen on the Lord's Supper*. Edinburgh: Banner of Truth, 2004.

Pelikan, Jaroslav. *Reformation of Church and Dogma (1300-1700)*. Vol. 4 The Christian Tradition: A History of the Development of Doctrine. Chicago/London: University of Chicago Press, 1984.

Peterson Sr., Robert A. *Calvin and the Atonement*. Ross-shire: Christian Focus Publications, 1999.

Pytches, Peter N.L. "A Critical Exposition of the Teaching of John Owen on the Work of the Holy Spirit in the Individual." M.Litt. dissertation, University of Bristol, 1967.

Rehnman, Sebastian. "John Owen: A Reformed Scholastic at Oxford." In *Reformation and Scholasticism: An Ecumenical Enterprise*, ed. Willem J. van Asselt and Eef Dekker, 181-203. Grand Rapids: Baker, 2001.

—. *Divine Discourse: The Theological Methodology of John Owen*. Texts and Studies in Reformation and Post-Reformation Thought. Grand Rapids: Baker, 2002.

Reid, James. *Memoirs of the Lives and Writings of Those Eminent Divines Who Convened in the Famous Assembly at Westminster in the Seventeenth Century*. Paisley: Printed by Stephen and Andrew Young, 1811; repr. Edinburgh: Banner of Truth, 1982.

Royston III, Holmes. *John Calvin Versus the Westminster Confession*. Richmond: John Knox, 1972.

Sell, Alan. F. Review of *Atonement and Justification*, by Alan Clifford. *Calvin Theological Journal* 27, no. 1 (1992): 116-117.

Schmid, Heinrich. *The Doctrinal Theology of the Evangelical Lutheran Church, Verified from the Original Sources*, eds. Charles A. Hay and Henry E. Jacobs. Philadelphia: Lutheran Publication Society, 1889.

Sheldon, Henry C. *History of Christian Doctrine*. 2 vols. New York: Harper and Brothers, 1886.

Sherman, Robert J. "Toward a Trinitarian Theology of the Atonement." *Scottish Journal of Theology* 52, no. 3 (1999): 346-74.

—. *King, Priest and Prophet: A Trinitarian Theology of Atonement*. London: T&T Clark, 2004.

Spence, Alan J. "John Owen and Trinitarian Agency." *Scottish Journal of Theology* 43 (1990): 157-73.

—. *The Promise of Peace: A Unified Theory of Atonement*. Edinburgh: Continuum International Publishing/T&T Clark, 2006.

—. *Incarnation and Inspiration: John Owen and the Coherence of Christology*. London/New York: T & T Clark, 2007.

Stam, F.P. Van *The Controversy over the Theology of Saumur, 1635-1650: Disrupting Debates among the Huguenots in Complicated Circumstances*. Amsterdam/Maarssen: APA-Holland University Press, 1988.

Stover, Dale Arden. "The Pneumatology of John Owen: A Study of the Role of the Holy Spirit in Relation to the Shape of a Theology." Ph.D. dissertation, McGill University, 1967.

Strehle, Stephen. "The Extent of the Atonement and the Synod of Dort." *Westminster Theological Journal* 51 (1989): 1-23.

The School of Faith: The Catechisms of the Reformed Church, Trans. And Edited with an Introduction by T.F. Torrance. London: James Clarke, 1959.

Thomas, G. Michael. *The Extent of the Atonement: A Dilemma for Reformed Theology from Calvin to the Consensus*. Carlisle: Paternoster Press, 1997.

Toon, Peter. *God's Statesman: The Life and Work of John Owen*. Exeter: Paternoster Press, 1971.

Torrance, James B. "Covenant or Contract? A Study of the Theological Background of Worship in Seventeenth Century Scotland." *Scottish Journal of Theology* 23 (1970): 51-76.

—— "Strengths and Weaknesses of the Westminster Theology." In *The Westminster Confession in the Church Today*, ed. Alisdair Heron, 40-53. Edinburgh: St. Andrew Press, 1982.

—— "The Incarnation and 'Limited Atonement'". *Evangelical Quarterly* 55 (1983): 83-94.

Torrance, Thomas F. "Predestination in Christ." *Evangelical Quarterly* 13 (1941): 108-141.

——. *The Mediation of Christ*. Exeter: Paternoster, 1983.

Trueman, Carl R. *The Claims of Truth: John Owen's Trinitarian Theology*. Carlisle: Paternoster Press, 1998.

—— "John Owen's Dissertation on Divine Justice: An Exercise in Christocentric Scholasticism." *Calvin Theological Journal* 33 (1998): 87-103.

—— "A Small Step Towards Rationalism: The Impact of the Metaphysics of Tommaso Campanella on the Theology of Richard Baxter." In *Protestant Scholasticism: Essays in Reassessment*, ed. Carl R. Trueman and R.S. Clark, 181-195. Carlisle, Cumbria: Paternoster Press, 1999.

—— "Puritan Theology as Historical Event: A Linguistic Approach to the Ecumenical Context." In *Reformation and Scholasticism: An Ecumenical Enterprise*, eds. Willem J. van Asselt and Eef Dekker, 253-75. Grand Rapids: Baker, 2001.

——. *John Owen: Reformed Catholic, Rennaisance Man*. Aldershot, England: Ashgate, 2007.

Trueman, Carl R., and R. Scott Clark, eds. *Protestant Scholasticism: Essays in Reassessment*. Carlisle: Paternoster Press, 1999.

Tucker, Thomas Jackson. "Safeguarding the Treasury: John Owen and the Analogy of Faith." Ph.D. dissertation, Aberdeen University, 2006.

Tylanda, Joseph. "Christ the Mediator: Calvin Versus Stancaro." *Calvin Theological Journal* 8, no. 1 (1973): 5-16.

—— "The Controversy on Christ the Mediator: Calvin's Second Reply to Stancaro." *Calvin Theological Journal* 8, no. 1 (1973): 131-157.

Wallace, Dewey D., Jr. "The Life and Thought of John Owen to 1660: A Study of the Significance of Calvinist Theology in English Puritanism." Ph.D. dissertation, Princeton University, 1965.

Ward, W.R. Review of *Atonement and Justification*, by Alan Clifford. *Journal of Ecclesiastical History* 42, no. 2 (1991): 326-327.

Weir, David A. *The Origins of the Federal Theology in Sixteenth-Century Reformation Thought.* Oxford: Clarendon Press, 1990.

Williams, Carol A. "The Decree of Redemption Is in Effect a Covenant: David Dickson and the Covenant of Redemption." Ph.D. dissertation, Calvin Theological College, 2005.

Williams, Gary J. "A Critical Exposition of Hugo Grotius' Doctrine of the Atonement in *De Satisfactione Christi*." Ph.D.\ dissertation, University of Oxford, 1999.

— "The Puritan Doctrine of Atonement." In *"Where Reason Fails...", the Westminster Conference 2006*. Stoke-on-Trent, U.K.: Tentmaker Publications, 2006.

Winship, Michael P. "Contesting Control of Orthodoxy among the Godly: William Pynchon Reexamined." *The William and Mary Quarterly* 54, no. 4 (1997): 795-822.

Wong, David Wai-Sing. "The Covenant Theology of John Owen." Ph.D. dissertation, Westminster Theological Seminary, 1998.

Wood, A. Skevington. Review of *Atonement and Justification*, by Alan Clifford. *Evangelical Quarterly* 63 (1991): 287-288.

Wright, Robert K.M. "John Owen's Great High Priest: The Highpriesthood of Christ in the Theology of John Owen, (1616-1683)." Ph.D. dissertation, The Iliff School of Theology and University of Denver, 1989.

Author Index

Augustine 25, 60, 76, 124, 171.
Ambrose 28, 55, 60.
Ames, W. 13-14, 20, 26, 60, 78.
Amyraut, M. 95-97.
Anselm 72, 139.
Aquinas, T. 41, 52, 77, 164.
Aristotle 147, 152-153, 159
Arminius, J. 33-34, 92-94, 102, 133-134.
Athanasius 16, 28, 124.
Barth, K. 3, 31, 42, 80.
Basil of Caesarea 28.
Baxter, R. xi, 5, 10, 114, 118, 126, 136-146, 148-149, 152, 170, 181, 183.
Bavinck, H. 33.
Bellarmine, R. 84, 115, 118, 126.
Beza, T. 68, 93.
Biddle, J. 60-62, 118, 128, 173.
Boersma, H. 53, 126, 136, 139-140, 145, 151.
Bolton, S. 97-98.
Bucanus, W. 25.
Calvin, J. 2-3, 5-8, 14, 16, 20, 33, 41, 52, 55, 59-60, 78, 79, 95, 152, 164.
Campanella, T. 152.
Campbell, J.M. 2, 10.
Cameron, J. 95-98.
Charnock, S. 66.
Chemnitz, M. 80.
Chrysostom 60, 124.
Clifford, A.C. 5-8, 10, 53, 95, 147-149, 151-153, 183.
Crellius, J. 130-131, 145.
Crisp, T. 125-127.
Cromwell, O. 10, 137
Cyprian 124.
Dickson, D. 34-35, 44, 55, 131, 139.
Diodati, G. 55, 131-132.
Edwards, J. 2.
Edwards, T. 11.
Episcopius, S.
Eusebius 124.
Essenius 33.

Gataker, T. 117, 119, 122.
Gerhard, J. 115.
Gillespie, P. 41, 47.
Gomarus 33.
Goodwin, J. 170-171.
Goodwin, T. 78, 117, 121.
Gouge, W. 131.
Grotius, H. 21, 61, 120, 131, 136-138, 142-143.
Hammond, H. 131.
Irenaeus 124, 184.
John à Lasco 60.
John of Damascus 76.
Jones, W. 55.
Kargius, G. 115.
Knapp, H.M. 4, 9, 49, 171.
Lawson, G. 55.
Leigh, E. 68, 131.
Leo the Great 124.
Maccovius, J. 102, 146.
Millington, E. 8.
More, T. 11, 15-16, 19, 22, 87, 89, 92, 99-101, 107, 112, 180.
Muller, R.A. 6-7, 9, 12, 24-25, 30, 33-35, 41, 56, 58-59, 65-66, 78, 80, 93, 96, 114, 126, 128, 135, 152-155, 164, 168.
Musculus, W. 25-26.
Origen 124.
Pannenberg, W. 3.
Perkins, W. 9, 20, 26, 32.
Peterkin, A. 34.
Piscator, J. 24-26, 41, 115-116.
Polanus, A. 66.
Poole, M. 68-69.
Prosper of Aquitaine 124.
Quick, J. 96, 116
Rehnman, S. 7-8, 65, 154
Rutherford, S. 11, 34, 41, 47, 164.
Saltmarsh, J. 126.
Schlichtingius, J. 130-131.
Smalcius, V. 118.
Socinus, F. 60, 120, 123, 142, 164.

Socinus, L. 60.
Suarez 146.
Spence, A.J. 4, 7, 63, 75-76, 81, 183.
Stalham, J. 11.
Stancaro, F. 60, 180.
Testard, P. 96.
Trapp, J. 68.
Trelcatius, L. 25, 41.
Trueman, C.R. 2, 7-8, 24, 34-35, 40-41, 45, 47-49, 54-55, 62, 69, 73, 81, 87-88, 131, 133-134, 136, 139, 143, 151-154, 164.
Turretin, F. 17, 20, 41, 98, 114, 136.
Twisse, W. 117, 164.
Ursinus, Z. 174.
Van Asselt, W.J. 2, 7, 26, 47, 102, 128, 168, 154-155.
Vermigli, P. 60, 79.
Voetius, G. 128, 146.
Vorstius, C. 115.
Whitfield, T. 11.
Wilson, T. 131.
Witsius, H. 33-34, 41.
Wollebius, J. 14, 17, 24-26.
Zanchius, J. 155.

Scripture Index

Genesis
1:2 26
1:26 46, 158
2:17 148
3 73
3:15 177
8:20–22 39
9:9–10 39
15:17–18 39

Exodus
24:5–8 39
34:28 40

Leviticus
16:21 127
16:21–22 127

Deuteronomy
9:11 40

2 Samuel
18:33 148

1 Kings
8:9 40

Job
5:23 40
33:23–24 37
33:24 38

Psalms
1:5 39
2:7–8 36, 38
16:2 38
16:8–11 148
16:10 38, 56
16:11 56
22:1 148
22:30–31 38
31:5 56

40:7–8 38
55:14 37
89:27–28 38
116:3 148

Proverbs
8:22 39, 68-69
8:22–23 67-69
8:23 69
8:22–31 27, 37, 46

Song of Solomon
2:4 172

Isaiah
4 172
4:1–6 171
7:14 73
9:6 37, 73
19:20 51
42:1 37
42:1–4 38
42:4 38
42:6 38
48:16 51
49:5 37
49:5–6 38
49:8–9 38
50:5 38
50:5–9 38
52 34
53:4 52
53:5 91, 130, 148
53:6 52, 125-126, 130, 148
53:8 36
53:10 37, 52
53:10–11 38
53:10–12 36
53:11 91
59:21 40

Jeremiah
33:20 40
34:18–20 39

Daniel
9:24 38

Hosea
2:18 40

Micah
5:2 78
6:6–7 37

Zechariah
2:8–9 78
6:13 37
13:7 37, 52

Matthew
1:23 73
11:27 27
13:44 11
13:44–45 11
25:31f 6
26:31 52
26:37 148
26:38 148

Mark
14:33 148

Luke
1:80 53
22:44 148
23:46 56

John
1:1 68
1:14 73
3:16 19, 143
3:35 27

5:20 27
6 34
6:46 27
8:58 73, 78
14:28 37
15:1–2 123
17:1 38
17:2 36, 38
17:4 36
17:4–6 38
17:9 38
17:12–16 38
20:12 57

Acts
2:24 139
2:24–28 148
2:33 176
13:33 38
20:28 73, 120-121

Romans
1:4 38
3:24–25 148
3:25 167
3:26 167
4:6–7 115
4:25 91, 107
5:6 130
5:6–8 129
5:8 130, 143
5:10 148
5:12 124
8:3 37, 148, 167
8:32 148
8:32–34 91
9:5 73

1 Corinthians
1:24 31
12:4 26
12:12-13 124

2 Corinthians
1:20 173
5:18–20 148
5:21 52, 125, 127, 129-130, 148, 167

13:14 81

Galatians
3:13 129-130, 148, 167
4:4 37

Ephesians
1:10 184
5:25–32 123

Philippians
2:6–7 37
2:6–8 38
2:7 36, 37, 169
2:8–10 135
2:9 36, 38

Colossians
2:9 73
2:15 177

1 Timothy
1:1 51
2:6 11
4:10 51

Titus
1:3 51
3:5 26

Hebrews
2:9 11, 148
2:9–10 37
2:14 148, 177
2:16 37
2:17 109
3:3 14
5:7 38, 148
5:7–8 120, 134
5:8 134
7 131
7:21 38
7:22 129-133
7:25 38
7:28 38
8:4 109
8:6 40, 78

9:6–7 176
9:7 49, 176
9:14 53-55, 120
9:15 33, 176
9:18-20 39
9:24 38, 110, 175
9:26 148
9:28 148
10:4 37
10:5 37
10:8 37
10:9 37
12:2 36, 37, 38

1 Peter
1:18 37
2:24 148
3:18 148

1 John
2:1 175
2:2 52
3:16 73
4:9 143

Revelation
5:6 70

Subject Index

Amyraldianism xi, 10, 19.
Angels 17, 57, 78, 107, 155, 169, 184-185.
Anhypostatic Christology 73-74 (see also "Incarnation"; "Hypostatic Union").
Anselmian tradition 72, 139.
Antinomianism xi, 4, 118, 125-127, 140-141.
Archetypal/Ectypal Theology 154.
Aristotelianism 5-6, 138-139, 147-148, 151-153, 182.
Arminianism xi, 2, 30, 10, 18-19, 34-36, 39, 41, 52, 55, 64, 87-89, 92-96, 98-99, 101, 102-105, 107-108, 112, 133, 136-137, 146, 164, 180, 182.
Attributes of God 30, 66, 70, 151, 153, 154-163, 164-167, 178, 184 (see also "God").
Augsburg Confession 117.
Bremen Confession 173.
Calvinism 5-6, 33, 95-98.
Catholicism xi, 63, 84, 88, 115-116, 118, 126-127.
Christ as Mediator 13-18, 22-23, 28-29, 32, 35, 38, 44, 48-51, 56, 58-86, 87-88, 103-105, 117, 119-123, 132-135, 139, 150, 151, 163, 165, 173-175, 179-181, 183-184.
Christ as King 14, 70-71, 78, 105, 109-110, 131, 163, 173, 180, 183.
Christ as Priest 14-20, 22-23, 34-36, 47-50, 51, 57, 58, 70-71, 78, 82, 86, 87-113, 114, 119, 129-133, 135, 142-145, 147, 149-150, 151, 156-157, 173-178, 179-184 (see also "Oblation/Intercession of Christ").
Christ as Prophet 14-15, 70-71, 78-79, 105, 110, 131, 163, 180, 183.
communicatio apotelesmatum 80-81, 84, 86.
communicatio idiomatum 58-60, 74-75, 80-81, 85, 139, 180.
communio naturarum 59, 74.

Covenant of Grace 3, 33-34, 41, 60, 79, 98, 172-173.
Covenant of Redemption (see "*pactum salutis*").
Covenant of Works 33, 98, 172.
Creation 13, 26-28, 46, 54, 67-68, 93, 155-160, 162, 165, 167, 184-185.
Divine Decree/Counsel 29-32, 36, 43-44, 97-98 (see also "Divine Election"; "Predestination"; "Reprobation").
Divine Election 10, 27, 30-32, 44, 93, 99, 182 (see also "Divine Decree/Counsel"; "Predestination"; "Reprobation").
Divine Justice 37, 44, 50, 52, 72, 124, 139, 149, 154, 156, 161, 163-169, 177-178 (see also "God").
Divine Simplicity 41-43, 155 (see also "God").
Dutch Annotations 55, 134.
Effectual/Ineffectual Redemption 18, 53, 77, 100, 173 (see also "Universal/General Redemption"; "Limited Atonement").
English Annotations 55.
Eternal Compact (see "*pactum salutis*").
Eternal Justification 4, 140.
Eutychianism 59, 74.
External Works of God 12-13, 24-26, 27-28, 32, 51-5, 68, 70, 155, 157, 167 (see also "God").
filioque 26, 31, 35, 46-47, 57 (see also "God").
God (see "Attributes of God"; "Divine Justice"; "Divine Simplicity"; "External Works of God"; "*filioque*"; "Internal Works of God"; "Order of Subsistence"; "Trinity").
Grotianism 50, 136-138, 142-143.
Heidelberg Catechism 174.
Helvetic Consensus Formula 98.
Holy Spirit 3-4, 13, 22, 42, 45-47, 51, 53-

57, 62-63, 68, 75-79, 99-100, 120, 124, 125, 128, 140, 143, 158, 163, 168, 170-172, 175-178, 180-184.
Humiliation/Exaltation of Christ 14, 17, 23, 49, 56, 87, 105-107, 110, 114, 133-135, 144, 149, 169, 175, 178, 179-181.
Hypostatic Union 56, 59-60, 62-64, 79-81, 85, 121, 123 (see also "Anhypostatic Christology"; "Incarnation").
Incarnation 4, 7-8, 10, 13, 15-16, 18, 24, 35, 43-44, 48, 50, 53-54, 58, 63-64, 66, 72-76, 78-79, 81, 85, 99, 105, 123, 169, 182-184 (see also "Anhypostatic Christology"; "Hypostatic Union").
Image of God 65, 96, 158-160, 163.
Imputation 84, 102, 114-130, 132-135, 140, 149, 174-175, 181 (see also "Justification"; "Union with Christ").
Infralapsarianism 94.
Internal Works of God 13, 25, 27-28, 29-50, 57, 155, 167 (see also "God").
Justification 2, 4-5, 7, 10, 31, 53, 61, 83-85, 91, 95, 107, 140-142, 144-147, 150-152, 171-172, 174-175, 181, 183 (see also "Imputation"; "Union with Christ").
Limited Atonement 2-3, 6, 10, 147, 182 (see also "Universal/General Redemption"; "Effectual/Ineffectual Redemption").
Lord's Supper 4, 58-59 (see also "Sacrament").
Lutheran Orthodoxy 56, 58-59, 63, 74, 80-81, 114-115, 119, 135, 180.
munus triplex 173.
necessitas ex suppositione 168.
Nestorianism 58, 63, 79.
Obedience of Christ 17, 20-22, 32, 35, 37, 44, 48-50, 56, 75, 79, 84, 105-106, 114-135, 136, 149, 160-163, 169-171, 175, 178.
Oblation/Intercession of Christ 13-20, 22-23, 35, 48-49, 53-55, 67, 88-92, 100-101, 103-112, 135, 143-145, 150, 156, 169-170, 173-178, 179-182, 184 (see also "Christ as Priest").
Order of Subsistence 13, 15, 26, 28, 46, 57, 75, 158, 163 (see also "God").

ordo decretorum 96-99.
ordo salutis 7.
ordo temporum 33.
opera dei (see "External Works of God"; "Internal Works of God").
pactum salutis 13, 20, 31, 32-57, 67, 73, 78, 121, 133, 141, 146, 149, 166-167, 170, 179-180, 182-184.
Perseverance 2, 9, 32, 98, 102, 118, 151, 159, 170-178.
potentia absoluta/potentia ordinata 164.
Predestination 6-7, 30, 93-94, 97, 99, 102-103 (see also "Divine Decree/Counsel"; "Divine Election"; "Reprobation").
Priesthood of Christ (see "Christ as Priest"; "Oblation/Intercession of Christ").
principium cognoscendi theologiae 9, 154.
Protestant Scholasticism 7, 9, 80, 95, 152-153.
Puritanism 1-4, 7, 9-10, 63, 125, 136-137, 145, 171.
Racovian Catechism 61-62, 64, 88, 108-109, 111.
reatus culpae/reatus poenae 126.
Recapitulation 184-185.
Reformed Orthodoxy xi-xii, 3, 6-9, 12-15, 17, 20, 22, 24-26, 35, 41-42, 47, 52, 55-56, 60, 66-68, 86, 87-88, 98, 102, 114, 116, 119, 122-123, 128, 154-155, 164, 168, 179, 181.
Remonstrant 94-95, 102-103, 133.
Reprobation 27, 30 (see also "Divine Decree/Counsel"; "Divine Election"; "Predestination").
Resurrection of Christ 13, 17, 35, 53-54, 56, 62, 99-100, 105, 107, 134, 184.
Sacrament 63, 142, 180 (see also "Lord's Supper").
Satan 64, 160, 175, 177-178, 181, 183.
Satisfaction for Sin 12, 14, 17, 20-23, 44, 61, 72 79, 82-83, 85, 114-150, 151, 161-164, 166, 169, 170, 176, 178-181, 183 (see also "*solutio eiusdem/solutio tantidem*").
Savoy Declaration 9, 32-33, 116-118, 172-174.

Saumurian Theology 95-99.
Scripture 4-6, 8-9, 14, 29, 33-34, 37, 39-40, 51, 60-62, 67-68, 73, 80, 85, 94, 99-101, 107, 120, 123, 134, 144, 148-149, 154, 157, 164, 170, 182-183.
Septuagint 39.
Sin 13, 16, 18, 20-22, 33, 48, 52-53, 62, 72-73, 75-76, 79, 82-83, 85, 87, 90-91, 94-95, 98, 100, 102, 104-106, 108-109, 112, 136, 138-145, 147-150, 151, 154, 157-158, 160-171, 174-175, 177-178, 179-185.
Socinianism xi, 36, 55, 60-63, 66, 82-83, 85-86, 88, 108-112, 118, 120-123, 130-132, 137, 141-143, 145, 164, 173, 180.
solutio eiusdem/solutio tantidem 136-139, 141-144, 147-150, 181, 183 (see also "Satisfaction for Sin").
Supralapsarianism 93-94.
Synod of Alençon 96.
Synod of Dort 53, 93-98, 134, 173.
Synod of Gap 116.
Synod of Tonneins 116.
The Death of Death 1-3, 8-22, 24, 29, 35, 47, 51, 53-55, 64, 87-90, 92, 99, 101-103, 106-108, 111-112, 129-130, 136, 138-140, 143, 151-152, 156-157, 159, 164, 170, 179, 184.
Two Short Catechisms (Owen) 104-106.
Twofold Catechism (Biddle) 61-62.
Twofold State of Christ (see "Humiliation/Exaltation of Christ").
Teleology 20, 147, 149, 151-153, 156, 178.
theologia viatorum 185.
theologia unionis 65.
Trinity 12-14, 19, 21-22, 24-31, 42-47, 51, 57, 66, 73, 76, 78, 82, 155, 158, 179 (see also "God").
Union with Christ 3-4, 7, 123-129.
Universal/General Redemption 10-12, 16, 18-20, 22, 35, 52-53, 99-103, 107, 112, 129-130, 142-143, 170, 180.
Universal Offer of Salvation, 53.
Westminster Assembly 1, 33, 56, 116-117, 119, 122, 164.
Westminster Confession 6, 33, 60, 80, 116-117, 172, 174.

www.ingramcontent.com/pod-product-compliance
Lightning Source LLC
Chambersburg PA
CBHW070400240426
43661CB00056B/2483